SOCIAL WORK AT THE MILLENNIUM

---

*Critical Reflections on the
Future of the Profession*

Edited by
June Gary Hopps, Ph.D.
Robert Morris, Ph.D.

The Free Press
New York • London • Toronto • Sydney • Singapore

THE FREE PRESS
A Division of Simon & Schuster Inc.
1230 Avenue of the Americas
New York, NY 10020
Copyright © 2000 by June Gary Hopps, and Robert Morris

THE FREE PRESS and colophon are trademarks
of Simon & Schuster Inc.
Designed by Deirdre C. Amthor
Manufactured in the United States of America

10 9 8 7 6 5 4 3 2 1

Library of Congress Cataloging-in-Publication Data

Social work at the millennium : critical reflections on the future of the profession /
edited by June Gary Hopps, Robert H. Morris
p. cm.
Includes bibliographical references (p.) and index.
1. Social service—United States. 2. Public welfare—United States.
I. Hopps, June Gary II. Morris, Robert

HV91 .S6247 2000
361.3'2'0973—dc21
00-024528

ISBN 0-684-83946-6

ISBN 978-1-4165-7692-1

*f*P

To my devoted family, especially:
William P. Gary, Grandfather
Ollie Colden and Homer Gary, parents
and Eleanor E. and Wallace Z. Gary, aunts

In memory of Sara Morris,
whose critical intelligence, patience and support
played so major a part in our work

Acknowledgments

There are many we wish to thank for their kind assistance in the development and realization of this book.

Scott Briar and Carol Myer, former editors of *Social Work*, proffered many ideas regarding the focus of the book. Both passed on before they were able to complete their contributions. All of us are deprived of their vision, ideals, and commitment to the advancement of the profession. Anne Minahan and Alvin Schorr, also former editors of *Social Work*, supported the project.

A great debt is owed to colleagues at Boston College: Mary Hogan, Regina O'Grady LaShane, Robbie Tourse, and Debbie Lynn for reviewing selected chapters of the manuscript; Linda M. McCarthy, Evelyn Aleman-Zuniga, Stephanie Neely, and Jo Connors for administrative support. Professor Ollie Christian of Southern University also reviewed the manuscript.

Finally we express gratitude to Free Press editor, Philip Rappaport, and William Morrison for support, insights, and shepherding of the project through all phases of development.

June Gary Hopps
Robert Morris

Contents

Part I: Context and Evolution of Social Work

Part II: Fields of Practice—The Challenge: Achievements vs. Unrealized Visions

Contents

Part III: Conceptual and Scientific Critiques

About the Contributors

David M. Austin, Ph.D., is Professor at the School of Social Work, University of Texas at Austin, and previously taught at Brandeis University. He has been a member of the Board of Directors of the National Association of Social Workers and the Educational Planning Commission of the Council on Social Work Education. He chaired the NIMH Task Force on Social Work Research (1988–1991), and prepared the Report on Progress in Development of Social Work Research in 1998.

Donald Brieland, Ph.D., is Professor and Dean Emeritus, University of Illinois at Chicago (UIC), Jane Addams College of Social Work. He served as the first Director of the Illinois Department of Children and Family Services. He was Dean at the School of Social Work, University of Illinois at Urbana-Champaign prior to going to UIC. Special interests are social work and the law and children's services. He was Editor of *Social Work* from 1976 to 1979.

Claudia J. Coulton, Ph.D., is the Lillian F. Harris Professor in the Mandel School of Applied Social Sciences, Case Western Reserve University, Cleveland, Ohio. She is also Co-Director of the Center on Urban Poverty and Social Change that was founded in 1988 to conduct multidisciplinary research, evaluation, and policy analysis related to urban poverty and community building. Dr. Coulton is the author of numerous journal articles, book chapters, and policy reports on urban neighborhoods, evaluating community initiatives, and welfare policy.

William M. Epstein, D.S.W., teaches at University of Nevada, Las Vegas. He has written extensively on social welfare programs and issues. His latest books are *Social Welfare in America* and *Children Who Could Have Been*.

About the Contributors

Ruby M. Gourdine, D.S.W., is Associate Professor and Director of Field Instruction at Howard University School of Social Work. Her most recent publication is "Teenage Black Girls and Violence: Coming of Age in an Urban Environment," *The Journal of Human Behavior and the Social Environment.*

June Gary Hopps, Ph.D., is Dean and Professor, Graduate School of Social Work, Boston College. She is a former editor of *Social Work* and co-author with Elaine Pinderhughes of the Free Press's *Power to Care* and *Group Work with Overwhelmed Clients.*

Demetrius M. Iatridis, Ph.D., is Professor of Social Policy Planning and Chair of the Planning Department of the Boston College Graduate School of Social Work. His recent publications are *Social Policy: Institutional context of Social Develoment and Human Services;* "Policy Practice," *Encyclopedia of Social Work,* 19th ed.; *Privatization in Central and Eastern Europe: Perspectives and Approaches,* and *Social Justice and the Welfare State in Central and Eastern Europe: The Impact of Privatization.*

Wynne S. Korr, Ph.D., is Professor of Social Work at the School of Social Work, University of Pittsburgh, where she serves as Co-director of the Center for Mental Health Services Research. She directed the doctoral program there from 1994 to 1999. She previously taught at the University of Illinois at Chicago, Jane Addams College of Social Work. Her major fields of interest are mental health policies and services and social work history. She and Donald Brieland have collaborated on other projects including ethics in social work education and children's rights.

Anthony N. Maluccio, D.S.W., is Professor of Social Work at Boston College, Graduate School of Social Work, Chestnut Hill, Massachusetts. His teaching and research interests focus on service delivery and outcome evaluation in the area of child and family services. In addition to articles in professional journals, he has authored or co-authored a number of books on the above topics, including most recently *The Child Welfare Challenge—Policy, Practice and Research; Together Again—Family Reunification in Foster Care; Teaching Family Reunification;* and *Reconnecting Families—A Guide to Strengthening Family Reunification Services.*

Robert Morris, Ph.D., worked for twenty years as program developer and social worker in various private and governmental health, welfare and social service organizations. He was for thirty years a founding faculty member of doctoral program for advanced studies in social welfare, Brandeis University, the first of its kind, and is also a former editor of *Social Work.*

Helen Rehr, D.S.W., is Professor of Community Medicine Emerita and consultant on social-health research, education, and program planning to the Department of Social Work Services and the Division of Social Work, The Mount Sinai School of Medicine and Medical Center. Dr. Rehr, the author, co-author and editor of more than a hundred published studies, reports, articles, chapters, and books, is the recipient of numerous honors, including Distinguished Social Work Practitioner for the National Academies of Practice, the Knee-Wittman Award for Lifetime Achievement, and the Ida M. Cannon Award of the Society of Hospital Social work Directors, the American Hospital Association.

Gary Rosenberg, Ph.D., is the Edith J. Baerwald Professor of Community and Preventative Medicine, Chair of the Division of Social Work and Behavioral Sciences, Mount Sinai School of Medicine, and Senior Vice President of Mount Sinai NYU Health. Dr. Rosenberg is Editor-in-Chief of the peer-reviewed journal, *Social Work in Health Care.* He has written or edited nine books and is the author of over fifty articles in professional journals.

David J. Tucker, Ph.D., is Professor of Social Work, School of Social Work, University of Michigan. His scholarly areas of interest include the formation, growth, and death of organizations; the structural analysis of inter-organizational service delivery systems; and the application of macro-organizational theory to the analysis of selected social policy issues. His recent work focuses on questions about the production and validation of knowledge. Dr. Tucker's recent publications include "The Institutional Ecology of Human Service Organizations" (with J. A. C. Baum and J. Singh) and "An Ecological Study of Dynamics of Foster Home Entries."

About the Contributors

Wendy G. Winters, Ph.D., is professor of sociology in the College of Arts and Sciences at Howard University and author of *African American Mothers and Urban Schools: The Power of Participation* and co-author of *The Practice of Social Work in Schools: An Ecological Perspective.*

Introduction
Robert Morris

The terms *social* or *public welfare* (or possibly *public well-being*) are commonly used to describe a major area of American civic life, although it is seldom clearly defined. Depending on how the term is interpreted, it can be said that perhaps a fifth of the gross national product and a quarter of government budgets consist of payment for an extensive array of services and programs designed to help not only the poor but middle- and low-income working families.

Social work, as a profession, has been identified with the growth of this area of civic life, although responsibilities and roles in it are not easily summarized. Professional social workers have usually had a much broader view of their responsibilities than relieving the poor or helping the troubled and confused. They have sought to address many of the difficult social and economic conditions in modern society that form the environment in which individuals try to shape their lives: poverty, race, discrimination, inequity. These conditions are seen as causing the individual case problems the field is expected to ameliorate or remedy, but their assigned responsibilities and their training seldom go so far as tackling the basic causes of distress.

The gap between aspiration and reality remains a dilemma that continues to be a challenge to professional thinking. As the field celebrates its hundredth birthday and thinks about its future in the next century,

Introduction

the editors had planned a broad synoptic review of past and future, with articles by many surviving editors of the *Journal of Social Work* whose tenures cover major changes in a turbulent twentieth century. This proved unfeasible because of the death or illness of some editors, and even more by the almost encyclopedic task of reviewing developments in the many kinds of work to which social workers have gravitated. In the end, the editors asked a sample of social work educators and scholars to sum up their thinking.

The result is a stimulating range of viewpoints that represent the dilemmas and internal conflicts and discussions with which the field is slowly assessing (not at all systematically) where it has come to in a hundred years and where it is likely to go in the next hundred years. Although daily tasks are focused on amelioration, the aspirations persist to address the broader issues of social justice and equity.

Hopps, very broadly, and **Korr** and **Brieland,** who are more focused on welfare reform and child welfare, consider the field's concern with social justice in a world where public policy wavers between more and fewer public entitlements. They discuss persistence of interest in broad social issues in tandem with narrower definitions of case practices where the social worker is expected to deal with both.

Austin looks to the twenty-first century after examining the past history of the field, stressing that families and children are the focus for social work. While the field needs to devise new approaches to fit the coming century, it still lacks an adequate research foundation upon which to draw evidence to shape them. The approaches developed during the twentieth century were based on social reform movements of the early part of the century, but they have not performed well in the changed conditions of the later years. Thus the need for critical evidence and different concepts in order to introduce more effective means.

Morris reviews the same history from the point of view of strategies used to develop as a profession. He concludes that over time, the field, changed its focus from the individual to the environment, concentrating on the interpersonal services, but without adequate scientific evidence to influence the organizational purposes and structure for practice. In the end, the field missed opportunities to realize its aims and has, for all practical purposes, abandoned the social change (social justice) goal of its origins even though it still espouses them rhetorically.

Rehr and **Rosenberg,** dealing with health issues, are the most precise in documenting the changes in health care, the achievement of a clear role and function for social work in health services, and for the many remaining problems the field will confront as health services change under the force of technology and economics.

Winters and **Gourdine** discuss the changing world of public education, especially the variety of family, behavioral, ethnic, and economic conditions that affect the education of children. They discuss the various proposals to expand the public education system to incorporate various social service functions (without specifying social workers as the personnel), including after-school recreation programs, counseling and health services for children, family visits, and more. They argue that social workers, if they are to play a role in education in the future, as they have tried to do, equip themselves for quite different tasks that are conventional, including taking the school out to families and communities. Whether this becomes a teacher or a social work responsibility in a teacher-administered system remains unresolved.

Maluccio presents an approach to a competence-centered perspective for family and child welfare practice that relies on variously formulated human developmental educational theories but makes it clear he believes the field must do better in addressing the external social and economic factors affecting what is actually done. In the end, he too stresses that the external factors of public choice and public policy determine what the practice will achieve.

Coulton returns to the persistent challenge faced by communities, and the forces that shape a healthy physical and economic environment for all, with which social workers began their hundred years of evolution.

Iatridis considers the field's position against the backdrop of global shifts in thinking about government and the private sector, or decentralization of federal public influence in welfare. His views reflect a confrontatonal approach between two ideologies—the state as the major repository of responsibility for individual and group well-being versus the economic market as the producer of resources with which individuals can satisfy their needs equitably. Indirectly he is critical of concepts as expressed by what most social workers do and their inadequacy in coping with the massive shifts in public thinking between the two opposing views. As with the other contributors, he has no concrete suggestions to bridge the gap.

Introduction

Tucker is critical of the paradigms for practice, especially in family and child welfare and mental health, on which the field has relied. It lacks a solid core for paradigm development and remains scattered and imprecise in concept. After reviewing the literature he concludes that it has relied on a concept of ecology to find consensus about the individual/environment interaction but has lacked clarity about how social, economic, and political conditions affect both organization and practices and about how social workers can deal with such human affairs in persuasive ways. He offers a crisp view about what a true ecology of social work requires: a clear statement about the different levels or circles of analysis, which move from concept to context to policy and program. The open-ended view of the past that "anything goes" and can justify diversity in practices has proven insufficient. Abstract knowledge is the foundation of an effective profession whose function is publicly recognized. We need to separate successful practices from failed ones as measured by outcomes and not input; empirical experience reports are insufficient. At the end he asks whether social work is ready to decide what "its question is."

Epstein carries the discussion further by a thorough review of all research on outcomes of practice. He concludes that most of the research is not scientifically justified, that its claims of successful practices are not convincing, and that the handful of studies that have tried to pin down the results have found only very weak evidence of success. He argues that this lack of solid, dependable findings has frustrated social work's efforts to be effective or compelling in influencing public policy or in establishing that its work produces desired results.

In sum, the authors, surprisingly, agree on the need for a critical conclusion about where the field has come from and what its challenges are if it is to become an effective factor in achieving the social justice it avows as its aim. The articles are, by turn, pessimistic and optimistic, but in the end they offer paths that will require professional aims and the steps needed to be effective in realizing them in the future. Where the field has concentrated its efforts, as in health care, its base is most secure; in family and child welfare, however, it is often unclear. The field has been least effective in realizing its persistent emphasis on poverty and social justice as central to its practice. In education there is a new opportunity to find its way.

Changes in thinking, in shaping agreement about core knowledge, and in supporting scientifically rooted research are recurrent themes. All these changes remain rooted in the original social work aim of linking individuals in a social context, but to be effective in making the link requires more than general assertions.

The authors, taken together, reveal the achievements and the unrealized high aspirations of social work—to become the profession able to manage the junction of individuals in their most diverse economic, social, and cultural contexts. It has successively narrowed the reality of the training provided and the areas in which its members play a major role. The aim is still to become the profession addressing current economic and social needs, but it lacks the concrete next steps to begin bridging the gap between high vision and modest capacity.

Part I

Context and Evolution of Social Work

1

Social Work:
A Contextual Profession
June Gary Hopps

Introduction

The turning of a century invariably draws commentators to a review of the past and speculation about the future. The impetus is heightened by the new millennium and—for social workers—observance of our centennial as a profession.

Although social work has had a long history of concerns (for example, child welfare, poverty, and family relations), it has not developed sufficient theoretical and empirical foundations and skills to address social ills comprehensively in an effort to impact and ameliorate problems. The profession must be attuned to its context of time, place, and public awareness if it is to be effective.

Precisely because of this contextual immediacy, we cannot simply invoke history for solutions to contemporary problems. Yet as noted so often, not to learn from the mis-steps and omissions of the past is to ensure their recycling. The centenary's Janus moment provides an opportunity to compare and contrast our circumstances with those of our founders, to note the benchmarks of progress and, most important, to take a candid look not only at the gaps and needs that invite rededicated action, but also at the radical changes in our world that demand major rethinking.

At first glance, the scope and complexity of conditions at the end of the nineteenth century, which convinced the reform-minded that traditional approaches were inadequate and that the times called for a new, interlocking set of insights and skills, bear uncanny similarities to our own.

The settlement house founders, family visitors, union organizers, "muckrakers," and community workers who formed the nascent social work community attacked the negatives in each scenario, exposed injustices, and advocated for those in need. They also wrote knowledgeably and movingly on social structures and types of responses that could ease or prevent recurrence of the suffering and waste they confronted daily.[1] Much of this century's progress was rooted in their efforts. Yet merely to list the topics, let alone the more specific housing, health, job, and education issues entwined with them, reflects our own experience all too clearly and raises fundamental questions.

Does the continuity or repetition of these problems a century apart indicate that they are, together with the underlying attitudes and triggers associated with them, simply intrinsic to human nature and impervious to remediation? Have reform movements themselves failed to assess the full dimension of the problems? Is their apparent intractability a function of successful efforts to eviscerate reform? (It does not require conspiracy theory to recognize that vested interests play off less powerful groups against each other to maintain or strengthen the status quo and retain power for particular in-groups.[2]) Can research throw further light on historical patterns?

Again it is our primary task to focus on what makes today's apparent déjà vu different from the previous incarnations. Does the growth in scale, as well as the rapidity of change, engender a difference in degree so great as to be a difference in kind? What aspects and dimensions of seemingly perennial threats to social balance and well-being can we approach in innovative and more sustainable ways? Reexamining some of the "common" themes a century apart clarifies the challenges to American society as we have known it, as it is changing, and as social work itself must change to be an effective agent of change.

With the end of the 1800s, not only cities but small towns were confronting shifts from a preeminently Anglo-Saxon population to polyglot ones; from a rural outlook to all the implications of a new age of industry, an unprecedented source of energy in electricity and new modes of transportation in the automobile and soon the plane. The twentieth century was also the first to bring world wars. A slower agricultural economy gave way to excitement, uncertainty, and a frenzied pace, to time lines and stop watches. Capitalism and industrial expansion were powerful forces affecting community as well as individual life. The parallels are striking as we prepare for the dawning of the twenty-first century and the impact of electronic technologies, a global village and marketplace, and unprecedented expansion of wealth for some juxtaposed with increasingly inescapable poverty for others.

The Paradox of Prosperity and Inequality

One of the underlying phenomena common to both eras is the country's ambivalence about wealth and inequality. American society expressed from its founding a contempt for excessive luxury, for the abuses of wealth and degrading treatment of the poor that characterized the European monarchies. The pioneer and entrepreneurial spirit would create a new median of productivity and comfort that would preclude the extremes common to the Old World, but this self-image was compromised in the Gilded Age. At the present time, we have apparent economic and job growth, coupled with the lowest inflation in forty years. At the same time there is the troubling reality that those at the low end of the economic spectrum are not connected to or benefiting from society's general prosperity.

In the course of the twentieth century the country flirted with progressivism, was impacted by World War I, the boom of the Roaring Twenties and economic chaos of the 1930s, enacted Social Security and other legislation as a hedge against financial insecurity, and rebuilt the economy during and after World War II, only to "discover" real poverty in the 1960s.[3]

Again, the important distinction is that this poverty still persists even in the face of unprecedented growth, and there seem to be no programs helping those below the poverty line achieve greater incomes and a better quality of life.[4] While highly educated entrepreneurs, managers, and stock holders are enjoying good fortune, the "faces at the bottom of the well" are experiencing manifestly poor fortune. The problem is compounded by a lack of nontechnological employment opportunities, the inability of certain groups to find and hold jobs,[5] and the absence of bargaining power due to poor education and low status. Not coincidentally, a deliberate policy approach has championed laissez-faire economics as evidenced by deregulation of many industries (airlines, trucking, telecommunication, railroads), union busting, wholesale reliance on imported manufactured goods, growing disregard for the need for and importance of safety nets, erosion of the value of wages,[6] and devaluation of the quality of child care and care providers.

It also cannot be denied that part of the poverty problem is caused by the long-term effects of racial discrimination, still experienced by many, especially the traditional U.S. minorities identified by dark skin: African Americans, American Indians, Puerto Ricans, and Mexican Americans. Reflecting on abandoned nineteenth century reconstruction initiatives to improve the lot of former slaves, W. E. B. DuBois noted in *The Souls of Black Folk*[7] that "the problem of the 20th century, is the problem of the color line . . ."

> "The problem of the twentieth century is the problem of the Color-line . . ."

The consequences of three centuries of discrimination still impact many lives, manifest, for example, by the fact that the number of African American males who were in college in 1995 (556,000) was almost matched by the number in prison (511,000).[8] The ripple effect is visible in the family life of millions of children who are increasingly trapped at a level of poverty that isolates them from opportunity because of an absent, unemployed, or even incarcerated father. Communities and institutions are hard pressed to provide the moral foundations that young people are expected to get through family life and education, which is also deteriorating.[9] In fact, child poverty is one of the most pernicious, unsolved problems of our time. What contributions social workers have made to the welfare of children in practice is one of the issues highlighted in this volume. Social work's role as the major professional player in the child welfare field will be increasingly challenged, unless we heed the need for change.

The Structure, Role, and Function of Families

The most basic social institution, the family, has changed. In the mid-nineties, 77 percent of families were headed by married couples. This represents a shift from the 85 percent that characterized the late nineteenth century.[10] The two-parent family in which the husband is the breadwinner and the wife the homemaker is not only no longer the norm but for many, neither a hope nor an ideal. "Alternative" styles now dominate, including the two-parent, two-earner family, the single-parent family (due to divorce or out-of-wedlock births), the blended family, the gay or lesbian family, and the common-law marriage with family. Even though the rate of increase in these pluralistic styles has slowed, their members indicate that people are significantly less affected either by traditional norms or by social stigma, and create family structures that suit their individual needs. Many others now simply defer marriage or remain single.[11]

The role and function of the family have changed as well, with much less time for nurturing and care giving. Though women are disproportionately low-wage workers, they constituted 57.4 percent of the labor force in 1991, and predictions are that they will constitute 63.5 percent by 2005.[12] Obviously there is even less time for child rearing or caregiving to elderly parents, roles traditionally and currently assumed largely by women.[13]

The formal social welfare system now being dismantled was developed with the expectation that it would function merely to supplement strong primary systems, such as the family and the neighborhood. The reality is that the family, in whatever form, is becoming increasingly unable either to give the traditional range of nurturing and care or to provide for economic necessities. Compounding the situation is a government that, with societal approval, has become less willing and less able to provide the financial supports and services that many contemporary families need.

Families in marginalized racial and ethnic groups have experienced a particularly sharp transition from the two-parent to the single-parent family, and poverty is a major challenge for them.[14] The rates of poverty are higher for women who live alone or with nonrelatives in every age group. Further, when a single woman heads a family with children, the chances for poverty increase substantially, one in two versus one in four for male-headed families.[15] Recently it has been reported that the birth rate for unmarried black women of all ages is at its lowest point in forty years, with the decline attributed to sex education, greater reliance on contraception, and emphasis on abstention, all conducted by community groups. The report is significant to national policy, since one of the arguments about causes of poverty in the African American community relates to the birth rate among unmarried mothers.[16] There is currently an increase in the number of children born to single white women resembling what occurred thirty years earlier among African Americans and spurring some concern about the possible emergence of a white "underclass" identified with young, welfare-dependent single parents.[17] Such shifts and changes in the role of family suggest that women are now forced to rely more on their own independence than on government support to buttress personal efforts. This is particularly troubling because these women share meager resources with their children.[18]

The social work profession must prepare to address needs of women who do not have the government supports that were available for the past sixty years. If these clients are to escape the cycle of poverty, this preparation should include a focus on education and employment opportunities in addition to the traditional clinical and macrointerventions. How to multiply options in a period of shrinking resources and empathy will test the ingenuity and influence of social workers.

Impact of New Waves of Immigration and Resettlement

Yet another contextual issue to which social workers are expected to respond is the range of demographic changes influenced by the extensive resettlement of displaced people, both immigrants and refugees. This cohort has nearly doubled since 1970.[19] The Center for Immigration Studies reported in 1988 that the greatest immigration in U.S. history was occurring in that decade.[20] As with the influx a century ago, displaced people have not been universally well received.[21] Established groups in various regions of the country and the general population are having to deal with new cultures, languages, and value systems (including, ironically, a previously respected emphasis on the extended family and the collective good that have since been outrun by individualism in our history) and—what calls for the most significant adjustment—to interact more and more with people of color.

Although refugees and displaced persons are motivated to work and improve their status, they are often viewed as siphoning off jobs, depressing wages, consuming public assistance, and draining social services. In reality, such perceptions are ill-founded.[22] Studies demonstrate that displaced persons are not as reliant on the U.S. welfare system as are native-born citizens. They tend to use kinship and informal networks more than formal supports and, when they do resort to public assistance, they view it as a step to self-sufficiency, which they frequently achieve within five years of arrival.[23] These facts notwithstanding, members of immigrant groups continue to be the targets of violence by those whose fragile toehold on identity and financial security appear weakened even further by the magnitude of social and economic change.[24]

Violence

How to prevent and manage violence has been a perennial issue for over two hundred years of national sovereignty. Compared to most other industrial countries, ours has been a violent society owing in part to the traditions associated with moving into a wild and difficult frontier, coupled with a diverse population (and a large number of poor people). The rate of violent crime has been higher than in those countries from which many have emigrated.[25]

Urban riots, which caused much concern in the twentieth century, have been a periodic part of the American scene since colonial times. In the latter part of the century, ethnic and racial problems developed into riots in many cities.[26] Earlier in the century, cities were affected by violence and corruption associated with prohibition. More recently, there has been a strong association between violence and illegal drug activity and labor racketeering.[27]

In addition to collective violence, small group and individual violence tears at the societal fabric to which the country and the profession must respond more effectively. Despite prolific studies on all types, problems are increasing in many spheres, though there is a modest decline in others, for example, homicide rates. One anomaly, however, is that juvenile crime, despite declines in overall homicide, ranks as the second highest cause of death among young people, and death from gun wounds is the leading killer of teenage males.

The Anglo-Saxon and successive white ethnic populations have often resisted persons of color, many of whom have been victims of hate crimes by the Ku Klux Klan, Aryan Nation, and skinheads[28] This phenomenon has been growing in this and other Western countries, as well as less known and organized groups.

Another destructive and complex area is family violence, although the actual extent is hard to determine. It is often cloaked in secrecy because of shame or because victims fear reprisal from the attacker.[29] While elder, child, and spousal abuse (as well as sibling violence) appear to be more prevalent, it is child abuse that has been more carefully documented in the last half of the twentieth century.

Yet a third area of concern is violence in the workplace, where much of the hostility is directed toward employers. The numbers for both men and women are escalating, with 1,000 people being murdered at work annually and millions physically attacked or threatened.[30]

This society knows that minorities are at greatest risk of violent victimization and death. (In the last decade of the century, blacks and Hispanics were 41 percent and 32 percent, respectively, more likely to be victims than Caucasians.) Homicide rates are also highest for minorities. While less is known about perpetrators than victims, both tend to share demographic profiles: largely male and disproportionately minority.

Social workers are concerned with all forms of violence and their cause, particularly those that have both psychosocial and socioeconomic ramifications. Aggressive and violent behaviors seem to be learned responses to frustration as well as cultivated for perceived goal achievement, but the role of models in both instances is critical. These are too readily available, and they are observed in family life, peer groups, mass media, pornography, and in the neighborhood environment.[31]

One of the hotly debated issues going into the millennium centers on whether more stringent gun laws or more widely legalized possession by ordinary citizens is the greater deterrent to crime. Baffling gun control proponents is the renewed argument for *More Guns, Less Crime.*[32] The argument inflames the discussion by maintaining that gunmen are more likely to attack individuals whom they view as weak (that is, unprotected) and that states enacting "shall-issue-laws" for guns have drastically reduced multiple-victim shooting episodes.[33] The extension of this reasoning would suggest that certain personnel in schools (and presumably other types of institutions in which there have been several recent multiple killings, such as social service agencies and hospitals) should have quick and ready access to weapons as a way of thwarting attacks. Given public frustration, the idealized western pop-cultural symbol of the "equalizer," and beliefs in exaggerated individual freedoms, the proposal may well become a rallying point. Professionals either have to pay attention to or be objects of the trend, as so many of our positions (both in terms of ethical stances and employment) are involved, it is impossible to remain neutral.

The Challenge of Racial and Gender Diversity and Leadership

At the turn of the nineteenth century, the predominately influential population in the United States was Anglo-Saxon, faced with adjustment to new ethnic groups and unresolved longtime color issues. At the turn of the twentieth century, the nation is in an uneasy embrace with a significantly more diverse racial and ethnic polyglot, that poses challenges in numbers and shifts in power structures. Several prominent cities no longer have a racial minority, as such, but a people-of-color population in the majority. Detroit, Los Angeles, and Gary, Indiana, as well as other urban centers, have or are approaching "minority" majorities. The results are political structures in which persons of colors hold top elective municipal and state legislative positions. Large peoples-of-color districts also send representatives to the U.S. Congress, where many have been in office long enough to hold key committee chairmanships. People-of-color communities are now in a position to insist on powerful executive appointments by governors and even the president. As much as proportions have changed, the growing numbers of minorities have not resulted in comparable everyday political clout and certainly not in economic power. Many of the gains noted above were the result of the prayer and protest model of change used by civil rights groups in the last half of the twentieth century. We can expect the goals of prosperity and local policy to be added to the model in the twenty-first century.[34]

In addition to people of color, women—marginalized as a group from public power in virtually all cultures—have demanded recognition and sought it mostly in the workplace. In the latter part of the twentieth century women challenged the "pink ghetto" and "glass ceiling," demanding more opportunities and respect as equals. Although the majority of women have faced discrimination based on gender rather than race, they have won protection through the laws achieved by the long civil rights struggle against the color bar and have benefited from the affirmative action policies now under attack. White males may be the world's numerical minority in comparison to all women as well as to men of color but they still hold political and economic sway. As with holders of power in any venue, many are willing to "give" a little, but few would give it up. There is much anecdotal report of conscious alliances to retain white male hegemony in corporate and political circles, but little documentation and less public awareness or discussion of the growing discordance between presumed ideals and actual practice. While individual patriarchy may not seem as overwhelming as in the past, it is structural patriarchy that must receive greater focus if issues of inequality and justice are to be resolved.[35]

An emphasis on ways in which power sharing can be seen as expanding the well-being rather than simply threatening that of the current holders is one that needs to be developed now if progress is to be genuine in the early decades of the new century. The setting for this recognition and debate will be largely in the workplace, including the political arena. Except for those born into great wealth, work has been central to class, status, and the mental as well as physical well-being of Americans. It has even been considered noble, but that image cannot survive if job categories continue to be structured and designated by race and sex.[36] We will also need to confront the continuing devaluation of women in the home when their caregiving work is neither reflected, valued, nor credited toward Social Security or accumulated resources that can lead to power.[37]

Power sharing in the workplace has not been sufficiently addressed and keeps blacks, other people of color, and women marginalized.[38] Women are not immune from oppressing other women, since in hierarchical organizations those who manage to obtain top positions can—and too often must—exploit those in lower positions if they are to retain their own. The same observation holds for women who employ domestics and child care workers. Women of color often sense a distancing from majority women who they feel exclude or distort their experiences.[39] Acknowledging such distinctions makes us more aware of the powerlessness that is associated with poor work options or the absence of work.

Historically, practitioners have overlooked the centrality of work in defining the extent of clients' self-esteem and life satisfaction.[40] This omission can keep practitioners and the profession out of an important political debate. It can also help ensure low rank and benefits for practitioners who are mostly nonminority women carrying out administrative policies of mostly nonminority males. Contrary to its goals, and however inadvertently, the profession helps to prolong the marginalization of a portion of the population and, therefore, needs to consider the extent to which it contributes to it.

Reexamination of the task ahead is not just for clinicians. For the future, we can expect marginalized people to seek out new paths for organizing and joining unions as a way to ameliorate their dismal workplace status. This presents an opportunity for the profession to use its macro-knowledge and skills to help facilitate change. For professional women, mostly Caucasian, the task involves transcending old status perceptions (salary/benefits, higher positions) and embracing the concerns of the poor and marginalized.

One cannot predict in the decades ahead whether schools of social work will be educating people of color in numbers sufficient to carry out the needed change strategy for improving work opportunities. Despite several decades of calls by the Council on Social Work Education for greater diversity, the response does not bode well. In most schools of social work, minorities comprise less than 25 percent of the graduating classes. This is not to suggest that only "minorities" can be of assistance to minorities, but it is one more demonstration of the need for cooperation by all in working for the good of the whole.

13

Increasing Longevity and National Goals

Another dramatic difference from a century ago is life expectancy, which was forty-seven years in 1900 and is now nearly eighty. The largest age cohort in America (those born from the mid-1940s to the mid-1960s) can expect still greater longevity and are demanding that the country give major attention to health and health care.[41] Hi-tech medicine is already prolonging aging beyond our ethical consensus for relevant decision-making on the meaning and quality of life. Questions have multiplied about the cost of quality and how best to manage the health care needs of individuals. Cost containment is a highly volatile issue posing ethical dilemmas about who gets what, when, for how long, and at whose expense.[42]

So far, longer life has meant extension of its most fragile phase rather than its most productive. For a society that values doing over being, the distinction is critical. Elders are viewed increasingly in economic and primarily negative terms, the healthier ones as holding on to jobs that prevent younger persons from advancing and the more sickly as leaving the ranks of productivity and multiplying the burdens on their juniors. The highly politicized and even misleading debate on proportions of expected reserves, contributors, and recipients for the future of Social Security polarizes discussion and threatens to contaminate intergenerational relations. Social work research can help restore perspective here.

As medical breakthroughs extend life, the range of choices and decisions multiplies; whose life is valued in society and who makes decisions regarding the access and distribution of medical goods and services are critical issues that influence all other systems.

Social workers, among others, have rapidly shortening time to influence perspectives on longevity, the ways it can be viewed as contributing to a different kind of productive opportunity,[43] the relational quality of human interactions, and a broad understanding of community that could be enhanced by those who now fear they will be seen only in negative economic terms. Critical to any resolution of this issue is the operating definition of productivity. If human value is limited to commercial utility alone, then the tendency will continue to reduce all considerations to material goods, bottom lines, and profits. Just as Oscar Wilde a century ago chided those "who know the price of everything and the value of nothing," we can challenge those who limit people's social worth to productivity for profit rather than for quality of human life.

More mature individuals are now, and will continue to be, available for compassionate as well as simply commercial roles. What this can mean for countering the mechanistic trends in schooling, medicine, social service delivery, and communities at large invites exploration.

Caring roles provide not just a mechanism for material help to others in need, but offer useful channels to apply knowledge and relational competencies in unique ways that make the process itself life enhancing.

Recognizing Spirituality

Social work has a substantial foundation in concepts of spirituality and, historically, in organized religion. The profession has been moving away from this orientation for some time. More recently, however, there have been growing tendencies, apparently responding to our oversecularized, impersonal, and corporate world, that challenge us to give more concerted thought to the spiritual needs of individuals and communities. This broadened awareness should not be confused with the fundamentalism of the religious right, with which it often has been in sharp contrast.[44] It has not been based on ideological conservatism or exclusivity but rather on greater fellowship and acceptance of all human beings. Spirituality has been defined as "the underlying dimension of consciousness which strives for meaning, union with the universe and all things. It extends to the experience of the transcendent and those beyond us."[45]

The desire to realize one's own nature, fully, and the need to connect with an entity greater than the individual self are two fundamental aspects of human nature.[46] These tendencies are recognized unevenly in Western psychology (with the focus on the individual) and Eastern psychology (with the focus on being part of a larger entity).[47] The effort to integrate these within the person and among cultures is seen as related to spiritual awareness.[48] Increasingly, social workers view spirituality as an essential component in the healing process.[49] Often, family and community supports are mobilized in the healing process in work with several diverse ethnic groups.[50]

The Road Ahead

In the late nineteenth century through the early twentieth, the Progressives and incipient social work professionals were among the few keenly aware of the irrevocable alterations to society following the industrial North's defeat of the agricultural South, the closing of the frontier, and the growth of urbanism as the dominant way of life. As our fin de siècle comparison indicates, however, neither they nor we foresaw how quickly or completely the subsequent social welfare mind set and monumental legislation designed to end the old inequities could be reversed. Child and sweatshop labor has simply been internationalized. Criminal trial of children as adults, thought to have been ended by Dorothea Dix ninety-nine years ago, is being reinstated. Immigrants are denied food, as are many indigenous poor. The mentally ill are returned to the streets, and other aspects of an 1890s déjà vu are too apt.

The pressing contextual concerns identified earlier will weigh heavily on the profession in the coming century. Collectively, too many demonstrate a decline in the fabric and "spirit of the American community."[51] What has to be undertaken in the years ahead is not just a reexamination of our roots and paradigms, but a commitment to pull together forces that redefine and rebuild community.

Not only compassion but enlightened self-interest and an awareness of fundamental human interdependence argue against the renewed indifference to the poor and to long-term economic reality. The cultivation of individualism has dulled that awareness. Social work's understanding of the necessary interplay of genuine autonomy and community can contribute greatly to the needed arguments. Asking people to surrender cherished ideas, perceived advantages, and hard-earned wages in the interest of an elusive equity is a formidable task. Arrayed against financial and physical forces, social workers and their allies have only the power of persuasion at their command. Authenticity is key.

The arena for decision making has changed radically. International conglomerates with no community loyalties, elective mandate, or accountability can intimidate or destabilize most governments. Few nation-states have the power or the political will to put the commonwealth, much less their neediest citizens, first. As the sensed but unfocused economic anxiety grows around the world, demagoguery and tribalism tend to drown out reasoned discourse.

How to reign in the irresponsibly destructive forces and maintain the desired economic benefits that accompany advanced economies while reembedding them and helping them to become more aware of and sensitive to undergirding cultures, is not only a central political task but a necessity. If social workers are to have a place at the drafting tables rather than the triage rooms, we will have to (1) incorporate in our decision making and practice far more in-depth study of economic realities that until now we have left to interpretation by others, and (2) develop new levels of sophistication in presenting our knowledge to a media-saturated and distrustful public. To be credible, that knowledge must evidence theoretical and experiential validity, backed by research that is relevant to the lives and quandaries of the real people being asked to fund and respond to it.

It may still be possible to help redirect and move to positive change, wrenching changes in our pet theories and priorities. How to maintain services to those desperately in need now, while mobilizing for a creatively new systems approach, calls for much wider cooperation within the profession as well as with other disciplines. The questions preparatory to practical engagement are largely ones of vision, ethics, commitment, and will. In their absence, what kind of society will we be existing in and fronting for—if there is to be a social work profession in the new millennium?

2

Greeting the Second Century: A Forward Look From a Historical Perspective

David M. Austin

The end of the first century of social work is indeed an occasion to look back at highlights of the history of social work and social work education. But the most important lesson to be drawn from an examination of history is that *we can never reenact history.* Whether the events of human history represent "progress," or some other form of social process, it is clear that the present and the future are completely different from the past in many important ways. The hundred years of social work that are being celebrated in the late 1990s tell an exciting and dramatic tale. But although the past is precursor to the future, *it is not the future.*

I begin this analysis by examining the emergence of social work—one hundred years ago—and the characteristics of the system of "welfare capitalism" that provided a framework within which social work education, and the organized profession of social work, emerged. I then look at some of the key developments in social work over the past half century, developments that I and other "social work pioneers" have taken part in. Finally, I examine critical issues that face social work at the beginning of a second century.

Presented at the National Professional Conference of the National Association of Social Workers, Baltimore, Maryland, October 1997.

The Beginnings

During the nineteenth century two competing paradigms emerged for the organization of the social welfare dimensions within industrial societies. One paradigm involved a strongly centralized system of government and a regulated marketplace economy. The second paradigm involved a central government with limited authority and a laissez-faire approach to economic development.

The first paradigm provided the framework for developments in Europe where there was a history of strong central governments, with extensive governmental regulations and control of economic development, under kings and emperors and also under parliamentary governments. Within this paradigm national social welfare systems emerged across Europe, beginning in the 1800s, designed, in part, to ensure loyalty to traditional national governments against the revolutionary challenges of Marxism and communism. In its most highly developed form under democratic, parliamentary governments this pattern of social welfare has often been referred to as "the welfare state."

However, there was an alternative paradigm, set forth by Adam Smith in *The Wealth of Nations*.[1] Adam Smith challenged the concept of governmental regulation of the economy and argued that a freer, laissez-faire marketplace economy could result in greater economic productivity and thus greater economic benefits for the general populace. What emerged in the United States was a pattern of limited and fragmented governmental authority, a dynamic laissez-faire marketplace economy with a very limited structure of governmental regulation, and a diverse, decentralized, nonuniform pattern of social welfare. This social welfare paradigm has been labeled "welfare capitalism." It is this framework of welfare capitalism that shaped the initial development of social welfare and social work in the United States and is still shaping the most recent developments in social policy at the end of the twentieth century.

There were two important dynamics in the last half of the 1800s when the pattern of social welfare began to take shape in the United States. The most important was the arrival of millions of immigrants from Europe, mostly crowded into cities that were overwhelmed by their numbers and their diversity. One result was the political control of big cities by political "bosses" whose power was based on the large number of new voters,

19

and the jobs and other "benefits" provided to those voters through control of the municipal finances.

The second dynamic was a broad-based middle-class movement for social and political reform—the Progressive movement. In part, this reform movement was a reaction to widespread corruption in both business and politics. And in part, it was a response to desperate living conditions among the immigrants, particularly in large cities, as well as a response to the increasing popularity among many of the immigrant populations of revolutionary socialist ideas coming from Europe.[2] One important characteristic of this social reform movement was the attention given to conditions affecting women and children,[3] issues which the rhetoric of Marxist socialism did not deal with.

But another very important characteristic of the Progressive Movement was that it included very little attention to the conditions facing colored citizens throughout the United States, including segregation and discrimination, and murder by lynching throughout the South. W. E. B. DuBois, a highly visible leader in the newly formed National Association for the Advancement of Colored People, withdrew from the Progressive Party convention in 1912 because the convention, including Jane Addams, who was a delegate, refused to support a resolution affirming the status of Negroes as citizens (for fear of alienating white working-class voters in the South). The Progressive movement also largely ignored the economic conditions of white tenant farmers in southern states and the ways in which the states of the South were treated as a colonial territory to be exploited for the economic benefit of the expanding economy in the North.

The combination of massive immigration and the Progressive Movement response created the conditions that led to the beginnings of social work education and the organized profession of social work.[4] The precipitating event was the economic collapse of the early 1890s, which created widespread unemployment and misery among big city families. The beginnings of social work and social work education in that period are often identified with individual pioneers: Zilpha Smith, Mary Richmond, Jeffrey Brackett, Jane Addams, Edward Devine, Porter Lee, Sophonisba Breckinridge, Julia Lathrop, Florence Kelley, Grace and Edith Abbott. These were outstanding and creative individuals, each of whom made a very distinctive contribution to the beginnings of social welfare and social work. But it is important to recognize that the beginnings of organized social work were actually shaped by larger sets of social forces.

One set of forces came from the development of the voluntary nonprofit philanthropic sector, created by the wide variety of religious communities and by the leaders of the business community. This development was represented by the organization of the National Conference of Charities and Correction, which began meeting in the 1870s.[5] It brought civic leaders and organizational managers together to share information about the management of voluntary charity agencies and other nonprofit service organizations as well as state and local custodial institutions. Social work as an occupation and social work education emerged in response to the staffing needs of these service organizations. The financial support of social work and social work education came from the wealthy families and business leaders who had created the institutions of private philanthropy, including private foundations. In large part the development of private philanthropy, consistent with the model of welfare capitalism, was intended to prevent the development of large-scale, tax-supported, politically controlled governmental social welfare programs.

A second set of forces affecting the development of social welfare came from the emergence of the social sciences as a part of the academic community.[6] The development of the social sciences was supported by the formation of the American Social Science Association (ASSA) in the 1860s. Within the emerging social sciences—history, economics, political science, and sociology—there was a concern with applying social science theory to contemporary social problems, particularly poverty, pauperism, and crime. There was particular interest in the concept of social insurance, which had its beginnings in Germany, as the answer to the problem of income risks and household poverty. A number of the early American social scientists also studied in Germany. For a time, the leading center of graduate studies in applied social science was in Baltimore at Johns Hopkins University.[7] This development of the social sciences was strongly supported by Daniel Gilman, the first president of the university and one of the founders of ASSA. Johns Hopkins was also the first university in the United States to adopt the German model of university-based graduate studies and the research-based Ph.D.

A third set of forces came from the establishment of private women's colleges (particularly in the Northeast), together with the expanding pattern of coeducation in the new public universities in the Midwest[8] and the expanding participation of educated women in public life. One result was an increasing number of educated young women looking for personal career opportunities other than the Victorian model of housewife and mother. Many of these women identified with the social reform causes of the Progressive movement. Since they were excluded from the traditional professions that many of their brothers were entering (law, medicine, the ministry, business) some of them took jobs in the voluntary, philanthropic, nonprofit service agencies. They created a new profession, called social work, which was both an occupation—a career and part of the Progressive movement for social reform—and a *calling*.

These three sets of forces came together around the beginnings of social work education, which was created before there was an organized profession of social work.[9] The wealthy leaders of voluntary, philanthropic organizations were looking for people to staff their organizations, particularly during the economic crisis of the 1890s. A potential pool of such persons was emerging from the women's colleges, most of whose students came from well-to-do families. The academic social scientists were developing a model of applied social science graduate education focused on theories of systematic social reform, including social insurance, within a capitalist society.[10] Their reform proposals fit the U.S. model of religiously motivated welfare capitalism.[11] The ultimate result of the initiatives of the applied social scientists was the Social Security Act of 1935 and, in turn, substantial federal involvement, for the first time, in the diverse and fragmented system of welfare capitalism.

Social welfare in the United States, and the profession of social work, developed within the framework of social reform welfare capitalism. Moreover, largely because of the financial base for those developments, social welfare and social work developed as part of the more conservative wing of social reform welfare capitalism rather than as part of the more radical and confrontational wing, which included the Socialist Party, the labor unions, and the suffragists.

These initial developments resulted in a series of dilemmas that became part of the development of social welfare institutions and social work during the twentieth century. One of the dilemmas involved the tension between the role of social workers as socially motivated organizational employees, primarily working in voluntary nonprofit service organizations controlled by the patrons of social work, and social workers as independent, educated, career-oriented women and autonomous professional specialists guided by general principles of professional practice.

A second dilemma involved the tension between addressing the problems of poverty and other social welfare concerns through individual, case-by-case services, dealing primarily with women and children (that is, "maternalistic" approaches) or addressing such problems through public policy initiatives dealing with broad labor force and employment issues (that is, "paternalistic" approaches) as advocated by the applied social scientists.

The third dilemma involved the tension between the concept of a comprehensive social welfare system established through governmental action, based on the emerging European model, and the concept of a diverse, decentralized, nongovernmental social welfare system dependent largely on the charitable initiatives of individual well-to-do citizens.

These dilemmas, which are reflected in the early pattern of social welfare and social work, have had an influence throughout the twentieth century, and are likely to continue to be significant for the future of social work.

Initial Development of Social Welfare and Social Work

The initial pattern of social welfare and social work included a number of distinctive characteristics:

• The development of the voluntary social welfare philanthropic organizations was primarily a response to conditions affecting women and children. The new social workers, who were mostly women, dealt primarily with women and children.[12] These early social workers worked in a variety of settings: charity organizations, early private child protection and foster care agencies, orphanages, out-patient clinics of privately financed general hospitals, psychiatric hospitals, and settlement houses.

• The development of voluntary social welfare organizations took place primarily in large urban centers in the Northeast and Midwest.

They were, at best, only a very limited response to the widespread problems of slum housing, contagious disease, family destitution, child abuse and exploitation, death and disability from industrial accidents, drunkenness, prostitution, and the economic exploitation of workers, in spite of the claims of such writers as Martin Olasky in *The Tragedy of American Compassion*[13] that this early pattern of voluntary initiatives is the only type of "social welfare" system that is needed in the United States today. In the South the social welfare initiatives that did develop were consistent with pervasive patterns of racial segregation. Rural communities throughout the United States had no systematic form of social welfare protection other than assistance provided through individual churches, largely for their own members.

• From the beginning, the basic services provided by social workers were services to individuals and families. "Social workers everywhere deal with individual human beings, deal with them most often under adversity, or surrounded by grave difficulties, victims of disease, poverty, appetite, harsh industrial conditions, or unfavorable living conditions but still individuals, grouped by nature and providence into families. . . ."[14] Organizational executives and members of agency boards of directors carried the active roles in social policy advocacy.

• Settlements were different from other social work settings in several important ways.[15] They were neighborhood focused, an early version of the "target areas" of urban antipoverty and economic development programs. The settlement focus was on social conditions within a central city community rather than on individual family situations. They were largely staffed by short-term, middle-class volunteers rather than paid staff. Settlement house leaders—head workers—were an important part of the early social welfare community and in some of the social reform movements.[16] However, they were not, from the beginning, a significant factor in either the institutional development of social work education (except in Chicago) or of social work as an organized profession.

• The women who were the new social case workers faced daunting conditions. They were employed in service organizations controlled by businessmen as board members, particularly by the board president, who was often the largest financial contributor. Many of those who completed graduate social work education and had careers as social workers were single women. Without birth control, middle-class women had a choice of either marrying and being almost immediately faced with the responsibilities of household management and child rearing, or remaining unmarried and childless. The men completing graduate studies in social work could combine career and family.

As single, employed professional women, the early social workers were outside the general social norms defining the role of women in American society. They were protected, to some degree, because they were viewed as carrying out maternal and nurturing functions, dealing with the problems of women and children.[17]

• The response of the employed social workers to their vulnerable position was to organize. Although social work began as an organization-based occupation, the diversity of employment settings required an organizing strategy separate from any single work setting. Employed social workers, many of whom had known each other as fellow students in college, and indeed, may have traveled in the same social circles as they were growing up, formed local social work clubs. Looking at the examples of medicine, law, the clergy, and academic professors, they began talking about social work as a "profession."

A great deal of attention has been given to the 1915 speech of Abraham Flexner at the National Conference of Charities and Correction,[18] which attacked the idea that social work was a "profession," as the spark that created the movement toward formal professional organization.[19] However, a careful reading of other reports at the 1915 conference[20]—the only one of the annual conferences at which there was a special section on social work education—makes it clear that the idea of the systematic organization of social work education and of the promotion of recognition for social work as a "profession" had already been extensively discussed.[21]

One of the most important sources of support for professional organization were social workers with positions in psychiatric hospitals and general hospitals[22] and the "visiting teachers" in public schools. Working in host environments, they were particularly vulnerable to being treated by members of male-dominated professional specialties as "go-fers," the in-between service linkers that Flexner had described, rather than as professional colleagues. It was the medical social workers (1918) and the visiting teachers (1919) who organized at a national level before there was a general membership association of social workers, the American Association of Social Workers (1921).

Schools of social work organized to create a national identity (1919)[23] and later adopted standards of accreditation to avoid being absorbed by academic social science departments. Practicing social workers banded together not to create an "elite" status but to establish an identity separate from any single employment setting and to gain respect from doctors, lawyers, professors, and judges—in many instances their own brothers, cousins, uncles, and nephews—and from the businessmen on the boards of directors in the social agencies where they were employed.

• From the beginning, the development of social work education and of social work as a practicing profession was shaped by the pattern of gender roles in the structure of society in the United States.[24] This was most clearly reflected in the separation that developed between education for social work practice and education for social policy analysis. The academic community in the last half of the nineteenth century was a community of men, except for the women's colleges. The development of graduate studies in applied social sciences in the universities involved men as faculty and as students, initially at Johns Hopkins and then in universities across the Midwest, as the Johns Hopkins social science faculty were scattered.[25]

Professional education in social work began as training programs attached to women's colleges, or programs that were initiated outside of the academic community but later became attached to universities as distinct units that protected the position of women with professional experience as social work educators. There were four classical examples of the way in which this separated, gendered structure developed: in Baltimore, Boston, New York, and Chicago. In each instance there was a separation between an emphasis on professional training for hands-on practice, primarily for women, and an emphasis on social research, social theory, and proposals for social reform, including social insurance, in male academic social science departments.[26]

• Baltimore had unusual significance both in the beginnings of graduate studies in applied social science and in the beginnings of social work education.[27] Male social science faculty members who were responsible for the graduate "social science seminary" at Johns Hopkins were members of the board of the Baltimore Charity Organization Society, where Mary Richmond became the general secretary and developed a systematic training program for employed staff and volunteers. Her training program was built around a medical model of individual case diagnosis rather than around general social science theory. Her predecessor as general secretary was Amos Warner, a social science doctoral student at Johns Hopkins. Graduate social science students were encouraged to volunteer at the charity agency to become acquainted with community conditions. Yet Mary Richmond was never invited to attend or to make a presentation to the all-male Johns Hopkins social science "seminary."[28]

• In Boston the initial training program for social workers was cosponsored by Simmons College and Harvard University. In 1916 President Eliot of Harvard withdrew the Harvard participation on the grounds that the person-to-person social casework being taught was not an appropriate activity for men, and moreover that men are not likely to be good at it.[29] In 1920 Dr. Richard Cabot (also known as the originator of medical social work) became the head of an applied social science, "social ethics," program at Harvard. The Kennedy School at Harvard represents the conceptual descendant of that social ethics/applied social science program.

• In New York the first full-time director of the one-year training program for social workers, appointed in 1907, was Dr. Samuel McCune Lindsey, an "applied" economics professor on leave from Columbia University.[30] By 1910 it became apparent to Mary Richmond, by that time a member of the staff of the newly established Russell Sage foundation, and John Glenn, the first executive of the foundation (a social welfare leader from Baltimore), that Dr. Lindsey's model for the curriculum (primarily applied social science) was not what they considered appropriate for the preparation of front-line social workers.[31] They complained to Edward Devine, the COS executive. Dr. Lindsey returned to Columbia, and Devine took over leadership of the program. It was extended to two years with an emphasis on social casework, the use of community agencies as training laboratories, and the employment of experienced social workers as full-time faculty members.[32]

• In Chicago Edith Abbott gained the support of William Harper, president of the newly created University of Chicago, for the program of social work training, which had begun as the Chicago School of Civics and Philanthropy under the leadership of Graham Taylor, head worker of the Chicago Commons. At the beginning of the twentieth century there had been considerable interaction between male social scientists in the university, including John Dewey, and the women at Hull House. By 1920, however, both Edith Abbott and Sophonisba Breckinridge were convinced they did not want a university-affiliated program of social work education to be placed in the University of Chicago sociology department.[33] And the male members of the sociology faculty knew they did not want those women in their department, a department that established a substantial reputation for male chauvinism during the 1920s.

In part, this gendered structure of educational preparation reflected a separation between an emphasis on social theory and social reform in the male-controlled graduate social science departments and an emphasis on the development of practice skills through professional education in the predominately female schools of social work. It was also a separation between "objective/descriptive" social science and "normative" professional education that included an explicit emphasis on "social justice."[34] One particularly critical result of this separation was the almost total absence from the social work education curriculum of any significant attention to *economic theory* and the economic analysis of social policy.

The Second Half Century

The formative events at the beginning of the twentieth century have continued to have important consequences for the development of social work as a profession and social work education. However, social work as we know it today has also been shaped by a series of events that began in midcentury. The second half of the social work century—the

1940s to the 1990s—really began with the passage of the 1935 Social Security Act, although the full implementation of that Act did not take place until the mid-1940s, after the end of World War II. Some of the most critical events in the decades that have followed include the following:

• The passage of the Social Security Act, which included both "paternalistic" policies (the social insurances) and "maternalistic" policies (the public assistance and child welfare titles). The public assistance and child welfare titles led to the creation of the *public social work sector* as embodied in the federal-state ADC/AFDC programs, the Aid to the Blind and the Aid to Aged programs (and later Aid to the Disabled and Medicaid), and the federal-state child welfare programs. The establishment of state public welfare programs in every state, first to administer emergency relief during the 1930s and then to administer the public assistance titles under the Social Security Act, dramatically increased the demand for individuals with social work education and the employment opportunities for such persons. The programs actually initiated through the Social Security Act were consistent with the general pattern of welfare capitalism and the existing patterns of racial discrimination. The social insurances were directly connected to employment. And initially employment in many low-wage settings—domestic workers, hotel and restaurant workers, and farm workers—was excluded, particularly affecting occupations with a high proportion of Negro workers. The means-tested public assistance titles involved shared federal-state funding but were administered by the states, with differences in eligibility and benefits among the states, reflecting both labor market and political variations. Social workers with prior experience in voluntary nonprofit service agencies often became the administrators of these public social welfare programs.

• There was a closely related development, supported initially by federal funding, of undergraduate social work education primarily intended to prepare students for employment in the public sector.[35] The development of undergraduate programs in public universities also opened social work education to a much larger number of men and women from families with limited income and from diverse ethnic and cultural backgrounds.

29

• The creation of the National Institute of Mental Health in the late 1940s was a very important institutional factor in shaping the graduate social work curriculum and the expansion of graduate social work education. Another development that followed from the establishment of NIMH after the initiation of the community mental health center movement in the 1960s was the dramatic expansion of the public mental health sector and employment opportunities for social workers.

• There was an organizational restructuring and consolidation of the structure of social work as an organized profession with the establishment of the Council on Social Work Education (1952) and the National Association of Social Workers (1956). This provided a framework for steady growth in social work education at both undergraduate and graduate levels, and for the structure of the organized profession and growth in official membership.

• The expansion of doctoral education in social work, beginning in the 1960s, was very largely a result of financial and institutional support through the National Institute of Mental Health. The development of doctoral education has been associated with the development of an expanding support system for practice-relevant research in social work in the 1990s.

• The New Frontier and Great Society programs of the Kennedy and Johnson years, respectively, along with other developments in the early Nixon years—Supplemental Security Income (SSI) and Title XX of the Social Security Act, the Social Services title—brought new federal initiatives and expanded federal funding for a wide variety of categorical social welfare programs, many of which were directed at the social and economic problems of central cities and the increasing costs of health care.[36] These programs were funded initially from the expanding federal tax resources that came from an expansive national economy. Most of these initiatives were either curtailed or eliminated in the early Reagan years. This was consistent with the underlying assumptions of welfare capitalism, which included an emphasis on wage and salary employment and employment fringe benefits as the fundamental source of economic security for all households. By then federal social welfare programs also had to compete for funding with the accumulated military costs of the Vietnam War and the cold war.

• The development in organized social work that perhaps had the most fundamental consequences for the structure of the profession was the emergence of a private practice sector.[37] The addition of mental illness coverage to group health insurance plans in the 1970s and 1980s dramatically expanded the opportunities for both full-time and part-time private practice in social work. The expansion of private practice, in turn, led to NASW initiatives to promote state licensing, to the creation of other forms of professional credentialing within the structure of the profession, and to other forms of professional organization such as the clinical societies. It also made social work practice part of the emerging structure of managed health care and managed behavioral health care. It is around the issue of the place of private practice in social work that it has become increasingly obvious that many of the assumptions of the professional education community in social work about the nature of the profession, and the assumptions of the National Association of Social Workers, representing practicing social workers, *are really quite different.*

• Another significant development was the entrance of an increased number of men into social work in the late 1930s and the 1940s. The first wave included men who were refugees from Europe, with academic and professional experience, who found a professional home in social work and psychology, in both the academic community and in community agencies. The second wave was the GI Bill generation of military veterans, mostly men. The GI Bill generation was significant because, after professional education and an initial period of professional experience, these men often moved rapidly into agency administration, particularly during the 1950s when the argument was advanced that social work needed male leaders to get increased public recognition.

A number of these men also became part of the first large generation of doctoral students in social work. More than 90 percent of the 1960s students in the Florence Heller Ph.D. program at Brandeis, then the largest social welfare Ph.D. program in the country, were "re-treads," men who were coming back to the university after an initial career in social welfare administration and social planning. Many of these men became senior faculty members, deans, and administrators in governmental social welfare agencies, leading to frequent charges that patriarchal men were taking control of social work. What is significant today is that that GI Bill generation of men, of which I am a member, has now largely disappeared through retirement and death.

• But the most significant development of the past half century has been the involvement of social work in the processes of cultural transformation, which has been reshaping the society of the United States since the 1940s. The 1930s left the structure of race relations in America much as it had been since the 1860s. Although the Social Security Act created new "safety-net" social programs, Negro citizens, in actual practice, were largely excluded. The military establishment was segregated, education and housing were completely segregated in the South and largely segregated in the North. Demands by men and women coming back from World War II, changes in employment patterns that had emerged during the war, the opportunities created under the GI Bill for Negro veterans to enter higher education, and then the relocation of millions of Negro citizens from the rural South to the urban North when cotton harvesting was mechanized created the dynamics that have forced far-reaching changes in American society.

The destruction of both legal and nonlegal but well-established patterns of racial segregation and discrimination became a high-profile social advocacy issue for social workers, in marked contrast to the neglect of this issue in the early days of social work. The social work profession became an important and expanding channel of opportunity for professional education for many women and men who would earlier have been excluded from access to professional education. The formal recognition by both NASW and CSWE of undergraduate professional education in social work in the 1970s was a major step in expanding the opportunities to become a professional social worker. Equality of opportunity and treatment across ethnic, gender, and sexual-preference lines—within the profession as well as in the larger society—became major moral issues for the profession in the second half century.

From the perspective of having been a participant in these developmental events over the past fifty years, I want to set forth some assumptions about probable developments in the larger society that will provide a context for the future development of social work.

The overriding assumption is that the basic paradigm of *welfare capitalism* will persist in U.S. society,[38] with its pattern of diverse and dispersed social welfare, with many innovations and new initiatives alongside many persistent examples of institutionalized neglect and oppression in a highly productive society with great economic resources. We will not replace welfare capitalism with a national comprehensive European style "welfare state." Moreover, within this system of "welfare capitalism" the same basic dilemmas in social work and social welfare that existed at the beginning of this century will continue to exist. The tension between the definition of social work as an occupation consisting of employees in nonprofit and governmental organizations or as a system of autonomous professionals who work in diverse organizations and independent settings will persist (For profit and economic, not welfare, as well). The tension between giving priority to providing professional services to individuals and families who are directly affected by poverty, oppression, and illness or giving priority to public policy research economic opportunities and systematic advocacy for public policies that might prevent or ameliorate such problems will persist. And the tension between addressing the problems of individuals and families through comprehensive governmental service programs or through voluntary proprietary and religiously based charitable initiatives will continue.

• There will be no catastrophic international war. If this assumption were to be incorrect, there would be no future for social work, or for the rest of society as we know it today. But assuming there is no such catastrophic event, it is likely that the process of devolution and decentralization of governmental responsibility for domestic social welfare programs will continue. The regulation of the U.S. *economic system,* however, will be increasingly centralized, including the regulation of those social insurance "entitlement" programs that are viewed as having similar economic and political consequences across the whole society. These include, among others, the social insurance programs for older persons and veterans' benefits, although the significance of veterans' social welfare benefits will be sharply reduced early in the next century.

Actual policy control of governmental human service programs in which social workers are employed, such as child welfare, mental health, family assistance, and public health will be exercised by state and county governments, even if some federal funds and regulations are involved. Moreover, there will be limited staff resources in the federal agencies to monitor those federal regulations that do exist. The shift from AFDC (Aid to Families with Dependent Children), to TANF (Temporary Assistance to Needy Families) has been the most dramatic change, *and that will not be reversed.*

New public policy initiatives intended to strengthen the economic position of low-income households with children will be focused on improving economic benefits from employment rather than on direct "safety-net" provisions of household economic support.[39] It is direct economic incentives that create the movement of individuals from dependency to self-sustaining employment, including minimum-wage standards, and the provision of day care, health care coverage, and real career planning and technical training, not psychological counseling or mandated job-search programs.

One important reason for the broad political support for the decentralization of personal social service programs is that this removes an entire set of divisive public policy decision processes from the federal political agenda and allows them to be dealt with piecemeal across 50 states and 3,000 counties. The result is political flexibility even though there is likely to be uneven, and often unfair, treatment of particular groups in certain states and therefore a continuous need for organized social justice advocacy. In particular, long-standing historical patterns of institutional racism may continue to have a significant impact on public policy.

• Health care and mental health care will continue to be restructured in ways that move away from independent practice by solo practitioners, whether doctors, psychologists, or social workers, and from the direct provision of such services by federal, state, or local governments. Various types of managed care organizations, including coalitions of employers, insurance companies, hospital corporations, and professional practice corporations, will provide the funding mechanisms through which the provision of health/mental health care will take place and through which health care professionals, including social workers, will be paid.

There will be, for the immediate future, a high degree of turbulence and conflict as these systems are put together. The end of the easy profits that for-profit firms realized from the initial cost-cutting initiatives will contribute to the turbulence. The health care delivery systems will include major for-profit sectors, but there will also be a number of non-profit organizations that will be aggressive participants in the health care marketplace. The managed health care/mental health care sector, including home health care, will most likely be the largest economic employment sector in the future for graduate level clinical social workers. There may, however, also be significant changes in the practice methodology of clinical social work.

Within the field of mental health services, the most dramatic change with continuing consequences for social work practice has been the paradigm shift from the definition of mental illness as a psychological phenomenon to a recognition of biological and genetic factors in mental illness,[40] the discrediting of open-ended psychoanalysis as a method of treatment for acute mental illness,[41] and the development of medications for the control of mental illness conditions.

There will be a substantial degree of consolidation in the for-profit health care industry. This will contribute to the development, at least initially, of both state and federal regulation of the industry. The ultimate result will not be the publicly managed health care system outlined originally by President Clinton, but something more like a *federally regulated commercial public utility* that will, in reality, have many of the system characteristics of the original Clinton plan. The end result is actually likely to be improved health care services for low-income households that are covered by the system. Ultimately, coverage will be close to universal, though low-income households will participate through one of a number of different types of coverage packages rather than being served by a single public system.

• The process of cultural transformation of American society will continue. The United States is the society in which the diverse ethnic cultures of the world—African, Asian, European, Latino—are meeting head-on to create a society for which there is no historical precedent. This process of cultural transformation will include changes in the ethnic characteristics of the entire society, with increasing numbers of individuals who have diverse genetic heritages, and diversity in commonly used languages; changes in the social roles of women; and changes in the position of gay and lesbian individuals within the society. All social workers will practice in culturally diverse environments. Their ability to be responsive to those environments will largely determine their level of professional, and economic, achievement.

The increasing numbers of children from African American, Latino, and Asian backgrounds will bring dramatic changes in the culture and the politics of the elementary and secondary education system, and ultimately in higher education, in spite of the short-term impact of the Supreme Court Hopwood Decision.[42] Public services in central cities, including health and social welfare, will increasingly be staffed by occupational and professional specialists who come from African American, Latino, and Asian backgrounds, with an increasing proportion of women across all types of the public service fields.

The process of cultural transformation also means changes in the pattern of families and households. Extended life spans; smaller numbers of children in each household; homosexual, as well as heterosexual, marriages; employment careers, even with interruptions, for both men and women; geographic mobility in employment—all of these changes mean that relatively few household/families will persist intact in a single geographic neighborhood across the sixty years of adult living.

The role of the family, and particularly the role of the extended family (which may be increasingly hard to define as marriages dissolve and are reconstituted) in providing continuous, dependable personal care will continue to diminish over time, as will the role of the stable residential neighborhood of caring and sharing neighbors. The role of organized human services to meet personal care needs of all types will continue to expand, as will the employment opportunities for social workers. The challenge will be to make those services relevant to the fundamental needs of individuals and households in such a period of social uncertainty.

The ongoing process of cultural transformation will also mean that there will be a continuous process of social and political conflict in local communities, including some violent confrontations, since there will also be persistent resistance to these changes. Social workers and social services may often be in the center of these conflicts either as advocates for change or as the target of protests against change. Collective support for individual social work practitioners through the organized profession will become more important rather than less.

• The federal political scene for the immediate future will continue to be dominated by the politics of the transformation of society in the southern states. Because the southern states were treated as a dependent, colonial society for a hundred years, with a social order that was essentially frozen in time during that period, the process of adapting to the social changes that have taken place in other parts of U.S. society will take time. Indeed, these changes will probably be strenuously resisted, including changes in the persistent patterns of institutional racism. Much of the political conflict will be around social issues rather than economic ones, issues that affect social workers and those served by social workers. The combination of traditional conservative Democrats who have become Republican voters, and strong, traditional religious movements in southern states will continue to be the most cohesive political constituency within the Republican Party. This political constituency will have a major influence on presidential policy making, regardless of the party label the President carries.

• As indicated earlier, one of the most important features of the pattern of welfare capitalism in the 1800s was the creation of the system of voluntary, philanthropic, nonprofit service organizations, separate from, and often in opposition to, the expansion of the public services. Today, the distinction between nonprofit and governmental services is increasingly blurred, as well as the distinction between both of these types of service organizations and for-profit, marketplace service organizations. With the ongoing process of privatization, or "contracting-out," many of the governmental service programs created by the Social Security Act and the Great Society programs of the 1960s and 1970s will be dramatically restructured, and down-sized. Governmental funds will be used to purchase goods and services through both nonprofit and for-profit human service organizations. Contract funding will become more important than contributions for many nonprofit service organizations.

But what are the implications of the changes taking place in American society for the organized profession of social work in the next century? My basic assumption is that social work will continue to be an expanding major profession, in spite of the dire predictions of some academics.[43] There may be fewer opportunities for long-term employment in traditional governmentally administered services but increasing opportunities in nonprofit and for-profit sectors. It will be a profession that is both an occupation and a *part of* ongoing social movements and the continuing struggle for social reform and social justice within our society.

The pattern of continuous social change and the increasing likelihood that there will not be lifelong continuity in household/family relationships, or of residential location, will result in an expanded sector of personal social services, although the priority areas of professional attention may change over time. Similarly, the specific social justice concerns to which individual social workers are committed may change over time.

• As a major profession, social work will provide professional services across the entire society, not just to one segment of society or in one type of community. The original exclusive association of social work professional practice with poorly paid employment in a philanthropic nonprofit social service agency serving only low-income households is increasingly outdated. Social workers are, and will be, employed in a wide variety of organizational settings across the entire spectrum of society.

• Social work will continue to be primarily a profession of women, providing new career opportunities particularly for women from families with limited income, as well as women who have experienced various forms of exclusion or oppression in their lifetime. The women who enter social work will be those whose primary concern is a professional career with adequate income and those whose primary concern is advocacy for social justice. Social work will continue to provide a greater diversity of career opportunities for women than either elementary/secondary education or nursing and will provide more opportunities for combining service and advocacy.

• The disappearance of the pattern of lifelong employment in a single organization will increase the importance for individual practitioners of professional education and professional credentials.[44] The ability to develop new competencies through a variety of work experiences and ongoing professional development will be more important than seniority within a single organization. Many professional careers will include varying combinations of organizational employment, participation in professional group practice, and self-employment. As important as public policy advocacy is within the traditions of social work, the future of NASW will depend on the effectiveness of the association in meeting the personal career development needs of the individual practitioner members of the association.

• Practice-relevant research will become increasingly important for professional practitioners, program managers, and policymakers as funding sources demand evidence that social work interventions, as well as other types of human service professional interventions, actually make a difference. *Outcome research* will be more important than organizational mission statements, along with the prompt dissemination of research-based information through professional conferences and professional publications.

• Social work as a profession, and individual social workers, will continue to be involved in conflict and controversy both because of the value commitments of individual social workers and because those who are served by social workers will continue to include the victims of social injustice. Social injustice includes not only poverty but other forms of discrimination and oppression, such as family violence, that are not always linked to poverty. And individual social workers with strong personal convictions will continue to advocate for their values within the profession and within the larger society.

• Women will provide most of the leadership within the profession of social work and in social work education. That leadership will continue to become more diverse in terms of ethnic/cultural backgrounds and lifestyle. A major challenge for social work as a profession, and social work education, will also be the recruitment of men, not because men are needed in visible leadership positions, but because men are needed within the profession to maintain the gender diversity that has been one of the strengths of this profession.

• Social work will continue to be a practice profession dealing primarily with the provision of services for individuals and families. That is what the majority of social workers get paid to do.

There will continue to be highly visible examples of social workers in public leadership positions, social policy analysis, social policy advocacy, community development, and for-profit entrepreneurship. But these individuals do not constitute the backbone of the organized profession. Moreover, without more attention to the central role of economic analysis and economic theory in human service management and social policy development, the influence of social workers in these areas of practice is not likely to increase significantly.

A major challenge for organized social work as the second century begins is to draw on the body of professional experience and knowledge to address institutional issues critical for the central practice areas that have always been a primary focus of professional practice: children and families.

Social work services for, and in behalf of, children is the service sector most clearly identified as a distinctive professional practice domain of social work. It was an important part of the earliest development of social work. The creation of the public child welfare system following the 1930s made it the largest public sector of social work practice. Today, the institutional structures in public child welfare services, a result, in large part, of the social welfare/social reform movements of the early twentieth century (protective services, family support services, foster care, adoption, residential treatment), are under sustained attack as often being ineffective in achieving their objectives, if not downright harmful. A 1997 report from the Government Accounting Office stated: "The Child Protective Services system is in crisis, plagued by difficult problems, such as growing caseloads, increasingly complex social problems underlying child maltreatment and ongoing systemic weaknesses in day-to-day operations."[45] In some communities there is a move, out of desperation, to substitute the police and the criminal justice system for social work family support services. The intensified training of existing child welfare staff is likely to have little effect on the actual experiences of at-risk children unless there is a new policy framework and new program models. Although there are now an increasing number of research studies in social work dealing with pieces of the child welfare service system, the crisis in child welfare services provides a good example of the fact that *without a systematic program of research, there is little policy-relevant information, and without policy-relevant information, there cannot be professional leadership.*

But most of the problems of children with which social workers are concerned are symptoms of a larger problem. The institution of the family is under unusual and increasing stress in our society. The appeal of the Promise Keepers movement, as well as the Million Man March and the Million Woman March, is an indication of the concerns about the institution of the family that exist across the country. Some of the stress on families is a consequence of poverty and institutionalized oppression. But there are other forms of stress that cut across society, across all income levels. Social work, in particular, faces the challenge of discovering new ways to protect and strengthen families under stress, not by reinventing the social structures of the past, but by developing new responses to the real dynamics of contemporary family life. Without effective responses to the increasing pressures on families, the demands on social work child welfare services may escalate indefinitely.

It is important to use the celebration of the beginning of the second century of social work to capture some of the highlights of history of the profession. But it is even more important to recognize that the past is not the future, and that, as perplexing as the beginnings of the second century of social work may be, it is the challenges of the future that must be dealt with by all the institutions that are part of the social work community.

3

Social Work's Century of Evolution as a Profession: Choices Made, Opportunities Lost. From the Individual and Society to the Individual

Robert Morris

At the millennium, it is difficult for social workers to recall how much their current status—with its numerous agencies, schools, professional associations, and hundreds of thousands of jobs—has roots in ideas, methods, and aims developed a hundred years ago by lay persons who had credentials from other disciplines or lacked professional credentials altogether. This essay sums up a personal understanding of the evolution since those days in order to better appreciate how fundamentally the objectives of social work, as a profession, have been transformed and selectively narrowed in practice.

Initial Modest Purposes Lead to Great Ambitions

The late nineteenth and early twentieth centuries were a time of turmoil and change as a consequence of rapid industrialization. The United States moved from an agrarian and commercial society to a world-leading industrial society. Family life was transformed as millions were uprooted from the farm to unready cities. The flood of immigration and internal migration was accompanied by great slums in the cities, with violence and crime, poverty and malnutrition, and high rates of maternal and infant mortality, along with great wealth in other parts of the same cities.

Some successful citizens, often the wives of the well-to-do, chose to relieve the worst conditions by charitable acts, helping individuals gain the moral or physical strength to climb out of wretched conditions. They worked through voluntary charities. Other citizens undertook a parallel effort to understand the life conditions of the poor and to help them take their own actions to improve their conditions collectively.

The parallel efforts were mutually supportive although very different in conception. Their proponents advanced core ideas that became a mantra for the profession in its evolution: (a) that the nation, the society, had a basic responsibility for dealing with the consequences in human lives of a rapidly changing and industrializing world; (b) that a system of agencies was necessary for the purpose; (c) that what had been a part-time citizen responsibility needed to become a profession; and (d) that this new profession would concentrate on the intersection between the education and psychological growth of individuals and the social and economic world in which they grew up.

This last concept—that the new profession would become expert in the life of individuals in their social/economic environment—can be seen in retrospect as a most ambitious undertaking, appropriate for a nation bursting with energy at the turn of the century. If ever carried out, this mission (the individual in society) would involve fusing contributions from economics, sociology, anthropology, psychology, political science and, later, science and technology.*

The effort was soon diminished by the practical demands of a service field with close ties to medical care and mental health and which soon embraced new psychiatric thinking, with its focus on the individual. But this early aim, without conceptual elaboration, has continued to be used by the profession to explain or justify its larger purposes.

The early social casework agencies began with the conviction that poverty was mainly a result of some personal defect, in either character or education. This led to emphasis on understanding each "case" by probing a family history and arriving at a social diagnosis.[2]

---

*It is only a small step to speculate that the roots of this ambitious idea can be found in the earlier work of the National Conference of Charities and Corrections, which brought together academics (sociologists, economists, and psychologists) as well as lay citizens concerned with human welfare.[1]

The parallel track of group work began with the settlement house convictions of Jane Addams and Hull House: that the poor were victims of economic and social circumstances that they, with their native abilities and with help from the more successful, could change. Joint and collective efforts were first directed locally but later moved to national issues. Out of this grew a tradition of helping groups help themselves.[3]

Over the past hundred years, in which these beginnings were modified by clear choices about how to develop a profession for the ambitious tasks of simultaneously ameliorating the lives of families and also of improving society, the profession has followed (not always intentionally) a clear path of evolution, which served it in surviving several catastrophic changes. Over this time the field made decisions at each critical juncture that diminished its ability to realize the aim of changing social conditions that injure the most vulnerable in the population. The consequences of these choices make up the baggage the profession carries as it looks forward to the next century.

The Argument Summarized

The argument about these consequences can be summed up as follows:

1. The tradition initially was part of a much wider interest in social change and human needs that had been expressed since 1860 through the National Conference of Charities and Corrections and the American Social Science Association. Scientific methods for human needs could, it was hoped, produce solutions for human and community social ills much as science had fueled great economic change.
2. The movement became a part of the later Progressive movement. The 1906 meeting of the Conference of Charities and Corrections (its thirty-third) viewed itself as part of a moral and political revolution in which the forces of good government would prevail. Its ninety-eight volumes of proceedings are a monument to the ambitious aims of early social workers, who hoped to create a profession that would simultaneously help poor and sick individuals and change social conditions contributing to their distress.

3. The early participants were multidisciplined, drawn from sociologists, nascent economists, other social scientists, lay community leaders, clergy, and workers in agencies.

4. Social work as a distinctive vocation soon concentrated on developing its position as a profession, with the apparatus of a social science: academic training to combine learning and practical experience and professional associations with accrediting authority.

5. The twin aims of individual care and changing conditions have been retained in the expressed aims of the field, but after 1935 the developments of the Great Depression and World War II forced the field to reconsider its future. Its equipment and resources did not enable it to do all it aspired to.

6. A series of choices, some taken almost unwittingly, were reinforced by the popularity of new mental health thinking and the compatibility of psychological theory with social casework, along with the great social and economic changes following the Depression.

7. By 1990 the field was primarily involved in interpersonal and mental health kinds of careers, while work to change conditions remained at the rhetorical level rather than providing jobs and institutional opportunities to work for change.

8. At the same time, social work as a profession was identified mainly with counseling help to individuals or as adjunct staff for organizations, rather than becoming "the profession" associated with any one service system. Many of these jobs required very little more than could be done by a well-educated baccalaureate.

The sympathy for others, which social work inculcated, probably did make social workers more effective in dealing with others and helping them adapt to difficult situations. Even that achievement is insecure, however: the field has not developed convincing scientific or other evidence that its work has changed the prevalence of the ills it works with comparable to the "cures of medicine" with which much of the field has identified. At best it can claim that many individuals seek and seem to get some hard-to-define benefit from social work.[4]

a) The track to change social conditions did not develop an intellectual foundation or technology suited for the times—which would have meant challenging the very institutional policies of individual amelioration. The social-change objectives became at best quiescent except for continuously calling attention to unmet needs. Theories and techniques for attacking the root causes were not well developed.

b) By 1997 the field had established itself as a profession with many career opportunities, but few of them are easy to attach to specific institutions other than state departments of public welfare. By comparison, other fields as diverse as medicine, nursing, teaching, and law were seen as being of value to all classes and citizens. Other services much in demand were rapidly added to become service systems with which the professions of nursing, medicine, law, and education could be quickly identified.

Conceptual and Educational Choices: 1900–1930

By 1900 the efforts at apprentice training were seen by volunteers as too narrow. In 1898 the New York Charity Organization Society began a summer training program that by 1904 was transformed into a one-year program at the New York School of Philanthropy. In 1910 the program was expanded to two years to provide training in the management of charitable institutions and in advising families. And in 1917 the school was renamed the New York School of Social Work, with limited affiliation with Columbia University. (Later, in 1940, the affiliation was made formal, and in 1963 the school was renamed the Columbia School of Social Work.)

During this era the Institute of Social Science was established as an extension program at the University of Chicago; it later became the Graduate School for Social Administration.[5] In 1900 Mary Richmond, a pioneer caseworker, and Simon Patten, an academic social scientist (who may have coined the term *social worker*), disputed whether the field should concentrate on advocacy for institutional and social change or on individualized services.

The two schools, Chicago and New York, became the two major sources for intellectual development: social administration and casework. By 1919 there were fifteen schools, nine under university auspices. Advocacy for change did not die out, but it became a minor part of more demanding curricula.

In 1915, at the National Conference on Charities and Corrections,

Abraham Flexner delivered his answer to a question put to him by social workers: Is social work a profession? His reply was influential, for he had already transformed the basis for medical education. He stated the opinion that social work was "not yet a profession." He urged training in a university with practicum learning linked to an agency providing clinical services guided by academic standards—basically the medical model.[6]

By the 1920s the work of Sigmund Freud had become popular. His emphasis on probing an individual life history fitted social work's tradition of taking a family history. In the succeeding years the interest in dynamic psychologies was used by most schools of social work to build their basic education, with its emphasis on interpersonal relationships.

Group work continued as an important function but with a more diffuse intellectual base than casework. It relied on social workers' relationships with the poor and working-class populations, most still close to their immigrant origins, with needs in education, housing, and job opportunities. Settlement houses, located where the poor lived, provided centers where residents of all ages could gather to develop their social connections with each other, take classes, and enjoy recreational activities. Social workers became, for them, facilitators in reaching for better living through self-improvement, education, and experience in creating their own organizations. In many ways the settlement houses were a bridge between a low-income working class and the economic opportunities to which they aspired while maintaining their varied ethnic associations. They provided places where the poor could find some social services or could organize to get them. These were a mix of services and community organizing activities. Over time, as the structure and financing of services became more complex, the organizing of wider community services became an important function to be learned, leading to an additional specialty in social work education.

At the end of the 1920s social work as a profession seemed well on its way. It had academic institutions, some theoretical foundations, and a set of ambitious values to improve both societal conditions and the capacities of the poor. It provided a professional core for leadership that combined voluntarism and one or two years of baccalaureate education, later expanded to postgraduate and doctoral training.

Other analyses of the evolution have been published by, among others, Lubove,[7] the Pumphreys,[8] and Chambers.[9]

The Depression Years: 1930s

The Great Depression produced a devastating challenge to social work and its institutions. The base function of relieving poverty on a case-by-case basis had been the foundation for helping individuals grow out of their troubles. Mass unemployment meant that almost all citizens were in such great economic trouble that the slim charitable agencies could not cope. The emergency introduction of public welfare with federal funding and administration was based on entitlement (because of definable conditions) and organization on a mass scale to provide income and public work to all in need.

For a time the private social agencies were used as one way to manage the relief flood with emergency tax funds. But that role was soon taken over by new public agencies, at first emergency in makeup, with most workers drawn from the unemployed and with a small cadre of trained caseworkers as supervisors and administrators. Large-scale organization, mass administration, and emergency improvisations became a new reality.

Out of the first reaction to a national crisis, social workers found it necessary to rethink social work's practice and structure, while retaining its commitment to both help the individual and improve society. In the end, the private social agency survived, but with shrunken influence in community life and with a casework staff primarily committed to understanding individual and family behaviors and how to help individuals cope with crises in their personal lives.

Public administration became the pioneer in the search for a new way to create a more secure foundation for all. Organization on this scale required not only new techniques—many of which had been developing in management, political science, and economics—but also very different sources of support. Social work was no longer dependent on philanthropically minded well-to-do citizens.

Unions and mass citizen movements of many kinds, including movements of the unemployed from almost all economic and social classes, had a stake in the new agencies. They found their own ways to express their needs directly to the state and federal governments, which responded with the experiments for which the era is remembered. The experiments included the Social Security Act and its almost universal social insurance to meet most economic risks, along with massive job-creation programs that included temporary public employment when necessary.

The education for such a different system would have to be different, but the schools of social work retained the interpersonal core for training. In time this choice helped casework and the profession to find new roles in the proliferating social agencies of the post–World War II era. Some social workers were attracted to the new organizations, but educational equipment was determined by the earlier training for helping individuals with personal adjustment problems. Apprentice or "clinical" field experience remained a dominant part of the curriculum, shaped by the opportunities for field experiences usually found in small private counseling and service agencies where most skilled counselors chose to work.

The response of the still-new profession to this crisis was anticipated in 1929 when Porter R. Lee, a distinguished social work educator of the time, restated the former Richmond/Patten debate as the dilemma the field faced between social reformer and social technician in his *Social Work: Cause and Function?*[10]

In 1928 the Milford Conference had proposed that social work, with all its specialty workers, was really a single profession in its report "Social Case Work: Generic and Specific." This, along with limited funding for training, led in time to an educational construct that, of necessity, focused on training workers as generalists able to function in many venues and areas but not developing depth in any one area, except perhaps the psychologies of human behavior.

The choice had to be made sooner than anyone expected. In succeeding years, this dilemma continued as the field tried to contain both casework and social reform as its purpose. Its training was increasingly dominated by a generic foundation in the individual case methodologies and theories. This carried over into many specialty services such as child welfare, chronic illness, etc., since teaching was mainly limited to social workers themselves educated in the basic approach. It was also influenced by trainee preferences for psychologically oriented skills. This tilt continued in the experiences of the educational system, although as late as 1971 the *Encyclopedia of Social Work* devoted about as much space to social group work theories as it did to social casework.[11]

During the 1930s individual social workers such as Harry Hopkins, Frances Perkins, and the Abbot sisters in Chicago were leaders in reforming the welfare system, which had become complex and included many new types of social provision. They had been organizers rather than caseworkers. The field hoped to maintain its level of contribution in the future, but after the 1930s the professional function continued to bifurcate, with the case technician doing better than the reformer in the academy.

It is interesting to recall that the two social workers who received a Nobel Prize were social reformers: Jane Addams (1931) and Emily Green Balch (1946), both pioneers in the strain of development that has since diminished in importance for the changing profession.

Thirty Golden Years of Growth: 1945–1975

World War II demanded most energies for four years but also opened up opportunities for social work to practice its individualizing skill in new territories—the armed forces (in their psychiatric and medical hospitals), the Veterans Administration, the Red Cross, and trade unions—usually working on individual problems. A few found careers in bridging the gap between trade unions of the mainly blue-collar workers and the social services. The few who entered the union movement in a search for better ways to change social conditions, such as Bertha Reynolds, Joseph Levy, and Jack Fisher, were caught up in labor organization as a professional career, which did not fit well with the career aims of most social workers, and few followed them.

After 1945 the country experienced thirty years of unprecedented growth. Taxes levied for the war now yielded surplus revenues, which encouraged Congress to authorize numerous programs to deal with social problems, which, if not exactly new, were different in causation and scale. These were the problems of average citizens, not of the dependent poor.

A national educational program helped discharged soldiers acquire new skills for a new technological era, and almost incidentally created a new middle-class-aspiring population. Racial discrimination took on a new urgency as part of the obligation to meet the rising expectations of minorities, and especially of blacks, following their military service. The workplace was transformed as married and single women who had become essential in the workplace now decided in increasing numbers to stay at work. Infrastructure in the form of housing and transportation, neglected during the war, was rebuilt with housing in suburban areas throughout the country, and a national network of highways provided work and helped shift populations away from older communities. The war and the new industries and work opportunities that it stimulated led to a major shift in population. Rural blacks moved from the South to the North and others moved west and southwest. Retirees before long began moving from the North to the Sunbelt. All created a massive migration.

New cities and towns grew up, birthrates boomed, and families had opportunities for a better life along with new tensions and pressures. Social workers did not play any leading role in these changes, but they did provide workers whose skill, limited as it was, proved effective in smoothing the rough transitions of change: helping communities develop new services and helping individuals and families adjust to new circumstances.

The new needs did not fit well with what had been the social workers' interest in treating the weak and helpless on the fringe of any community. By now the changes in society had produced numerous public services helpful to all citizens, not only the poor: institutions and programs for the major hazards of illness, loss of a wage earner, poor education, and a changing economy. These served a population that did not see itself as dependent and needing guidance (except in certain areas of behavior). Programs were available without the hint of personal "inadequacy." Clients became customers or consumers more than petitioners.

At the same time, problems inherent in personal and family dysfunction, substance abuse, discrimination, aging, and violent or aberrant behavior became more troublesome. Dealing with them called for a deeper understanding of these socially defined "ills"—their causes and consequences—than any profession could claim. The generic training for social workers was not sufficient, but it was all there was. More research and thoughtful analysis became necessary to understand causation and to test methods experimentally. The resources were not available to move from case observation to scientific study.

In many ways the years were heady with hope but troubled by the addition of new social problems. The rapid changes forced by technology, by a vigorous but mobile economy, by new population diversity, and by freer ways of thinking about family life were accompanied by changes in family structure, the increase in numbers of single-parent families, juvenile delinquency (which soon became defined as juvenile and youth crime), and persisting turmoil over race. With economic growth favorable, social agencies of many kinds proliferated, offering work and careers at a faster pace than social work education and practice could keep up with. Resources came easiest to relieve a crisis—to help individuals—but not much for research to examine the effectiveness of services, which was taken for granted. This trend was to grow with the speedy optimism of the times.[11,12]

Both health and welfare agencies found it useful to have social workers as intermediaries between their services and their clients/patients—to interpret what services are available, to explain how to use them, and to screen for entitlement. Social work case training fitted this need well, but did not satisfy the field's desire to find a niche to be professionally competent to treat this clientele in a therapeutic sense.

Proprietary agencies began to offer many previously nonprofit services: child care, child adoptions, personal or vocational counseling, and nursing home care to name only a few. The efficiency claims of the proprietary agencies slowly invaded the nonprofit sector so that by the time the era of expansion slowed down, the distinction between proprietary and nonprofit welfare organizations began to blur.

What was changed from the 1930s was that very few of these jobs needed people interested in social change. The services, as defined, became ends in themselves. There was little evaluation of the extent to which problems were reduced. As long as growth and public funds were available, there was little incentive to question cause and effect or to change basic conditions that just might be causal. Thus, there were few jobs for the social change half of social work's purposes. It became assumed, subtly, that even minor amelioration of a condition was an end in itself, not reduction in the scale of the problem. It was not until later that public concern over persisting ills and rising costs became serious.

Effects of Growth in Employment and Service Financing

The profession flourished in these years, measured by increase in university education, by the number of graduates, by the number of certified social workers, and by the dispersion of social workers to many new kinds of service agencies. Social workers found work staffing new health and disease agencies (birth defects, cancer, mental health), health insurance agencies, and corporate personnel and personnel benefits offices. Later, recognition of Alzheimer's and HIV/AIDS contributed to the proliferation of ameliorating services and professional opportunities. Private practice of "clinical" social work increased (often on a part-time basis), with private fee charging.

The number of credentialed social workers with an M.S.W. or B.S.W. increased rapidly, although finding a firm number is complicated by differing definitions of whom to count and by the absence (until recently) of any national labor force information. Clues are found in the exponential increase in full-time enrollment in accredited schools awarding an M.S.W.: from 2,421 in 1941 to 13,311 in 1970.

By 1983 the U.S. Labor Department estimated there were 407,000 employed social workers; in 1993, the estimate was 586,000. These numbers include many whom the profession would not consider "qualified." In recent years the NASW has reported about 150,000 members of the association, which included 21,000 unemployed, retired, or holding only an associate degree. Over a third of the members (54,215) were Accredited Clinical Social Workers, whose A.C.S.W. title opened the door to certain jobs in public and private agencies and to private counseling practice to which many school applicants aspired. In sum, the field has a variety of professionals, but their numbers represent only about a quarter of all those employed in what the public considers social work. At the same time, the expanded welfare system is no longer limited to the poor. It has expanded to a whole range of income maintenance and other services. The amount of public spending (investment) in welfare increased from $23 billion to $493 billion in constant dollars between 1950 and 1980, or over twentyfold. Per capita welfare spending increased by 340 percent. Public spending for welfare increased from 8.9 percent to 18.7 percent of the gross domestic product. The federal share tripled, and the local tax spending almost doubled.[13]

As funding and the scale of social needs grew and changed along with the much wider distribution, the profession made some clear choices about how to respond. It chose to consolidate its organizational base by creating the Council on Social Work Education in 1951 to standardize the quality of education while still hoping to find room for innovation. It also succeeded in 1955 in merging a number of specialized social worker organizations (psychiatric, medical care, group work, community organization) into a single national association in order to concentrate resources and have more influence in public policy making and in resource allocation.

One unintended consequence was the slow erosion of professional specialization in group work and community organization. The unified profession encompassed many functions, but its unified resources did not grow commensurate with the challenge of unity. Other organizations (ethnic, cultural, economic, and political) and their members made up the political mix that really guided service and resource allocation. Social workers were valued as employees but not as shapers of policy.

Bearing in mind that the 1960s were also a time of change and protest about civil and welfare rights by many citizen organizations, and later the so-called War on Poverty of the federal government, it is striking that 85 percent of the students in schools of social work chose casework as a concentration, while only 3 percent chose community organization. This reflected what the schools continued to treat as the core or base for their generic approach to the profession and very likely what students preferred for a career. Or it may have reflected the interests of agencies willing to help finance education through field appointments for students, mainly the casework agencies. Or it may only mean that, since faculties continued to consist only of social workers, they chose to educate themselves within the basic interpersonal model, their preferences influenced by the preference of students.[14]

Whatever the explanation for the continued emphasis of social work education on the interpersonal case foundation, graduates found ample career opportunity to work with individuals. But the twin approach with which the profession began in the early years—to improve society and deal with the adverse conditions with which individuals cannot cope single-handedly—had lost significant ground.

The public systems with major welfare financing did attract social workers as administrators, but their education concentrated either on relieving the poorest or on treating personal adjustment problems. Even for this, the nature of counseling and the results remained poorly defined. The profession now had careers but had difficulty in communicating just what its explicit skills achieved. It did not succeed in being identified as *the* profession on which the public systems depended.

The daily life of most social workers was lived out within the confines of the existing services. They applied their generic education concepts to clinical practice as well as to administration and policy formation. As a profession they retained a belief in their mission to speak and to work for social change, but that belief was expressed merely in the articulation of broad objectives by the National Association of Social Workers, which lacked the technical capability to realize them and could not have generated sufficient support to realize them. For a time, a handful of unusual social workers played key roles in major policy development: Wilbur Cohen, Ellen Winston, Jane Hoey, Charles Schottland, Elizabeth Wickenden, Alvin Schorr, and Mel Glasser, among others. And a few such as Grace Marcus, contributed as expert technicians, to thinking about practice in public administration. But they were atypical. The voices of other special interest groups—for the aged, for children, for minorities, for the disabled—usually led the way, both in creativity and in advocacy. They had more activist followers, different resources. Often social workers acted as individual citizens in responding to changes going on about them. But it cannot be said that social work became recognized as essential leadership in such citizen organizations or in the fields they represented. Social workers were welcome but not as inevitable leaders. Their role in the mental retardation movement is instructive: the driving force for change and improvement came from clients and lay citizens, whom social workers helped but did not lead.

A Failed Opportunity for Social Work to Administer Public Welfare

Despite its limitations, by 1962 the profession had sufficient acceptance for its work in the larger public arena for social workers to be given an unusual opportunity to deal with the AFDC program, whose growth had begun to alarm public officials. In that year a social worker, Alvin Schorr, was an assistant secretary of Health, Education and Welfare. Legislation with funding was enacted, opening the door for testing the belief that skilled individualized casework could slow or even reverse the increase. A demonstration and research budget was passed offering states three dollars of federal help for each state dollar to introduce skilled services to help dependent mothers move off welfare and into work or sustainable marriage. Promised were reduced caseloads, reduced spending, and control of public costs. The program was based on previous small, unevaluated projects that claimed success.

It was a brave effort, but not fully thought-through. There were not enough M.S.W.'s in the nation, let alone recruitable for public welfare, to fill the jobs, and turnover of less skilled workers was very high. Less than 4 percent of the public staff consisted of trained workers. The costs to the states in salaries and transitional income support was higher than most states were willing to invest. After five years of the trial, dependency had not been reduced, but had increased, and AFDC functioning was not improved. The project was terminated.[16]

There are many explanations for the failure, none of them attributable to social work. The worst that can be said is that the profession gravely misjudged the limits of its skills, or its resources, to deal with dependency problems of this magnitude. But that is just the point. "A profession which claims great competence needs to be able to demonstrate its expertness in something particular" (attributed to Dr. Richard Cabot, 1915, an early supporter of social work). In this example, social work lost the chance to become a major actor in public income maintenance as it had once been in philanthropy before 1930.

What Was and Was Not Achieved in the Growth Years

This brief review has been critical of what happened in the 1960s, and it is worth a brief detour to comment more positively, before considering what happened before and after 1975.

By 1930 social work was well enough respected for leaders of the American Correctional Association to advocate that social workers enter into the management of correctional agencies. Social workers refused, asking instead for a separate department within corrections for them to treat prisoners. While supporting corrections reform, they preferred to remain in their counseling and advisory corner. It may be going too far to ask whether the field could have combined its individual and social change ends if they had replied differently.[16]

In some major welfare institutions social work did carve out a clear role for its professional aims as a recognized and important part of that institution's functioning. The Veterans Administration Social Service flourished after World War II. It successfully resisted efforts to break up a unified social work service into separate VA medical services, which would have eroded the basis for a general social work professional role in the overall VA structure

In time the consolidated service pioneered in developing and managing major programs to provide services in the community rather than in hospitals (in the late 1930s before the rest of the country caught on to community-based services) in the health and mental health fields. VA social work was no longer only adjunct to physicians.

Later its members successfully led in training multidisciplinary teams in treating complex medical conditions with social needs, in helping families assume caregiving responsibilities, and in moving into management positions covering many departments and disciplines. It also supported risky but professionally responsible research. By 1950 the service established an M.S.W. degree as the basic entry qualification, an important victory. But by 1960 the service observed that many tasks performed by M.S.W.'s might be performed as well by lesser-trained staff. It launched a three-year pilot project with evaluation and found that a quarter of M.S.W. tasks could be as safely performed by others with, say, a B.S.W. It was a courageous self-critical action to minimize costly overqualified professionals.

Perhaps the field's greatest achievement was secured at the cost of diminishing its role and voice in the social-change half of its original purposes. The profession survived by carving out useful support roles in various activities and ensuring careers by regulations that require an M.S.W. for employment or advancement in most public agencies. In time this was supported by the Institute of Mental Health program for social work training for public welfare and mental health. Whatever their limitations for training middle-level administrative staff, some graduated into executive positions.

Social workers proved adept at entering new kinds of employment and making themselves valuable in representing an agency to its clients and supporters, in managing interpersonal staff and intergroup relationships. Its members were useful in educational and medical institutions as well as corporations, performing a variety of ancillary functions. Hospitals needed social work departments, initially to handle the problems of treating indigent or poor patients, arranging for aftercare, and helping the poorly educated understand the attention their illness required. During the 1960s and later, as hospitals were forced to reduce length of inpatient care as a way to control costs, social workers were given broader mandates to arrange discharge plans with patients from all economic classes.

One unfortunate consequence of these successes has been that social work increasingly was recognized as being skillful in facilitating activities, but not yet in administering major services or in reducing the prevalence of social ills, an objective that a pragmatic cost-and-outcome-conscious society values. Social workers were helpers rather than leaders.

Unfortunately, most social workers in medical facilities, when queried, preferred counseling patients on their sickness rather than planning for aftercare, so that few of them understood the hands-on job of arranging suitable aftercare for the chronically ill, or of seeing to it that such help was made available. This was not considered the best use of their presumed clinical skills. They filled the jobs but missed the opportunity to lead in the later evolution of home health and home care and, more broadly, in planning for chronic illness, as the Veteran Administration social workers had already done. Social workers established a firm place in health services, but in supportive or ancillary roles rather than as the profession ready to lead any major segment of health care.

Social workers were also employed in mental health, mental retardation, and developmental disability programs; the major innovations and leadership, however, came from others. Social workers remained valuable ancillaries and coordinators, not the profession people turned to automatically to lead, manage, or guide in any part of these fields. They have done well in the support tasks of sustaining community living with social means, beginning with a counseling foundation and learning organization on the job. But they are not identified as leaders in developing understanding about retardation or in testing new approaches, which usually came from other sources.

The same was true when it came to the need for hands-on social services in nursing homes or in arranging for home care. Nursing homes have frequently been criticized for not having qualified managers. In the end, nurses and business managers filled that need, not social workers, who might have done so but who preferred to keep to a counseling role. They did give voice to imperfections, but did not generate solutions to deal with them.

In mental health, during the deinstitutionalization drive of the 1960 and 1970s, social workers in California were offered key responsibilities where there was a shortage of physicians and where their clinical skills were recognized—namely, to share responsibility for the mentally ill living in the community. This carried with it authority to decide when a sick patient needed to be rehospitalized because of behavioral changes. The profession declined, either because it was really unsure of its capacity or because it feared the risk of malpractice. The opportunity to test out leadership in a major socially oriented mental health policy was missed.

It is especially noteworthy how far the profession had distanced itself from work in the major income-related public social services, which, since the 1930s, have been the major resource for improving social conditions. A 1996 NASW fact sheet boasted that only 1 percent of its members work in public assistance. In so doing, the field signaled how it was adapting to the changed society in which it was forced to function. It seemed to consider it good that *fewer than a third* worked in any state or local or federal agency, but it was a matter of pride that its members provided *half the mental health therapy services* in the nation.[14]

The field was reacting to the market forces [it descried as demanding results equal to investment,] using demand and supply criteria. It justified its choice of personal counseling by the large numbers willing to use their services or by the numerous kinds of agencies willing to employ them. Is only social work responding to market force? For some years U.S Labor Department projections listed social work as a growth vocational field.

So after many years of change, social work succeeded in keeping a foothold in many fields, relying on its generalized skill in managing interpersonal and intergroup relations, but without taking on major organizational responsibilities as a profession. Of course, individual social workers did take on greater tasks, learning by doing for the most part. The importance of "social services" continued to be recognized and advocated, but from the point of view of professional thinking, it appears that the field chose only that segment of "services" for which they were most thoroughly trained: interpersonal counseling.

They began to use "services" as meaning "social worker services." The blurring between the two meanings has had important consequences: What does social work counseling achieve and what do other services achieve? It meant a failure to evaluate results as a process for improving conditions or for innovating with better methods through critical evaluation. Conceptual development as a foundation for a profession has been malnourished.

End of the Growth Years, Beginning of Internal Criticisms

By 1975 the steam behind the era of exponential welfare growth was running out. Much has since been written about the feared, or threatened, dismantling of the welfare state and the reason for the cumulative changes in how the nation views its social needs. This is not the place to review them, except to mention the main sources. Prior to 1975 there were numerous organized pressures to expand social benefits, and there were available tax resources that voters were prepared to see allocated for social purposes, not only for the poor but for the middle class as well.

Beginning in the 1970s, important changes took place, none by plan. Social workers rolled with the changes, adapting while objecting. They seldom generated ideas about new policies, which could have produced services better suited to the new conditions.

1. The political balance became more conservative. Voters became, not necessarily less generous (although that emerged by the 1990s), but less willing to pay taxes without seeing who benefited and how much. Confidence in the national government's ability to manage problems eroded with skepticism.

2. The population was not only different, it was much more new middle class, much more diverse ethnically, and older. This population was encouraged by our national freedoms to develop an increasing variety of special interests, each devoted to its own wants more than those of the collectivity. It was uneasily self-satisfied and increasingly critical.

3. Class differences began to count in an economic sense. There was a growing divergence, after 1975, in the distribution of national in-

come, with the top 5 percent getting larger shares and the bottom 20 percent receiving less income over time, not more.

It might have been expected that social work could find in these inequities an opportunity to revive its earlier commitments to changing social conditions. But the training in conceptualization and in social change had not kept pace with the times. The broad public welfare systems were the nation's primary instrument for relieving inequities, and public welfare had so little appeal for most social workers that they did not demand such education from their schools. Personal counseling remained more attractive, especially for a less dependent—or more independent—population.

4. The number of single-parent families grew, some temporary from serial divorces, some long-term for teenage mothers with illegitimate children. These were confined to poverty in the main, since one-income middle- and working-class families are less likely to earn enough to insure a life commensurate with popular expectations. Social workers are drawn to these needs, but their effectiveness is caught in the uncertainty, whether they are due mainly to personal deficiencies or to environmental pressures.

5. Economic conditions were changing. A long-term slowdown (until the middle 1990s) in the growth in Gross Domestic Product led to limits on expenditure.

6. A slowly aging population with earlier retirement and longer life, both healthy and ill, were dependent on insurance payments from the successor working population, which would need to pay more taxes to sustain benefits—a consequence of the dynamics of any insurance scheme, which call for regular adaptation as conditions change.

Few of these macro social and economic trends have been in the educational base for social workers, whose social action efforts were based mainly on evidence consisting of who is injured in the major changes going on, but without analysis of what can be done other than spending more through an increasingly dysfunctional welfare system. The most that can be said is that these trends were rather superficially described in the curriculum without in-depth analysis about what, if anything, could be done about them, or even how these trends could affect the professional base. Such analysis was well beyond the limited resources with which the field made do for its education. A few social work educators began to criticize the parochialism in outlook of the profession, some doing so very sharply, others mildly.[16,19] The profession had viewed public aid as not professionally appealing because it was an income redistribution system (which it was, of course), but it could be much more, and the profession missed that distinction.

In 1971 Gilbert Steiner of the Brookings Institution published a critical analysis that anticipated later critiques. Reading it now makes clear how accurate was his analysis thirty years ago. After a decade (1960s) of steady expansion of social and welfare programs to improve life for families with dependent children, three successive presidents (Kennedy, Johnson, Nixon) began by continuing the growth, but very quickly retreated pragmatically in the face of institutional resistance to any major change. New or bold new policies for helping the poor were given low priority. They fell back on trying to "rehabilitate" or stimulate clients to do more for themselves, much as did the 1994 repeal of the Aid for Families and Dependent Children Act and replacement by the Welfare to Work policy.[17]

Steiner did not deny social work's interest in better outcomes, only its failure to move beyond the limits of case education and the narrowness of understanding about the complex of forces with which the profession must deal if it is to improve society instead of merely bearing witness to its defects.

On the way he identified the myths under which all welfare seems to operate, namely, to explain the preference for easy solutions that obscure the deep-rooted factors that produce economic dependency. Coordination, a common remedy, overlooks the fact that each public program is part of a larger system in which each program tries to game the system to its advantage by getting someone else to pay the costs. For example, the food-stamp program, a popular remedy for economic trouble, is also a way to handle agricultural surpluses. Federal and state governments go through a revolving door as each tries to shift costs of doing anything to someone else. The very "busyness" that occupies workers is mainly a way to satisfy the numerous organized constituencies resisting institutional changes not to their benefit, with little attention paid to more general well-being.

Social work can be held responsible mainly for failing to develop its own capacities to understand the elements involved in the problems it chose to deal with that lie outside the reach of interpersonal psychology. These include understanding political and organizational actions, economic bases for welfare, and the processes and limitations of large-scale administration. Even worse, the field really minimized any confidence in human potential to grow out of dependency with a combination of personal and social supports. Above all, relying on service inputs (counting staff and visits), rather than on evaluating outcomes of services delivered, has had a debilitating effect for social work's intellectual foundations. Although their numbers were small in public agencies, some social workers were in positions in several public welfare programs either to change policies or to acknowledge that the task lay beyond social work's aspirations, and with that self-criticism to ask the profession to evaluate itself.

Social work, had it taken another course, could have gained recognition for daring in recommending where money should be spent and what institutional reforms should be made—even if unpopular. Since the social efficiency approach seems to reject such social engineering, social work has chosen a more cautious approach: promising help through personal counseling as the least costly approach while being effective. It is a promise not yet realized. The intellectual, scientific, and educational framework is lacking.

Reversing the Welfare State: 1980–1995

As the twentieth century ends, social work has grown unevenly. It has survived major changes in American society and transformations in the role of national government. But the trends identified in 1970 continued after 1980 with a more radically conservative character. The election of a Republican White House and Senate provided a favorable environment for those who believed that basic welfare state concepts were flawed—entitlement detached from personal responsibility and the use of government to alter the distribution of income. This swing was accompanied by other efforts to use welfare as a way to promote conforming moral behaviors. Those—especially the dependent poor—who engaged in "deviant" behaviors were not considered entitled to public help. These views made for a potent political brew and found wide support among a great many people.

For whatever reasons, the next fifteen years produced an about-face in national policies. Taxes for many purposes, but especially for social improvement, were opposed by a majority of voters. Quick cutting of benefits was delayed, since so many in all classes benefited from them, but funding to cover population growth and the rising costs of all goods and services was progressively reduced. These projected cuts did not take into account the twenty-year stagnation in incomes for the lowest fifth of the population and the increasing pressure on incomes of middle-class families due in part to the costs of new medical technologies.

By the early 1990s it was clear that a real sea change had occurred in American society. Leaders of both political parties were in basic agreement (often reluctantly) that the time had come to:

1. Replace lifetime guarantees of public support with policies to ensure that all able-bodied adults would have to find work in the private sector or, in extreme cases, in public employment if private jobs were not forthcoming. It became acceptable policy to prefer that the dependent poor live in poverty working full-time at low pay rather than live in poverty "on the dole" paid for by taxes.
2. Reduce public (especially federal) spending.
3. Devolve most responsibility for social ends to the states, the private sector, and families. In this view the problems the nation confronts should not be entrusted primarily to the federal government.
4. Make a balanced budget—rather than human conditions—the mantra for policy. A balanced budget was deemed essential to avoid a future catastrophe. If political stalemate meant that cutting had to begin with welfare for a start, so be it. In fact, cuts were made across the board but unevenly, if ability to absorb cuts was factored in.

The sharpness of this shift caught social workers and welfare advocates by surprise. The ground had shifted. There were fewer allies and friends in either party. Decisions had to be pursued in fifty states, not only in Washington.

Social work was not equipped to advance remedies in the face of such a change, let alone grasp its implications. The first response to shrinking resources and devolution of authority was to roll back the tide. They were slow to face the changes that had taken place in American society: changes in population, in class structure, in family life, and in public beliefs about social services. Appeals to the evils of poverty would not be enough. Voters and policymakers were looking only at evidence that paying collectively brought valuable collective benefits. Attitudes were of course influenced by political rhetoric, but the underlying facts could not be so easily ignored. The expectation grew that a balance between rights and responsibilities also meant work for all who could, even at low pay and even if children would have to do with limited or inadequate day care.

To deal with the new environment, social work faced radically different choices than in the past. It now had to face the erosion of its ability to act to change life conditions. The baggage of the past—to concentrate on the case dimension—needed to be matched by equal investment in economic approaches to a welfare system as well as compassion.

In effect, public welfare became the testing ground for the field's "individual in society" construct. Income maintenance is a social support, but the varied capacities of able-bodied adults to plan their own futures involves psychological as well as environmental forces. Social work did not lead in trying to transform or reform a welfare institution, as it had done in 1960. The current opportunity is not only dangerous, but seems to exceed the constricted capacities the field had developed over its hundred years.

Internal professional self-criticism has not been welcomed, but it has taken two lines.

The price of concentrating on a generic casework core and interpersonal skills was the failure to also equip itself with an education specializing in policy, economic, and political analyses, which now were central to changing life conditions. This criticism is illustrated by Specht and Courtney's book, *Unfaithful Angels,*[18] and by others over the years. The "change society" subjects are touched upon, but in so thin a manner that graduates could not compete with others, who spent more time than the entire casework curriculum ever provided to acquire the necessary skills. The consequences can be partially explained away by the curriculum processes and by the limited academic resources social work had succeeded in acquiring. Faculty and curriculum are weighted by teaching counseling and interpersonal skills, theories, and methods. There is precious little left for other in-depth teaching.

The emerging doctoral-level programs have, with a few exceptions, been poorly funded and have merely refined and elaborated on the masters-level curriculum. They have also depended too heavily on social work educators, with insufficient depth in political science, economics, and management or organization sciences as they could be applied to welfare. There are too many doctoral programs for the resources the field can mobilize, and perhaps too many graduates, who compete for the available jobs against graduates with more depth from other disciplines. Protecting the generic base for social work education without developing specializations has proven counterproductive. It is very different from the medical model the field has tried to emulate. If there is to be doctoral education, it should produce scientifically trained researchers capable of critically studying the outcomes and results of social work services.

The decision to concentrate on the psychological, the interpersonal, and case methods has been seriously weakened by the absence of rigorous research to assure supporters that the social problems addressed by these means are alleviated, not just relieved for individuals. The field's research has been weak and unconvincing by contemporary research standards. Even when the research finds positive results, they are weak and inconclusive for policy purposes. Early work like "Girls at Vocational High" consistently found that control subjects did at least as well as treated experimental subjects. This has been found true of almost all mental health therapies if one excludes the most severe psychoses.

Unfortunately, much of social work's response to this internal criticism has been defensive, understandably so since so many social work programs are engaged in a constant struggle to stay alive. But it has not been enough.

Achievements and Deficiencies with Which to Enter the Twenty-First Century

As a profession social work has alternated between periods of high hope and of nearly disastrous external changes. It has survived all of them. But in the late twentieth century the tide has turned, unfavorably for a field still counting on the conditions of the growth years to continue. It has two main choices.

It can build on its core case foundation, which, in the short term, is fairly safe. Many kinds of organizations still need workers to perform ancillary tasks in nonsocial-worker environments. They will staff the private social services dealing mainly with mental health and behavioral problems. They are also helpful to the health system, to educational institutions, and to some corporations, to smooth their handling of inter-personal and behavioral problems and to build bridges from impersonal institutions to citizens they hope to serve. Thus far there seems to be an inexhaustible demand for such personal help by individuals who find it difficult to cope in an impersonal world.

But in the longer term, these services will continue to be demanded only if those who must pay for them find that the results are worth it. Will individuals pay from their own pockets? Will the public pay if the social problems of family disorganization, child neglect, deviant behav-ior, and poverty are not, over time, reduced or cared for at a cost voters deem good value? To protect the longer term, social work in this option will need to substantially reexamine how it will handle the demand for results and outcomes. The older appeal that compassion requires acting on and that "we will take care of the problems for you, the public" will face a more demanding, and even harsher environment.

To retain ground gained will call for a self-critical look at the concep-tual and scientific foundations for professional practice and at the effec-tiveness of the present training and accrediting system. This has not really taken place despite an elaborate history of studies and committees. Prob-ably the cold shower that Flexner threw on claims in 1915 and that led to the case/academic system, will have to be repeated by those brought in from outside the profession to introduce independent analyses for the profession to absorb. A first step would be to open the scientific exchange with disciplines other than mental hygiene. Such serious cross-discipline exchange has been taking place in the policy world as well as in the phys-ical sciences. The twenty-first century may see some such movement as a major source of social change.* What is still lacking is a professional structure willing to invite this kind of criticism.

Most likely social worker education would have to produce a few grad-uates interested in crossing over to work with the many other disciplines trying to unravel the mysteries of human behavior. Biologists have al-ready set the tone by exploring the evolutionary and biological founda-tions for behavior. It is doubtful that many social workers have either the

---

The Economist of 4 October 1997 discusses signs of extensive changes in higher education. The trend is away from discipline and department barriers to broad collaboration across dis-ciplines not necessarily on one campus. Another major shift is toward new forms to link ba-sic and applied research to early operational testing through as well as public authorities.

interest or the means to join in this basic science enterprise, but most will in time be influenced by the outcomes of such research. Can social work's educational structure embrace enough new knowledge to affect practice on the front line? In the long term, perhaps; in the short term, not yet ready? This option effectively drops major attention to changing society.

An alternative is to correct the absence of a social work specialty skilled in the highly developed (if not always successful) arts of social change. This may involve bringing into the social work academy those who have specialized in the economic, demographic, and political aspects of policy making and change. Or the field could radically revise its own doctoral training to produce staff able to perform these same functions. The experience of the Heller School for Advanced Studies in Social Welfare at Brandeis University is worth studying (note that its name uses "social welfare," not "social work"). This writer acknowledges a bias for this approach, which is a model that the field has not yet taken seriously, although other scholars and public officials have.

Either approach would involve a major development of additional educational resources in a restrictive era *and* a reallocation of existing resources. This would not be easy, for it would threaten the dominant position of casework faculty in most schools and would mean the reallocation of time and curriculum space, recruitment of interim teaching personnel, the acquisition of new sites for policy field experience, and probably a lengthening of the time for acquiring qualification.

Is there professional discipline to focus and allocate educational resources, resources on two skills, quite different in content, rather than relying, as professional groups have, on a base generalist foundation (casework with emphasis on interpersonal relationships), which has been assumed to be adequate for entry into the profession. Subsequent postgraduate specialization was influenced by the basic foundation in interpersonal relationships.

True that the demand for such dually trained social workers is largely untested and additional resources for a more complex educational base lacking. Still it is encouraging that some schools like Columbia have begun to fund chairs in policy. But it is not yet clear whether such prestigious chairs will be filled by clinically trained social workers or by those trained in more relevant disciplines of economics, political science, or even anthropology. For the present, few schools have the means to try any significant elaboration in educational bases.

Greenberg and Skocpol have proposed trying to create a New Majority that concentrates on the common sense concerns of most citizens: income, access to education and careers, and affordable housing and health care. Such a majority of voters would believe in the power of government to make a real difference by commitment to collective, not individual, efforts to achieve broad social goals. The 2000 election campaign has not yet produced evidence of such a majority.[22]

Another approach was developed by Mimi Abramovitz of Hunter College.[23] It is an eloquent appeal for various "welfare reforms." Can this one lead to the Greenberg and Skocpol future? Unfortunately, it probably could have served better in the turbulent and growing 1930s and the 1960s; less so in the restrictive public and economic environment of the 1990s. For example, the report calls for jobs with benefits and a living wage and income support for those the market does not absorb. Social work's hundred-year history makes it clear that such an approach has very little appeal to its practitioners, who still seek to improve their professional status along interpersonal adjustment lines and not along economic ones.

All of these appeals call for economic concepts and ideas to start with. At a minimum, social workers can wait for others to produce the ideas and then support the ones they like, in which case the field is no leader in dealing with changing social conditions; its members act as other citizens do. It ends up relying on its influence in supporting ideas of others. But its influencing resources are meager. The running will be led by the new politics for which Greenberg and Skocpol call. It is less likely that social work is equipped just now or ready for so ambitious a task.

These options will seem daunting, and they are. This author has hope that the field can play some part in the future by rediscovering its dual purposes and taking decisive action to replenish its capacities. After all, it has survived alternating periods of hope and consternation. But it has yet to decide what part to emphasize (the individual and society or the individual), and it is not clear that it has the will to equip itself to carry out the choice in the changed environment the twenty-first century brings. If the field is to flourish, it will need less doctrinal passion, more intellectual skepticism. But it will also need determination, not cynicism or pessimism.

The Likely Future

This excursion into development and trends leads to one most likely conclusion: that social workers will continue to have a place in the social institutions of the nation, but not as shapers of policy, as managers, or as policymakers. Social work, with its generic education core, might continue to produce midlevel facilitators.

Social work's future in a clinical and therapeutic practice will depend on whether its educational foundation can introduce a sufficient self-critical evaluation of the outcome results of its practices. It will need to demonstrate credible effectiveness in helping with resolution of individual human needs. For this it will need to produce evidence to users and payers that the service gives value, not vouched for by the provider alone. The value may be to individuals willing to pay for the cost because they find it helpful. Or the value may be to society, which sees that certain troubling social needs are effectively (not only inexpensively) taken care of.

As to the shrunken aims to lead in social change, social work will most likely perform best by bearing witness to the needs it discovers through its daily work, while leaving to others the crafting of the changes to be tried out. To do more would require a major change in social work education—by the introduction of learning from other fields—far beyond any demonstrated ability to do so.

It is not a matter for dismay, only regret, that the 1998 social work celebration of its one hundred years has adopted the slogan "Take Charge of Change" with so little recognition of how meaningless the slogan is, given the field's current lack of means or self-awareness to carry out the charge. It indicates that the field is in danger of continuing on the circumscribed and minimal course suggested above. The constricted thrust of a century of professional evolution has its own survival power.

Part II

Fields of Practice—
the Challenge:
Achievements vs.
Unrealized Visions

4

Social Justice, Human Rights, and Welfare Reform
Wynne S. Korr
Donald Brieland

The United States has always reflected differing views of the poor and differing views of help giving: Are the poor responsible for their own condition? Are they entitled to assistance or should they have to depend on charity? (We consider assistance as public responsibility and charity as a private endeavor.)

Other key questions: Which levels of government should pay for assistance (federal, state, or local) and in what proportion? Then, which of the three should set the policies and which one should administer the programs? Should Americans in similar circumstances be treated similarly, or should states and local jurisdictions have the freedom to devise programs as their own constituents wish?

Social Justice and Human Rights

This chapter first describes a philosophy of social justice based on a human rights perspective. The social work profession highlights social justice in both the Code of Ethics and in the standards for the education of new professionals.[1] Models that would inform practice based on social justice, however, have received little attention.

From the Social Security Act to Welfare Reform

Next, the chapter reviews several court decisions on entitlement since the Social Security Act of 1935. The cases selected pertain to issues relevant to current welfare reform. We also offer a critical analysis of mandates affected by recent shifts from entitlement to disentitlement reflected in reform legislation—the Personal Responsibility and Work Opportunity Reconciliation Act of 1996 (PL 104-193).

The Personal Responsibility Act combines Aid to families with Dependent Children (AFDC), emergency assistance, and work programs into a single block grant under Temporary Assistance to Needy Families (TANF). Unlike previous open-ended federal funds for the states, block grants providing fixed appropriations to them are based on 1994 spending levels.

Social Workers View Social Justice

Several social workers developed conceptualizations of social justice that have influenced the profession.

In *Common Human Needs,* Charlotte Towle analyzed the place of public assistance in a democracy.[2] Writing near the end of World War II, she saw that the ultimate resolution of conflict would come after the war in how nations dealt with ensuring human dignity and individual worth.

> Public assistance laws and other social legislation are the culmination of a democracy's conviction regarding its responsibility for human welfare. Such laws provide a way for us to work with individuals in meeting their needs. . . . Day by day ours is the opportunity to carry forward and to make real the aims of democracy.[3]

David Gil developed a theory of social policy that began at the same point as Towle.[4] For Gil, social policy and systems of social order emerged to address basic human needs. Like Towle, he saw the fulfillment of human needs from the material to the spiritual as necessary for healthy growth and development.

Prevailing social policies may obstruct and violate individual and social development by thwarting the realization of basic human needs and real interests, even though perceived needs and interests may be realizable for many people. To overcome and prevent such ills and problems, prevailing social policies would have to be transformed into alternative policies, conducive to the fulfillment of basic human needs and real human interests.[5]

Gil's view of transformation is more fully developed in the critical perspective espoused by John Longres, who used critical theory as a model for praxis, making social transformation and social justice central to practice. Critical theory assumes that individual problems are often social problems. He then presented a theory of practice "in which the everyday services [that] social workers provide for troubled clients could, by extension, bring about the changes necessary to improve the ability of social institutions to secure the common good."[6]

Josefina Figueira-McDonough proposed a social-justice-oriented policy practice based on principles developed by John Rawls, who examined the interdependence of freedom and equality and the tensions between them. He posited that to have personal freedom, basic social goods had to be equally distributed.[7] Figueira-McDonough sees social justice as a value—a commitment to ensure equal access to basic social goods for all. A commitment to social justice begins with policy analysis to identify elements that need to be redressed "using criteria of equity, adequacy, self-determination, and efficiency.[8] The policy analysis serves as the basis for legislation, reform through litigation, and social action.

Social Justice and the Constitution

The rights of American citizens were derived from a unique understanding of the individual and the government when the Constitution was framed. That all men are created equal and enjoy the right to life, liberty, and the pursuit of happiness are paralleled by positive and negative obligations including government's duty to promote the general welfare and to allow freedom of information and religion.

Most school children learn first about equality of all men. Later, however, they may find out the historical facts about equality concerning gender, race, and social class. Women, for example, did not get the right to vote until 1920, and American Indians got it only four years later. African Americans and other poor citizens in the South were prevented from voting by poll taxes and tests administered by officials until the Voting Rights Act of 1965. Most people are unaware that a slave was counted in the census as only three-fifths of a person.

For centuries, we have struggled to refine and revise our understanding of the rights of citizens and the proper responsibilities of government. But first, we should recall the criteria that defined who was human. While the answer may seem to be simply biological (all homo sapiens are human), defining "human" in relation to rights is an evolving social construction. Women and children were possessions of husbands and fathers. Children are still regarded as possessions because they cannot survive without the help of adults. Among adults, workers are considered more human than "sturdy beggars." Poverty gets sympathy; pauperism does not. The current abortion debate centers on when one becomes human—whether rights should be accorded at conception or at birth.

Frameworks for Rights

Models focusing on human rights also provide frameworks for social-justice-oriented practice. They consider the rights of persons with mental illness and children, most notably, the United Nations Convention on the Rights of the Child.[9] In considering the rights and responsibilities of individuals, families, communities, and governments, the models can help people to understand public policy shifts determined by amendments to the Social Security Act. The models are equally applicable to understanding new policies in current welfare reform.

A variety of frameworks have been developed for understanding human rights. Positive and negative rights provide one model useful for social work.[10] Positive rights pertain to obtaining some social good such as treatment in the least restrictive environment. At the same time, people have the right to refuse or avoid unwanted treatments. Negative rights based on the liberty interest, avoiding undue confinement and on Fourteenth Amendment principles of due process, are more fundamental and have a clearer constitutional base than positive rights. *Lessard v. Schmidt* specified due process rights in civil commitment, and *Price v. Sheppard* established guidelines for obtaining informed consent to electroshock and other intrusive therapies.[11]

Brieland, Fallon, Korr, and Bretherton developed a model to conceptualize children's rights that can be used more broadly within social work.[12] We defined three domains: affirmative freedoms, entitlements, and protections. These domains help translate social work values while linking them to policy. Affirmative freedoms encompass the right to self-determination, but that right is not absolute. Self-determination comes with responsibilities to society and with limitations imposed by resources. For example, individuals do not have the freedom to act violently against others, nor do they have an absolute right to jobs or housing.

Entitlements are those affirmative rights that one can expect from society; for example, society must provide children under age eighteen with a free public education. Protections are obligations of society to protect vulnerable members; for instance, society seeks to protect children from abuse and neglect. Commitment statutes provide for involuntary treatment of those with mental illness who are a danger to themselves.

In an ideal system working toward social and economic justice, entitlement and affirmative freedoms form the basis of the individual's expectation of access to adequate social goods so he or she can develop to full potential as a citizen. Of the three components in our model, entitlements and protections are more frequently the subject of American social policy than are affirmative freedoms. Constraints on the individual that facilitate freedom for others are more clearly specified than individual freedoms. Consequently, Americans emphasize citizen responsibility over entitlement.

Now we turn to the major strategy of current reform: the goal of work. Exploring the model in relation to work raises the question, Are adults entitled to employment? No. In our society, paid work is seen as a responsibility. Adults (first men, and now women, as well) are expected to work to support themselves and their families. Once people are working, however, they may enjoy major entitlements including health insurance and contributions toward a pension. Also, once employed, they can file suit when they are fired without cause.

Both devolution and disentitlement stand in contrast to human rights principles that promote equity, yet both reflect long-standing traditions in American welfare and are based on English Poor Laws enacted beginning in the seventeenth century. Joel Handler presents a useful analysis of the relationship between English law and American welfare.[13]

The Poor Laws as Poor Laws

Freedom of movement (the right to choose where you want to live) is an example of an affirmative freedom. The Poor Laws included mandates on settlement. Assistance could be obtained only in the place of birth. A person who became indigent was returned there. Woodcuts from the period portrayed dependent women about to deliver a child being taken by ox cart across the parish boundary to give birth. This tactic ensured that their offspring would not be the fiscal responsibility of the mother's jurisdiction. The settlement policy became more restrictive with industrialization and greater mobility. The Poor Laws were amended to require "less eligibility"; the poor could not receive more aid than the income of the lowest wage earner. This kept benefit levels low. Although never legally specified, less eligibility has characterized American welfare since colonial times.

Failure of Localism

Localism was a major principle in the American Social Security Act as well as in the English Poor Laws. Our Social Security Act established three aid categories in 1935: Old Age Assistance, Aid to the Blind, and Aid to Dependent Children. Aid to the Disabled came twenty years later. Conflicting policies and varying benefit levels created inequities from one jurisdiction to another. As a result, Congress rejected this dimension of localism in 1974 by federalizing three categorical programs into a Supplementary Security Income program (SSI). It provided nationwide eligibility standards making benefits much more equitable.

AFDC, which had been charged with promoting laziness and immorality leading to illegitimacy, was left out of SSI. Examples of differentials in AFDC benefits: large industrial states generally had the most generous levels; rural states with a large proportion of racial minorities provided the smallest grants. This scenario highlights the failure of local discretion in program operation and points out the unwillingness of the states to standardize welfare grants for a constituency considered to be unworthy.

Public education provides the clearest example of problems of inequity created by localism. Government has attempted for several decades to equalize funds from one school district to another with only limited success.

Social Justice and the Supreme Court

Important disentitlements for welfare recipients were removed by Supreme Court decisions in the late 1960s and early 1970s. Three of them relevant to the present welfare structure are reviewed here. A fourth decision is of particular interest to social workers because it deals with home visits to recipients.

SHAPIRO v. THOMPSON

The Social Security Act did not require that eligibility be limited to the place of birth, but at first it permitted the states to establish residency requirements making newcomers ineligible for assistance. They were expected to continue to receive benefits from the jurisdiction in which they had lived for a stated period. At least one state set a five-year period for ineligibility, a policy that was met with demand for change. Residency requirements were primarily imposed where higher benefits or a favorable climate allegedly encouraged migration. Restricting aid to newcomers came to an end in 1969 in *Shapiro v. Thompson* when the Supreme Court outlawed residence requirements for public assistance and affirmed the fundamental right to interstate movement.[14] This decision was unpopular with state governments because Congress appropriated no federal funds to cover the added cost of support for needy newcomers.

History is repeating itself. Several states have tried to restrict movement by eliminating the incentive for migration in response to higher benefit levels. They established waiting periods for eligibility or proposed to discourage migration of recipients by paying no more than they had received in their former state of residence. These policies were repudiated by the federal district court in at least one state, Pennsylvania.

GOLDBERG v. KELLEY

Another important decision from the same period, *Goldberg v. Kelley,* established the right of due process review through fair hearings for recipients who received notice that they would lose their welfare benefits because they no longer met one or more eligibility requirements.[15] Previous to the *Goldberg* decision, recipients usually lacked the right to appeal. The decision applied only to those who received welfare, not to new applicants.

Following *Goldberg,* the previously accepted recipient received a notice of pending termination that included entitlement to a fair hearing. He or she could go before a hearing officer in the assistance agency to make the case to be retained on the rolls. The decision accorded due process to recipients who would not have filed suit because they could not afford to go to court. Fair hearings did not require a lawyer. Since current welfare reform provisions reject the concept of entitlement, fair hearings are not authorized. The unlikely step of going to court is apparently the only recourse.

TOWNSEND v. SWANK

Welfare policy toward higher education raises a social justice issue. Stereotyping the poor by restricting their opportunities for higher education is not new. The United States Supreme Court dealt with discrimination toward AFDC recipients in *Townsend v. Swank.*[16]

To save money, the Illinois Department of Public Aid amended its rules to terminate AFDC benefits to students ages 18 to 20 if they went to college. "To fit students for gainful employment," however, they could be continued on the welfare rolls if they chose a "vocational or technical training school."

A Chicago legal assistance agency, citing constitutional violations, accepted the request for service from mothers acting on behalf of several college students affected by the Illinois rule. The mothers lost in the lower courts, but on appeal, the U.S. Supreme Court ruled unanimously in their favor. Under federal welfare regulations, the Illinois policy was held to be discriminatory on two counts: it violated (1) the Supremacy Clause in Article Six of the Constitution, which established the primacy of federal laws over state policies, and (2) provisions of the Social Security Act, which established AFDC.

The decision did not rule on the third issue that the plaintiffs raised: violation of the Equal Protection clause of the Fourteenth Amendment. However, Chief Justice Warren Burger in his concurring opinion saw Equal Protection as a relevant issue:

A classification that channels one class of people, poor people, into a particular class of low-pay, low-status jobs would probably raise substantial questions under the Equal Protection Clause.[17] If a state did not maintain eligibility for college students from 18 to 20, it had to terminate AFDC benefits for all children when they reached age eighteen.

The new welfare reform law does not provide adequate opportunities for poor people to become self-sufficient. Too often it denies a living wage and the opportunity to seek higher education, which provides an effective means to better oneself. While Americans do not hold that everyone has the right to a job or to higher education, most people would endorse a right to "opportunity" and object to barriers to getting ahead.

The dollar value of a college education is a critical question in determining welfare policy. Data from the City University of New York show that, compared to a high school diploma, a college degree adds about $700,000 to lifetime income.[18] Support for higher education is a bargain for both society and the recipient, because everyone in this popula tion who has graduated from college has the best chance to move to self-sufficiency with an adequate income and thereby to qualify as a taxpayer.

A parallel to the philosophy of limiting poor children's ability to obtain higher education is found in welfare reform that limits access to higher education. Now, welfare is no longer an entitlement and higher education is no longer an approved choice under the Personal Responsibility and Work Opportunity Act. The result will be more extensive discrimination than that caused by the youth policy in the *Townsend* case. Formerly, many recipients with the help of AFDC and support from educational institutions used higher education as the route to financial independence for themselves and their children. Today, most adults receiving assistance who may see higher education as their way out of dependency cannot realistically meet current work requirements, fulfill parental responsibilities, and be enrolled in a college-degree program—all at the same time.

Unless waivers are granted or state funds used, welfare reform can deny higher education to hundreds of current and prospective students from welfare families. For an individual to maintain welfare eligibility, the law requires twenty hours a week of work activities. High school attendance or twelve months of vocational education are acceptable alternatives to work, but higher education is not. Recipients are considered to be worthy of vocational education but not to attend college.

WYMAN v. JAMES

The question of whether recipients should be entitled to social services has an interesting history. In 1962 new amendments provided resources for social service to all recipients. The purpose was to give people support to get off the rolls. Unfortunately, during the next five years the rolls increased and the initiative was ended. Instead, payments and services became responsibilities of separate staff members. Social workers tended to approve the change because they agreed that recipients by and large did not require case work. They were also disappointed that availability of services had not reduced the number of recipients.

Wyman v. James involved a challenge by a recipient of the rule requiring home visits as a condition of financial assistance.[19] Visits were an entitlement that she didn't accept. The agency hearing officer concluded that her benefits would be terminated if she did not comply, but the district court disagreed. The U.S. Supreme Court overthrew that decision and held that visits could be required, that they were not an invasion of personal privacy and did not violate the Fourth Amendment concerning searches. By this time, however, visits tended to be discontinued because social services were no longer required and visits involved risk to the safety of social workers in many areas.

Social workers are concerned that the only provisions for social services in the new welfare reform law are work-related. Apparently other services will have to come from voluntary organizations.

Other Disentitlements

What are other new concepts of welfare reform related to disentitlement? Examples involve teenage mothers and elderly legal aliens.

Following a tradition of restricting the movement of poor adults, restricting the movement of minors who seek benefits is consistent. Negative attitudes toward teenage mothers are reflected in welfare reform. To be eligible for welfare, the current law requires a mother under age eighteen to live at home with a parent or legal guardian.

The provision may achieve three purposes: to save welfare money by disqualifying those who refuse to live at home; to discourage sexual activity by teenagers, thereby preventing pregnancy; and, if a child is born, to promote release for adoption. Abortion will be an unintended consequence.

The requirement rejects the best interest principle in favor of a hard and fast policy that is clearly undesirable for some family members. It also may challenge a long-standing right that motherhood conveys legal emancipation, including choice of where to live.

We know that early pregnancy and parenthood get a variety of responses from other family members. Probably in the majority of cases, living at home is the best plan, but the requirement will force some mothers and children to stay in a hostile family atmosphere. Mother and child may even face physical abuse.

Welfare reform provisions also reflect a policy of nativism—rejecting claims of noncitizens. Most people favor this course of action toward undocumented aliens, but denying food stamps to elderly legal aliens seems unnecessarily punitive. This situation creates a serious hardship not only for the elderly, but also for their children, many of whom have only limited means. While other restrictions on legal aliens were eased in the Balanced Budget Act at the end of 1997, this provision of the Personal Responsibility Act remained unchanged.

Conclusion

Since the proposal of a social insurance program in the 1930s, social workers' and society's views about the proper response to poverty have changed several times. Many social workers followed the tradition of the Charity Organization Society in opposing social insurance as a form of public outdoor relief that encouraged pauperism. By the Kennedy-Johnson era of the 1960s, social workers, like most other citizens, supported Social Security, civil rights, and the federal poverty programs. Social workers have maintained their liberal stance. In the 1980s and the 1990s, however, Americans demonstrated increasing commitment to self-support, limited government, and voluntarism. They expressed opposition to redistributive programs. The Contract for America and welfare reform reflected the attitude changes.

The current conservative mindset leads people to focus on welfare, whereas the more significant issue is poverty. The United States is unlikely to go back to welfare as we have known it, but we are skeptical about loss of entitlements, substitution of block grants, and extension of local control that raise social justice questions.

Both motivation and education are major issues to which this reform contributes little. Fortunately, some states are willing to use their own resources to provide the aid for recipients who attend college.[20]

We are skeptical, too, about the stringent work policies that succeed best in a period of prosperity. When an economic downturn is felt, are states going to be willing to assume a greater burden to provide assistance, health care, and nutrition aid, or will they establish waiting lists?

We question whether business and industry can solve the welfare problem, let alone the larger poverty problem. The skills of recipients do not match the demands of the good jobs that are currently available. Employment policies, too, often include social justice issues if they involve a strategy of part-time employment with lower wages and no benefits. Subsidies for hiring welfare recipients threaten to lead to replacement of lower-level employees by those who are subsidized. At best, welfare reform may help the majority of recipients who get off welfare, and join the working poor who already make up two-thirds of the Americans in poverty.

NASW through its Code of Ethics and CSWE through its curriculum standards have joined in a commitment to social justice. While social workers no longer play a major direct service role with welfare programs, their advocacy of social justice on behalf of the poor is essential. An examination of economic justice in welfare reform should be a major step in that effort.

5

Social Work and Health Care Yesterday, Today, and Tomorrow

Helen Rehr

Gary Rosenberg

Today, health care is in a state of flux. As we enter the twenty-first century it is hard to predict what the American health care delivery system will look like: what range of social and health care services will be needed, available, and accessible; who will provide these services; and how they will be paid for. In the current deregulated and competitive climate, capped costs for prescribed benefits are becoming the dominant payment mechanism. Managed care—benefit prescribed capitated systems—have come into vogue and appear to be favored as cost control mechanisms. Although the majority of Americans have some form of coverage for their care, more than forty million people are without insurance (ten million of whom are children) and thus limited in their access to needed care.

Technological advances in science and medicine have been remarkable in the 20th century, reducing the incidence of disease, enhancing diagnostic and therapeutic directions, improving the quality of life for many, and extending life for the severely chronically ill. On the other hand, extending life via new technology and medications has not always enhanced its quality. Often, invalidism and disability have required ex-

Excerpted from *Creative Social Work in Health Care: Clients, the Community and Your Organization,* by Helen Rehr, Gary Rosenberg, and Susan Blumenfield. (New York: Springer, 1998).

tensive social, emotional, and financial aids, both from informal and formal sources that are difficult to obtain.

The changes in the health care industry have been profound since the end of World War II. There has been a growing shift from the dominance of physician services to alternate means of care, and from a voluntary not-for-profit to an extensive for-profit system in which demonstrated accountability for care delivered is expected. Limited access to care, rationing of services, religious and philosophical beliefs emphasizing forgoing treatment, and people's changing lifestyles and accompanying social-environmental impacts, are additional forces affecting the "to whom," "when," "where," and "how" of medical and social work services.

Social work has been markedly influenced by changing social forces, organizational development in the medical arena, and availability of resources. It has a history of more than one hundred years in medical and psychiatric institutions, paralleling the history of physicians, who became creditable professionals in the United States at the beginning of the twentieth century. But social work in health care began to secure its professionalism only in the last fifty years, starting during World War II, and is perhaps more vulnerable to the process of change than organized medicine.

Early History

The history of American social services in relation to medicine begins with the early stages of lay charity services for the sick, in their own homes and in a range of institutions. Social services and hospitals as we know them have their beginnings in America in the late nineteenth and early twentieth centuries. However, ministration to the "sick poor" has existed in one form or another since the beginning of recorded history.[1] There are recorded experiences in the Middle East of Damascus, Baghdad, and Alexandria as well as in Spain, where the Saracens founded hospitals of opulent luxury, patterned in Europe by the returning Crusaders, who then opened these medical institutions with a social service overlay to the sick poor.[2]

If one has to allot a date to the somewhat more formal beginnings of medically focused social services, one could select 1636, crediting Vincent de Paul "as the patron saint of all hospital social services."[3] From 1636 until the time of the French Revolution, the hospitals of Paris had full-fledged social service auxiliaries. They served as fund raisers seeking essential financial support; as visitors who brought "material and moral aid" to those on the wards; while as home visitors, informed by the ward aides about the requirements in each case, they made domiciliary visits and advised, directed, and assisted convalescents.

During the French Revolution, the system was abandoned, but reestablished again first as a Hotel de Dieu, the French euphemistic term for the resting place where the terminally ill would make ready to meet their Maker. (The beginnings of the respite hospice movement for the dying.) But soon hospitals were reformulated and each had a form of social service auxiliary.[4] Sir William Blizzard is credited with a comparable organized effort on behalf of the sick poor in the development of the London Hospital in 1791.

Shortly after the creation of the London Charity Organization Society in 1869 to improve conditions of the poor and to repress mendacity, doctors protested the abuse of "free care" in clinics by those "who could and should pay" a private fee. In 1874 the Royal Free Hospital asked the London Charity Organization Society to investigate outpatients as to their "social position" in an attempt to exclude ineligibles. Charles Loch was responsible for suggesting the need of a "charity assessor" (the hospital almoner to be) to deal with financial eligibility screening for the hospitals. Patients in need were referred to the Charity Organization Society, and those who could pay a small fee were referred to Provident Dispensaries, which were fixed-fee clinics, set up to deal with the "abuse" problem. The English hospital almoner was formally recognized in 1895 when for the first time an experienced social worker from the London Charity Organization was stationed at the Royal Free Hospital, "to review applicants for admission to the dispensary and to exclude those unsuitable for free care."[5] Thus, in England, one of the first roles of medical social services was to serve doctors as financial screening agents to exclude those who could pay for private medical care.

A later innovation in the medical social services in England was created by the hospital almoners themselves when, while screening for eligibility, they began to identify other social needs related to welfare relief and illness. The National Health Insurance Act of 1911 was responsible for broadening the scope of the social services given by the almoners to the sick who utilized medical institutions.

In the United States

The eighteenth- and early-nineteenth-century history of nursing and medical care in this country is glaringly black, with only small pockets of innovation brought about by the medical and social leaders of the different periods (for example, Benjamin Rush et al.).[6] The proprietary type of medical institution was indigenous to the New World, where unprecedented rapid expansion of the population over enormous territory created a demand for doctors long before facilities for their training existed. Thus, the country created thousands of doctors with little knowledge and skill, trained in commercial medical schools set up for profit. Hospitals set up by municipalities, religious organizations, and philanthropic groups for services to the poor were also the apprenticeship locale for doctors in training.[7]

Medicine and social work crawled into the twentieth century with no organized base, and with a belief founded on Social Darwinism's "survival of the fittest." The American doctor at that time was a product of diploma mills, whose only requirements were the ability to read and write. Medicine in this country was without a scientific base and its ministrations had little therapeutic benefit. Doctors and hospitals were avoided by rich and poor alike. Science, however, had begun to enter European medicine, where new discoveries, new understandings of disease, and new techniques were developing. As the twentieth century began, this knowledge was also transferred to those American medical establishments affiliated with universities.[8] Medicine's role in the United States moved from the custodial to the remedial under the drive of these elite institutions.

Social ailments of the time included a depression, economic uncertainty, the influx of a massive immigration from all parts of Europe, the development of a new capital class, and a growing labor class of people. Along with breakdowns in the social environment, these ailments also were reflected in the growing patterns of illness, disease, and disability.

These social factors *may* have contributed to the changing character of medicine, and they certainly affected social welfare. The social break-down resulted in the rise of a social reform movement fostered by social work's early leaders and socially minded citizens.[9] The emphasis in the early years of the twentieth century, supported by the social reformers (many of whom were women) was on environmental and material needs. It was these pioneering volunteer women who brought a social and humane orientation to the medical institutions.[10]

The social services in American hospitals, formally initiated in 1905 at Massachusetts General Hospital, were evolved from the work of lay women who facilitated the development of organized social services and nursing by prodding the male-dominated medical institutions to be re-sponsive to the social needs of the poor.

At the end of the nineteenth century and beginning of the twentieth, physicians such as Adolph Meyer, Richard Cabot, William Osler, Francis Peabody, and Charles Emerson, with nurses and lay leaders, created the After-Care Movement in Psychiatry. The social worker served as the investigator and gatherer of information for doctors, who functioned with the belief that social and environmental factors were responsible for given diseases. Those beliefs led to the development of home supports in the form of home care and social services to patients and families. These leaders brought to medical education the need to expose their students to the community environment, working conditions, and people's homes to search out the etiology of illnesses. Medical students worked alongside the new medical social service workers as "friendly visitors." The emphasis was on the family, the neighborhood, and the workplace. The charity organization and the settlement house movements revealed the vast social and health needs of people living in crowded, deplorable urban conditions. Prevention and improvement of the social-health aspects of individuals surfaced as the means to deal with social problems. This resulted in a social reform movement directed at legislative and community levels, led by the leading social reformers of the era, such as Dorothea Dix, Jane Addams, and Edith Abbott[11] and joined by physicians who held similar beliefs.

Medicine, and later nursing, separated the clinical from the public health. Similarly, the social reform movement led to separating the clinical and the social welfare within social work. The medical, nursing, and social work professions moved to claim the clinical in the care of the individual as their primary function, and social-health policy as secondary. This disparity in emphasis between the clinical and social policy and the multiprofessional wish to dominate the clinical arena continues today. In the performance of their social services, workers in the medical area were frequently directed by bureaucratic or physician-determined expectations. Control of the who, the what, the how, and the when was not always in the primary aegis of social workers, who, like nurses, frequently were referred to as "handmaidens" to doctors. Both fields, female dominated, had to find ways to "control their performance." Autonomy was sought by nursing and by social work.[12] The issue of professional autonomy versus administrative authority is still common in the health care arena. It, along with interprofessional conflicts, surface over and over in many forms. Turf conflicts are still prevalent between doctor and nurse, doctor and social worker, nurse and social worker, social worker and hospital administrator, and between those dual authorities responsible for institutional service, the medical and lay boards. Roles and functions of the many health care professionals in the institution continued to become more confused and overlapping.

The Early Twenties and the Current Scene

By the mid-1920s social work, already studied by Flexner (1915) who identified its many problems, had attempted to formalize a scientific base to its services.[13] Mary Richmond (1917) had written *Social Diagnosis,* and social workers were attempting to integrate social diagnoses into medical diagnoses.[14] Social and environmental conditions were recognized as contributing to given diseases. However, by the late 1920s and early 1930s social work moved to accept a psychoanalytic framework for its casework services. The 1929 Depression reintroduced the need for a range of welfare benefits and concrete services.

In the 1940s a major shift in emphasis began in social work from psychoanalytic theory, which dominated social services from World War I to World War II, to the social sciences, which were beginning to achieve status. Social workers began to reintegrate a broad social concern into their philosophy as they witnessed people's problems and needs. The neighborhood and the community were seen as the loci for services for individuals and groups at risk. Social workers introduced group services and community development efforts in health care settings as well as in the community.

In the 1950s, the proliferation in major cities of homeless persons, illegal aliens, the uninsured sick, and an aging population led to the largest demands ever on the resources of the health care system. Diversity rather than homogeneity became the norm in communities. In addition, work environments were constantly changing, affected by the newest technology that touched not only the work environment, but also the workers' health status.

In the 1950s and 1960s, although there were some periodic fiscal concerns, there was a burst of affluence that resulted in major social and health care change. The civil rights movement, the women's movement, the drug culture, the sexual revolution, and more technologic initiatives were introduced than ever before. An explosion of federal involvement in the medical and social work fields resulted in provisions like the Hill-Burton Act for the construction of hospital beds, an expanded Public Health Service, a burgeoning Veterans Administration, the Health Professions Education Act, Medicare, Medicaid, the Maternal and Child Health Programs, and active support of biomedical research in the field by the National Institutes of Health. Rehabilitation, developed by Dr. Howard Rusk during World War II, began to come into its own, as physical medicine was introduced for the growing numbers of disabled adults and children. Poliomyelitis, the scourge of the fifties, adopted rehabilitation as a significant treatment modality. The recognition that parents were essential providers of care for children with chronic illnesses was instrumental in the beginnings of family therapy, a concept also extended in the case of the mentally ill.

The benefits of the fifties and sixties are fast being constricted as a result of fiscal crises and a taxpayers' revolt that furthered conservative limitations in support of existing social benefits and major changes in social policy. In health policy the national focus in the seventies, eighties, and nineties shifted from governmental commitment to ensure high quality comprehensive care to a so-called safety-net to capped limits in medical care, which resulted in less service for the most needy.[15]

From 1980 to today the reshaping of health care continued, with responsibility for payment of services falling more and more to the individual. Increased premiums, larger deductibles, cutbacks by the federal government in all its programs, and curtailment of employment-based health benefit programs have meant more out-of-pocket costs for everyone and created a population of between thirty-five and sixty million Americans without any insurance or very limited coverage. Those affected have been persons with marginal incomes, including people of color, those in uncovered work situations, millions of children of these marginally employed people, the poor elderly over sixty-five, and the homeless.

The fiscal crisis affected hospitals as early as the mid-1970s. The shift from per diem reimbursement for a length of stay to the diagnostic-related group (DRG) payment changed the hospital pattern of care from in-patient services, irrespective of length of stay, to a prescheduled hospitalization and a greater emphasis on ambulatory services, including the development of a multitude of one-day surgical programs.

Deregulation of health care, a 1980s phenomenon, changed health care from a public social utility and voluntary care system to a commercialized system. For-profit health enterprises entered the marketplace adding a third tier of care to that of the voluntary and public hospitals. The traditional charitable support for hospitals has been incorporated into a "charitable cost" factor in the reimbursement provided by third-party payers. Today, it is being challenged. With the privatization of hospitals came a practice of "creaming off" the private or well-insured patients, generally less sick than the medically indigent. This resulted in cost benefits to the for-profit hospitals and severe fiscal impact on the voluntary and municipal hospitals.

All governments, federal and state, put caps on what they would reimburse, and thus the "de facto" rationing of care became commonplace. Not only were benefits and services changed, but beds (and hospitals) were closed when occupancy rates were considered too low to support them. In the mid-1980s, while many beds and even some hospitals in urban areas were closed, the AIDS epidemic hit the major cities, resulting in a severe shortage of hospitalization for this population and a lack of acute and long-term care.

Two major societal trends will affect social work services and education in the future: the changing health care environment and its financing, and the changing demographics of society.

The Changing Health Care Environment

The United States is witnessing the most drastic industrial reorganization since the nineteenth century. The corporate takeover of American health care is a primary example. The not-for-profit medical institutions have begun to compete with those in the for-profit marketplace. The falling occupancy rate, cutbacks in reimbursement, and the resulting impact on revenues have moved the most enterprising medical institutions into market-driven enterprises sponsoring programs for wellness and fitness, behavioral medicine, drug and alcohol abuse, and eating disorders. A specialty emphasis on specific chronic illnesses with a "one-stop shopping" focus is the growing trend. Chronic illnesses and disabilities are being treated in multiservice centers. Specialty services are in vogue, such as those focusing on women's and children's social-health needs, including a host of counseling modalities, health education, and health maintenance. The programs are multiprofessionally staffed, and a growing interdependence among health care professionals is evidenced. Hospitals have created or joined in community/regional public health endeavors with their actual and would-be consumers of care to address current needs of sick individuals and families[16] and the social and political health care issues. In addition, health education and prevention programs are being introduced into neighboring communities with the assistance of local residents. A growing partnership between hospital providers and consumers is more in evidence than ever before.[17] Diversification and new organizational approaches have come into play along with a growing emphasis on how to keep people "well" and keep those over eighty years of age in the community. Managed care programs have proliferated, and many are commercial enterprises with a cost containment rather than quality of care focus. While many of the managed care programs have been sought by industry to control utilization of services, there has been some growing concern about their cost superimposed on the customary costs of services, and their occasional denial of services professionally deemed necessary.

Businesses and governmental agencies that pay for health care have organized to force their insured populations to use designated providers. By and large, patient freedom of choice has been exchanged for controlled benefit plans and lower costs. The health care system will be influenced in the future by four characteristics that will affect the way systems operate:

- The system will be vertically integrated. From preventive services, wellness programs, and health education through primary care, secondary and acute care to long-term care; all services will be obtained through one unified system.
- Regional system coverage will replace local catchment areas as the dominant form of targeting patients, resulting in a wide geographic area of people being served.
- Payment by capitation. The health care system will share the risks and potential rewards and will be paid a flat fee per covered life or per covered service/package.
- Costs will be lowered below the present fee-for-service market prices.

To increase the scope of health care services while decreasing the costs of health care, the new delivery system will have to require redeployment of major resources and people from inpatient acute care to ambulatory care, from specialist settings to primary care programs, and from tertiary care to early diagnosis and prevention programs. Because of fiscal concerns and the drive for higher levels of productivity, an increasing number of hospitals are restructuring by expanding into health care systems, shifting away from professional to cross-functionally trained personnel, and flattening the administrative structures of the system to create a horizontal system of management. With the downsizing has come reengineering of the inpatient services, with the introduction of team-organized patient-centered care units drawing on in-house trained personnel.

As a result of downsizing changing the way work is done and eliminating unnecessary work have become essential. First, the superfluous work must be identified.[18] In an organizational design, organized around core processes rather than functions, the health care environment is expected to be seamless, uncluttered by boundaries among departments where discontinuities can occur and where difficult and unnecessary work processes can appear.[19]

As a result of restructuring the health care environment, health care professional groups have had to justify and redefine themselves to administrations and to each other. The professions maintain that practice expertise is specific and unique to each discipline and that organizations benefit from centralization. Present-day systems involve removal of professional boundaries through cross-trained staff. To bridge divergent perspectives, new structural models must mesh the values and goals of the designs and the professions. Patient-centered care units do not always achieve the values and the goals.

The introduction of the DRGs in the eighties reduced the average length of stay of hospitalized patients and the number of hospital admissions. In addition, it resulted in a major increase in ambulatory visits. In contrast to the past, voluntary and municipal hospitals now serve a greater concentration of sicker in-hospital persons, which places heavier demands on the health care providers. Thus, more persons are leaving the hospital in need of a great deal of at-home support services. Such services, however, are limited even for those who can afford them. Shortened hospital stays reduce the cost of hospitalization but not the overall cost of illness. The discharged patient also is affected by the additional costs of direct services at home and the indirect social costs to his or her family members who also provide services.[20] However, there has been at least one major social benefit from the introduction of DRGs in that discharged patients do have the advantages of an early return to familiar surroundings, which may be more supportive than that of the hospital.[21] Social work has played an ever-increasing role in assisting with early discharge planning and attempting to secure optimum "assists" for patients and families.

As health care delivery and payment systems change, the industry needs to redefine roles and functions. For example, the elderly have been major users of hospital services and will continue to be so. However, chronic illnesses and age-related problems require a multitude of services. Linkages with community support services both voluntary and private are being negotiated, and in-house and at-home rehabilitation, both in physical and social functioning, are being used for early intervention.

The major changes in how medical care is reimbursed have thrown all the health care professions into turmoil. Tensions have grown among physician groups and among the different health care professionals. Boundaries have become fuzzy as competition and turf battles bring on instability. In addition, there has been a proliferation of nonmedical personnel entering into the counseling, support, and fringe health services or providing alternative therapies. These new providers create an expanding health care industry of nonsupervised and nonregulated enterprises ranging from well-known interventions such as diet/exercise/behavioral change programs to untested pseudo-health-related programs. Self-help groups are multiplying for alcoholism, substance abuse, person abuse, specific diseases, and bereavement. These programs, overwhelming in number, set up their own support services, more often than not without professional guidance, and drain billions of dollars from a worried, stressed, and anxiety-ridden public. There is little documented evidence of these programs' benefits.

In addition, there is increasing medical technology that is not always cost-effective and is frequently provided by inadequately trained personnel. Many costly procedures, such as heart transplants, are available only to very few, and the technology tends to lead to more depersonalization of care. On the other hand, there are biomedical breakthroughs that have and will continue to revolutionize the care of some. For example, technological advances are responsible for the shift from lengthy hospitalizations to one-day ambulatory surgery. New biomedical knowledge also brings new awareness and knowledge about one's physical and personal self, which can result in better self-care, health maintenance, and quality of life. The caveat is that sound self-care requires an educated and motivated public prepared to be responsible for its own health maintenance.

The most prominent demographic trends today are the changing nature of the family, expansion of the population over sixty-five, growth in the number of children eleven years of age and under, and increase in out-of-wedlock pregnancies. These demographic factors affect the focus and educational underpinnings of social work practice.

Social-Health Problems and Social Work Services

People's behaviors and their areas of interest reflect demographic trends, societal patterns of the times, and specific concerns of a region or a locale. Related social ills and medical illnesses command ongoing professional commitment, because in spite of many public health gains, social health problems of the most vulnerable populations have proliferated.

Among the most severe are

- inequities in health services, such as barriers to access, affecting millions of uninsured, underinsured, and minorities who "fare more poorly than the general population";[22]
- problems of poverty, homelessness, and hunger, which undermine individual health;
- social disorders reaching near epidemic proportions, including person abuse, violence, accidents, suicides, and substance abuse;
- social diseases resulting from lifestyle, environmental, and work conditions including AIDS, cirrhosis, emphysema, and coronary disorders;
- inappropriate use of services, such as seeking medical care late, arriving with advanced illness, and misusing emergency services;
- sicker patients with multiple and severe chronic illnesses making greater demands on hospitals and their staff;
- thirty-three million people with functional limitations that interfere with their daily activities, and more than nine million with limitations that prevent them "from carrying normal functions;[23]
- lack of preventive and health maintenance services;
- limited and costly at-home care resources in the community;
- growing numbers seeking care for stress, fear, and anxiety arising out of stressful daily living patterns and work situations;
- growing numbers of people with disabilities;
- increasing numbers of developmentally disabled.

Vulnerable people present in vast numbers to medical institutions and to providers. Medical care has been the prevailing means of service to relieve symptoms, but that care is frequently fragmented, neither coordinated nor comprehensive. Treating these populations requires a more focused social-health approach, including "counseling, support services and health education leading to self-care and to motivation to change existing lifestyle patterns."[24] The social and environmental ills affecting large numbers of the population require cooperation among many professionals, consumers, business, and government to develop and implement effective social-health policy.

Social and political events have affected the place of social work in the domain of service to people. During World War II social work gained status in the military, in world-based organizations such as the Red Cross, and in veterans' programs. After World War II a period of general affluence gave rise to one of the most progressive periods in governmental programs in American history. A plethora of social-health programs were created in which social workers played key roles.

The federal government advanced social work's status in health care via its legislation in the 1960s, which endorsed medical social services for recipients of government-supported health services to military personnel as well as to beneficiaries of Medicare, Medicaid, and maternal and child health programs. However, although social work in health care gained some prominence, it never gained power. Because the biomedical model dominated health care, social work's roles were largely incremental. Social workers worked alongside physicians in a medical model of care that has been individual-patient focused and in the medical institutions that have been essentially dominated by physicians. In the last half century, social work has striven to bring a biopsychosocial focus into medical care by demonstrating the impact of psychological, social, and environmental factors on patient and family attitudes and behaviors, diagnosis, treatment, compliance, and self-care. As medicine has begun to better value the biopsychosocial components, physicians and institutions have moved from a purely disease-and-disorder view of medicine to a more comprehensive social-health approach to care.

With incremental changes in health care philosophy and delivery growing, social work found itself in a more collaborative partnership with other health care professionals. It began to seek autonomy, with the right to regulate and control its own activities. It sought professional status and emphasized a knowledge base (values and skills) sought licensing and accreditation, supported an association, and controlled the education for the field. The health care field had gained tremendously in what it had to offer individuals in dealing with disease, disorders, and disabilities. But the tide began to turn starting in the 1970s, when the country suffered a brief recession, and accelerated in the 1980s, when social events, social problems, and a fiscal crisis furthered a public mood of increasing conservatism and a conservative government. Deregulation, privatization, and corporate supremacy became the political vogue. An overspent government gave industry leeway to privatize much of the health care system shifting it away from a voluntary, public health, social utility model.

In spite of today's fluorishing economy, and ultra-conservatism toward health care provision is still evidenced in corporate American and the federal government. It has produced another period of uncertainty and even conflict among the different disciplines. Currently, only a tenuous cooperation exists among them, as all aspects of the health care field have been and are continuing to be threatened by severe cutbacks and reorganization. Survival is today's major concern.

Although social work has found a key place in health care in spite of waves of crises, it will need to find new ways to hold and enhance its position. The rationale for maintaining social work services in health settings is based on a number of assumptions:

- A biopsychosocial focus is required to deal with the needs of individuals who are sick and disabled.
- A multiprofessional program, which recognizes biopsychosocial factors and cultural diversity in the care of individuals, is essential to quality care.
- A working partnership between professionals and consumers of care is essential for informed decision making.
- Services should be accessible, available, and affordable to all in need.
- Services should be comprehensive, coordinated, and continuous, to allow individuals to achieve maximum benefits.
- Prescribed opportunities to asses and reassess performance and programs should exist.

Shared professional and consumer responsibility for planning and implementing needed health care services is essential to improve the health status of the community and public social-health policy.

These assumptions support the premise that care of the sick and prevention of illness requires a social-health formulation involving a health care system that balances components. Shown is a model of a future-oriented health care system.[25] The model contains roles and functions for social work within the health care system even as that system changes.

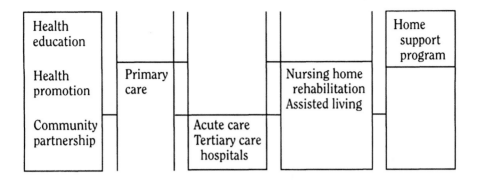

Social work has made many contributions, but more will be needed in the future. It has already played an important role in

- acute care of patients, by providing quality discharge planning, counseling, and resource information, which reduce length of stay;
- primary care, by providing psychosocial assessments for integrated care and facilitating patients' access to needed community services;
- counseling patients and supporting family members in response to the illness and expectations, and assisting with decision making;[26]
- emergency care by crisis intervention, triaging, and referring patients to appropriate care sites, and assisting in seeking entitlement benefits;
- ensuring access to needed services by outreach and case finding, eliminating obstacles, and providing financial counseling;
- health promotion, maintenance, and prevention, by identifying those groups at high social risk, and assisting in developing programs to support health education;
- long-term care, by providing social work treatment and investment in informal and formal support services within a design of continuous care;
- contributing to the development of a comprehensive and integrated social-health delivery within medical institutions, and by serving as case managers to coordinate needed care;[27]
- providing counseling to medically ill psychiatric and developmentally disabled patients;

- providing care within a patient-family focus, including end-of-life decision-making, bereavement and grief support services.

The government's debt crisis became a paramount issue in the 1990s. Our legislators moved to reduce the major social benefits designed for selected groups, and health services have continued to be on the agenda for cuts, including social work services in health care. Across the country, social work programs have been downsized, eliminated, or reengineered into new service formats.

Why has social work been unable to find a permanent and more fundamental place in health care? Because it has been difficult to find voices for its services. Social work's objectives are to improve individual and family life and mitigate social-health ills, at least in the individuals it treats. The lack of public recognition and status is determined by many factors.

- associates with the poor and needy, and this is seen as functioning primarily in the welfare arena;
- labors with those who have little or no voice in society;
- relates to physicians who hold the reins and are chary of competition in health care;
- has not demonstrated its cost-effectiveness;
- has not been active in affecting public social-health policy, such as working in the political arena toward addressing multicaused social problems;
- has not found an effective collaborative role with other health care professionals in addressing social-health issues;
- has been largely a charity and government-based supported service;
- has its own internecine battles (academics versus practitioners).

All of these factors have led to a general unease about the profession and uncertainty about its purpose and direction. For example, in the health and mental health care fields (which have the largest numbers of social workers and are responsible for the majority of counseling services), social work has not contributed sufficiently to cost-benefit and effectiveness of its services.

Future Domains in Social Work

Social work practice in health care will take place in the community as well as in the hospital. It will focus on the person and given populations; it will be a mix of social service provision and short-episodic and long-term counseling; it will take place in teams of multidisciplinary professionals and paraprofessionals. Social work services might not be centralized in the traditional sense, but social work consortia and coalitions will influence social work practice and the institutional social-health programs for vulnerable populations. Supervision as it is known today will not exist. Maintaining high standards of practice will require new modes of education and continuous learning. Social workers will need to be increasingly autonomous and self-directed.

Programs to Enhance Community Health

Community health programs are based on the concept of developmental provision, as need is uncovered. Social work will help provide "those social utilities designed to meet the normal needs of people arising from their situations and roles in modern life."[28] Social work along with other professions helps provide the social architecture for enhanced community living.

The interaction of the increasing rates of societal changes—shifts in technology, more crowding (population density), information overload, stress—will play a role in creating new disease patterns. Social work practice will be based on the following concepts:

- An integral relationship exists between people's health and their environment; just as confronting the actual infective and causative agents of disease is critical, so are the changing social and physical environmental conditions that permit disease onset.
- Vulnerability to new waves of health risk is greater for the economically disadvantaged in every community, so that improvement in living conditions becomes, by definition, a social-health promotion strategy.
- Physical and social functioning of individuals in relation to their in-

formal and formal networks is more significant than disease patterns themselves.

Using social epidemiology and survey methods, health care social workers will be helpful in identifying and reducing health risks. As they contribute to health promotion, social workers will add to community strengths. In part, the move to this domain represents a return to social work's settlement-house roots, which emphasized amelioration and reform from an empowerment perspective, social science as an integral part of practice, a comprehensive response to complex problems, and cross-functional program management. In this domain, social workers will

- respond fully to the organization mission, dealing with the constraints, while translating policy into programs that focus on individual and familly need;
- help institutional leaders develop the capacity to reach out to their communities and learn about their strengths, needs, and wants;
- help institutions respond to the needs of communities by identifying models of service, distilling research knowledge, linking the institutions with others that have similar dreams, brokering resources with other institutions, developing the social technologies to be tested and refined, and engaging in an efficient collaborative planning process;
- build the capacity of local institutions to initiate comprehensive programs;
- increase the accountability of institutions;
- increase citizen participation in and control over institutions.

One gain social work has achieved in health care is the ascendancy of its leaders to administrative levels in medical institutions. These leaders brought about increased emphasis on social-health and person-focused services. They have applied their professional values to socializing the institution, individualizing care and drawing on family support. They also sought necessary changes in the environment to provide service for emergency needs while strengthening overall health care delivery. To continue to be successful in the new health care system, social work leaders and their colleagues will need to rely on a solid foundation in practice to continue to effectively apply social work values.

Leadership matters, and good leaders will be critical to the future of social work in the new health care system. Roles and functions must be rethought, and a new pattern for social work must be set. Leaders will have to share their visions and work effectively with other professionals as institutions expand their roles and functions in the ambulatory arena and in community-based services. Institutions are extending ambulatory linkages to primary care, home care, respite, end-of-life decision-making and hospice care, life care residencies, and nursing homes. They are affiliating with a range of community-based social agencies and community hospitals. Because integrated ambulatory care is seen as cost-effective, financial support for services will come from a host of payers. The new primary care focus will be structured around triage and for the entire continuum of care. It will provide access to medical care either by designated physicians or other health care professionals who will follow preventive care and selective services.

New Models of Social Work Service

Social work has already begun to move away from its primary traditional role of working with hospitalized patients and families and planning their discharge and aftercare. As financing of medical services shifts to outpatient arenas, there is evidence of support for social work services; insurers, government, and individuals are beginnings to recognize social work's value and cost-effectiveness. However, the new financial arrangements demand that social work develop new organizational and service delivery and evaluation patterns. Reimbursement revenues are finite; capitation and managed care benefits will fix the dollars available for care, and social work will have to document its claim to dollars with cost-benefit data.

Social work will be expected to provide viable services within specific, often brief, time frames that focus on a contract with the client for shared responsibilities within a projected visit and/or time frame. Because of shortening lengths of hospital stay, the shift to ambulatory and prehospital and posthospital care, and the introduction of a range of one-day ambulatory surgeries and technological treatments, social work will be expected to develop new organizational arrangements that address the needs of diverse populations in diverse locations. Preadmission and fast-track triaging will be used to identify individuals with potential aftercare risk. Contractual arrangements with managed care organizations will set prescribed service allocations.

Social work leaders are already introducing models of mixed social work service that include combined salaried and private social service for private pay and insured patients, coverage for clientele of group practice physicians, community organizing services, and social work services for affiliated health care providers. In the institutions, social workers will be assigned to selected medical arenas (patient-centered care units, for example) to be available to clusters of patients with special needs, such as severely ill children in pediatric care, and their parents.

Integrated Services

Social workers will serve as case managers, facilitating use of services and resource allocation. As case managers, they will review service determinants to learn whether client-provider contracts with Medicaid and other insurers are being implemented or require change. Such individual and collective case reviews should lead to new knowledge and to development of new treatment models.

Social workers will become community-based clinicians with one foot in and one foot outside the institution as they provide direct services and serve as consultants about the social-health needs of clients within the community social work services network.

Collaboration will lead to networking among social and health agencies, and services will be drawn from many sources. The health care system may support "bundling" of community and health services coordinated by the hospital. Consortiums with "packaged care" are already in the marketplace. Because of the breadth and scope of its services for the geriatric population to women's health to rehabilitation, social work will continue to contribute to the design, organization, and implementation of integrated services.

Cost-Effectiveness of Service

Social workers will need to look at how their services can help reduce provision of unnecessary and costly medical services. The worried well, the stabilized sick, and those with social ailments will be redirected from medical care to less expensive social services. Social work can demonstrate that their services enhance physician productivity and efficiency. Social workers will have a responsibility to define vulnerable populations (high-social-risk screening will be expected). Preventive services and those that eliminate unnecessary hospitalizations could be offered. Since they offer health promotion and health education services as well as counseling, social workers will have to demonstrate cost-effectiveness in developing a more motivated, educated group of patients.

Shift in Focus

Social work will shift from a diagnosis/disease-illness focus to one that stresses individual physical and social functional capacities. Concentration on social risk factors as they affect health status will require specialized knowledge of the etiology, treatment, and consequences of disease and disability. Major emphasis will be placed on those risk indicators related to chronic illness in the elderly, the physically and developmentally handicapped, children who are acutely and chronically ill, individuals who are terminally ill, and bereavement services to related kin. The family and/or the informal network will be critical components affecting how the individual copes with illness. Because resources for social work are diminishing in the formal service community, much care will be provided by family and will draw strongly on clients' informal support systems. Social workers can facilitate this involvement because they are trained as family-focused therapists. Involvement with patients will be focused on social and functional diagnosis and enhancing motivation, discharge planning, support of home care, rehabilitation, and linkage with essential community-based facilities.

Case Managed Care Framework

Social work will find a role in case managed care programs, particularly in those that it has designed, such as adolescent health services, rehabilitation, employee assistance programs, and wellness and prevention programs. Social work will continue to provide a range of brief services, concrete and environmental, for those clients who require limited intervention. Inpatient discharge planning services will be time-limited and brief for those who have positive family and environmental support systems. Triaging and screening will facilitate case finding among those at high social risk and those who need long-term care. For certain targeted groups, a continuum of care will have to be prescribed, including services such as information and referral, mental health counseling, support services, prevention, environmental assistance, and home care. These functions should be negotiated as covered services because social workers' knowledge of community social agencies and their ability to network with others will be a requisite for efficient managed care programs. Caregiver training and services will be critical.

As care most likely will be prescribed, limited in service, and limited in the number of contacts, services are likely to be packaged or bundled with defined reimbursement rules. Social work providers will set critical pathways for patient care. They will set standardized patterns of care and guidelines for service delivery in prescribed situations. Like physicians, however, social workers will argue for the "art of practice" as an essential component in individualizing client care.

Hospitals will serve a more critically ill population as well as persons with social disorders such as substance abuse and person abuse, focusing on dollar-productive, reimbursable services. These services will be provided by a multiprofessional team of administrators, nurses, doctors, and social workers. Because of the biopsychosocial factors inherent in social disorders, leadership of these programs most likely will be nonmedical.

Special Service Programs

To assist in establishing wellness and health maintenance programs, social work will need to identify vulnerable and at-risk individuals. Employee assistance programs will grow as institutions recognize the need for keeping their staffs well and productive by helping them and their families during illness. Such services will be reimbursable and will involve a large number of social workers who will be invested in the problems of the workplace: substance abuse, elder care, child care, stress management, and bereavement. Hospital employers will seek skilled counselors with business acumen and financial management skills to run such programs.

Counseling services that are endorsed by managed care programs will not be open-ended. No payer will cover ongoing, unlimited care. Clinical focus will be on a "strengths" perspective, which tends to shorten the need for service, and payers will expect goal-focused, time-limited, capped services. Providers will have to substantiate the benefits of services or they will not be reimbursed. Payers will expect meticulous documentation of screening, assessment, goals, plans, services provided, and outcomes. Utilization limits will be established, and the professions and their clientele will have to address how much care is enough and find new cost-effective methods. Although government support of scientific studies in medicine will be reduced, research will continue, as will development of new technology to enhance diagnostic ability and introduce new treatments. But to be incorporated in the new health care system, new technologies will need to be proven more cost-effective and beneficial than current procedures and technologies.

At-Home Services and the New Technology

Computer use will be driven by information needs of social work clinicians and administrators. Information will be used to enhance individual provider performance and integrate departmental requirements. Data will be used for studies that affect service planning. Telecommunications and telephone counseling will be major clinical interventive tools with clients at home or in institutions. The benefits of those tools have been demonstrated and will need to be covered by insurance.

Specialization

Although the trend toward task-oriented and product-trained teams is developing, social disorders such as person abuse and substance abuse will require specialized professional care. In addition, many victims of chronic illness will require ongoing specialized assistance to achieve a reasonable quality of life. For example, the field of geriatrics has demonstrated that a multiprofessional team is needed to address the myriad problems the elderly face.

Community-Based, Patient-Family-Centered Care

Social work will build on collaborative models of service, achieving team leadership and partnership in a community-based, patient-family-centered care system. Staff will be culturally diverse and trained to work with cultural diversity. The focus will be on helping clients achieve quality and optimal living patterns. Social workers will work with colleagues in like-minded organizations, networking, building consensus, and setting priorities for community needs. Priorities will be based on research that informs projects for programmatic change. Multifocused accountability to clients, the institution, regulators and payers, and the profession will be predicated on pro bono publico as well as on the good of the individual.

Health Education

Most health insurance programs of the future will require health education. Many large corporations already support employee wellness and fitness programs. Self-care education will be a major function of social work practice in employee assistance programs, with self-help groups, and as writers for popular magazines.

Fee-for-Service Social Work

Although fee-for-service medical *care* will decline as group capitation practices show steady growth, social work compensation for service (even within capitation plans) will continue to grow as medical practitioners seek psychosocial counseling for patients. Because managed care and other insurers support mental health counseling, the majority of which is performed by social workers, these providers will need to learn how to contract for services with clients, clarify client and provider responsibilities, and set time frames and fees for service. Social workers also will have their own group practices with linkages to medical group practices.

Marketing

Social work will need to invest in marketing its services and learn to do so effectively. It will have to strengthen its identity recognition among constituents and encourage clientele to acknowledge its value. Institutional providers, community residents, and organizations that pay for services to insured members will demand to see the cost-benefit of social work services. The visibility of these services and their recognized benefits will facilitate marketing.

Quality Improvement, Client Outcomes, and Satisfaction

Comprehensive, continuous quality improvement programs will be expected. Such activity requires systems to gather relevant data, and social workers will need to conduct applied studies by gathering and analyzing these data.

A major means of ensuring the cost-benefit of client services is to measure social-health outcomes that reveal the effects of care on patient physical functioning, stress, and social functioning, and on family and others. While Patient and family satisfaction studies concerning social (and other) services may be considered subjective, they have been revealing to

111

both payers and providers. The consumer will be asked "what he perceives, his expectations, what he believes is happening, did happen, and his satisfaction with the outcome." Correlating client satisfaction and provider satisfaction will be customary. Case finding and high social-risk screening to identify vulnerable populations will be expected. Documenting and understanding the outcomes of social work services should lead to new treatment models, enhance productivity, and uncover the need for continuing education. Practitioner feedback will be essential to ensure continuous improvement in the quality and cost of service. Studies of satisfaction and outcomes will influence reimbursement as payers will tie reimbursement to demonstrated effects of therapies.

Participation in Epidemiological Studies

To address populations at risk, social workers will need to be in multidisciplinary coalitions with public health professionals and other disciplines. Studies of at-risk populations facilitate disease control by uncovering vulnerable individuals and groups. To permit setting priorities, studies should be regionally based, multidisciplinary in nature, and should include community residents and industry partners. Epidemiological studies can help the institution and social work define programmatic needs, case-find prospective users, set guidelines for service and evaluate cost-effectiveness. Findings should influence social-health policy deliberations and the linkage of social-health care to new knowledge.

Leadership

Social work leaders will need to be strong and committed to the integration of social-health care in a context of multiprofessional collaboration. Social work leaders will no longer be solely caretakers of social services but will be collaborative organization builders, seekers of information, partners with staff and colleagues. They must be able to set priorities and encourage staff to join in new visions. They will need to prove, encourage, and facilitate cost-benefit studies in order to ensure ongoing support for social work service in an integrated social-health system.

Knowledge

What has been critical knowledge for social work practitioners in the past remains critical for sound social work services today and tomorrow. Clinical interventions are vital components of the social work enterprise. They will continue to be the essence of practice, but will be refined in the context of new roles and functions. As financial issues escalate, triage and assessment skills will need to be enhanced and practice interventions modified in order to service more clients in shorter time frames. New models of treatment will develop with experience and study. While they will continue to focus on individuals and their families in an environmental model, social workers will also need to master the case manager function as well as oversight of caregiver services. A study of Fortune 500 corporations[29] found that personnel managers and insurance carriers supported social workers as efficient case managers for mental health services, and nurses for medical care. To effectively assume case manager roles for disease- and disability-related services, social workers will need to develop better "strengths-based" approaches.[30] Because it emphasizes what an individual and/or family members know and can do, strengths perspective lends itself to outcome-focused practice.

Social workers are effective in preventing the overuse (risk exceeds benefit), underuse (failure to use services), and misuse of health services. How do social work services add to the quality, effectiveness, and appropriate use of the health system? How does social work contribute to achieving a desired health outcome consistent with current professional knowledge? Social work has developed and implemented the following:

- high social-risk screening as part of standardized assessments;
- health social work protocols that standardize known treatment techniques that are proven effective;
- information systems that capture and evaluate outcome data and provide feedback about effectiveness to providers and payers.

Social workers also will need to become more knowledgeable about disease, disability, and mental illness, including their direct and indirect consequences, etiology, diagnosis, treatment, and the social and physical functioning potential over time. As they study their practice and engage in selected case finding, social workers will find themselves more knowledgeable about risk factors and more involved in disease- or disability-specific groups, particularly the frail elderly, and in new women's and children's programs.

Collaboration and the Multidisciplinary Team

These will remain the sine qua non of social work in health care. The ability to collaborate requires professional self-realization and a stance that supports patient advocacy. Social work will need to continually clarify its role in an interdependent relationship with other health care providers, not only in service delivery but in program and policy deliberations. For example, experience with patient-centered care models is likely to prove that task-focused services do not sufficiently individualize patients' needs. Social workers along with patients, families, doctors, and nurses will raise concerns about task-oriented care, and consumers will pressure institutions to reintegrate a comprehensive professional service that ensures socially oriented, consumer-friendly care.

Education of Social Work Practitioners in Health Care

Professional social workers have a long history of self-education, and of collaborating with other disciplines in encouraging and promoting education in all the health professions and the public. The social work profession is responsible for:

- continuing the education of social work practitioners so they can offer services that are relevant to the social-health problems of the times;
- developing tomorrow's social work professionals through investment in collaborative partnerships with schools of social work and the provision of sound practical education in health care settings;
- transmitting social work values and knowledge to other health care professions in order to enhance their understanding of social-health concerns and service delivery;
- educating others, such as volunteers, about the nature of social work services so that they can help make services available.

Continuing Education

Every professional social worker, regardless of field or modality, requires continuing education to develop social work practice, skill, and expertise. No field of service can remain constant or static; it must reorder its practices and priorities in terms of societal and organizational changes. In their efforts to improve the quality of their service, agencies should offer orientation for new employees and in-service training to inform practitioners about agency policies and programs and to enhance their practice skills. When linked to schools of social work, agencies often establish clinical relationships or research partnerships with academics. Continuing education is essential because it;

- facilitates application of new knowledge to practice concurrently;
- maintains currency in clinical content and enhances professional status;
- stimulates research and innovation in practice by group learning;
- promotes professional standards;
- improves economic potential;
- enhances vendor reimbursement levels.

Continuing education is the responsibility of the individual social worker, the professional association, the professional department of social work, and the agency in which practice takes place. These associations are the bridge between practice assessment, in which areas for improvement are identified, and program assessment, in which recommendations for improvement have been applied.

Social Work Student Education

Academic social work education does not fully prepare professionals to work in the wide range of health care settings. To date, it has done little to introduce health content or to emphasize health promotion and maintenance.

To function effectively in health care practice settings, social workers must have current knowledge of the health care delivery system and must understand dynamic changes in the system and how to deal with them. To practice effectively in complex health care systems, social workers must also understand the intricacies of the organizational structure, health care financing, and its correlation with service delivery. Moreover, as social workers begin to practice in disease-specific arenas, knowledge of disease, disorders, and disability is required. The social worker requires self-awareness about the impact of a client's illness on himself or herself and needs to know about the social and physical limitations that might be the consequences of illness and of the individual's social environment. A working knowledge of social-health diagnostic and therapeutic processes and the relevant resources are key to service in any setting. Finally, the multiprofessional organization of social-health care demands skills in collaboration and team work.

To collaborate successfully requires professional self-realization, a willingness to advocate for one's patients, and partnership with other health care professionals. Although the new graduate is not expected to be fully prepared to handle complex situations, the new graduate *is* expected to understand that sickness and medical care are the phenomena of daily living.

Education of Other Health Care Professionals

Since its beginnings in medical settings and in mental health programs, social work has contributed to and been influenced by sociology, medicine, and psychiatry. In its earlier form, social work brought a social-environmental component to medical and psychiatric diagnosis and treatment formulations. Over time, a biopsychosocial frame of reference was developed as the philosophical base of patient care, and social work participated in this formulation.

A clinical social work staff can participate in required and elective educational programs providing learning opportunities for medical students, social work students, and students from other health care professions. The curricula can include information about:

- the effect of social and personal needs on health status and on access to services;

- societal provisions for promoting and maintaining health and pre-venting disease;
- patterns in health care planning, policy development, financing, and the organization of services;
- the emergence of consumer concerns in a voice for quality health care;
- quality improvement and professional accountability;
- a social-health frame of reference for all aspects of health care;
- an epidemiologic approach to understanding persons at risk;
- the place of community social services in the support and care of those in need;
- the impact of the complex health care delivery system on patient care;
- the partnership between patients and providers;
- interprofessional service delivery as a tenet in social-health care.[31]

Social work needs to assume a major role in medical education within the medical school. It should participate in determining educational policies and practices, developing curriculum, and determining social work content for providing medical students with a wide range of experiences from graduate education to internship and residency programs to continuing education of practicing health care professionals. In addition, social work needs to enter into full collaboration in research with many different medical social issues. It should also play a key role in a partnership with the community in the planning and delivery of community-based services. In teaching institutions, clinicians carry out these functions in their practice or in their specific teaching responsibilities in medical education.

Social work achievements in student education, continuing professional education, and the education of other health professionals requires that practice and programs must be of good quality and must be provided in valued settings. But social work cannot rest on any laurels. It is vulnerable in terms of service delivery and in education. Because its scope encompasses management, program development, community networking, and new functions and roles wherever clientele in need are found, education for social work practice must expand beyond its present boundaries. The skills social workers have today may not suffice for tomorrow. The current system for educating social workers may not be adequate to build the skills required in the coming decade. It may be necessary to also teach them about:

- organization dynamics and translation of policy to program (services) focusing on the individual and family;
- ways to deliver social work care in primary care practices, and community-based settings, rather than solely in hospitals;
- methods for drawing on consultation from social work and other disciplinary expertise;
- work in a wide range of fiscally structured programs such as managed care, fee-for-service, and group practice;
- developing collaborative skills for a multiprofessional practice and program planning;
- ways to evaluate one's practice and services for outcomes and drawing conclusions for change as well as professional accountability;
- participation in educating social work students and other health care professionals;
- recruiting and retraining minority social workers and those who wish to advance in the field;
- collaborating with academic social work;
- understanding the value of information and its utilization;
- designing and participating in applied studies;
- assisting in better distribution of social work services in underserved and rural areas;
- participating in community-based activities and being aware of community needs and relevant data;
- participating actively in outreach programs;
- educating the public about how to use a health care system and what to expect from it;
- educating the public about self-care, health maintenance, disease prevention, and diseases and their consequences, with emphasis on social and physical functional limitations;
- working with the elderly, disabled, vulnerable, and other major users of health care;
- developing greater awareness of social illnesses;

- defining the role of social workers in service and in social action;
- entering into coalitions to enhance the social-health of the community.

Market forces affect schools of social work and health care organizations. Each has responded to these forces in different ways. Health care agencies and schools of social work have reciprocal needs. It is vital to create a set of educational processes through which schools, the field, students, other health care professionals (including public health practitioners), payers, and clients forge a new set of relationships that provide bridges to the new world of health care and social services.

Educating for social work in health care requires a consortium made up of the multiple parties involved in health services to create curriculum and practice for today and tomorrow. The implementing structure should allow for joint deliberation, decision making, and appropriate participation in

- developing curriculum and determining educational goals;
- making available opportunities for field testing innovative programs;
- making available opportunities to teach in the appropriate locus, broadening the concept of the campus to include the agency setting;
- relating to the realities of a complex multprofessional system;
- making available a wider range of agency programs and activities including a range of processes and functions as learning opportunities;
- offering continuing educational opportunities;
- permitting an exchange of staff between school and practice, on lend-lease sabbatical, or planned arrangement on agreed-to objectives;
- developing a set of guidelines and expectations for experiential learning, shared with students, and made a conscious component of curriculum;
- developing standards for instructional centers and field educators with recognition through awards of faculty rank;
- making research principles, methodology, and applied studies a conscious process by the joint development of (a)measurements of

educational effectiveness; (b)methods to assess social services, their utilization patterns, quality, and cost allocation, with particular emphasis on professional accountability; (c)methods to assess the utilization of differential manpower; (d)studies to enhance knowledge and skills in looking at the implications of program change
- making overt the costs of all aspects of the educational expectations, both academic and field, and jointly seeking support mechanisms;
- making available to lay groups the understanding and the knowledge relevant to achieving the common goal and to enlist appropriate lay representation in the deliberations.[32]

Conclusions

Make no mistake. Changes in health care have been dramatic and pivotal. Market forces are transforming the system, and how it is financed will affect what will be provided. Social work must be vigilant against the medicalization of its services. In the basic triad of public health (medicine, nursing, and social work), medical care remains significant for the sick, but health promotion becomes more meaningful. The most important determinants of health status are preventive services and quality-of-life standards.

As the health system changes, social work in health care has three possible alternatives: decrying change and portraying it as diminishing in quality; sharing the plans of others for change; developing innovative programs in partnership with health care colleagues and the community. Evidence exists that social workers can take any one of the three pathways. However, creative social work leadership in partnership with creative social work staff can be the catalyst for innovation. Creative leadership will help support an informed public, particularly consumers of social work service, who will agree to and lobby for quality professional care. Professional social workers, particularly in academia, have always argued for a scientific base for practice, but this has been as difficult for social work to achieve as it has been for all behavioral sciences.

The professional status of social work in health care is neither prescribed nor tidy. Just as the health care delivery system is changing, so too must social work, for if it does not, it will have little reason to exist. Change should mean expanded roles: contributing to institutional status, resources, revenues, and programs while supporting access for prospective clients, eliminating fragmentation and obstacles to service, advocating for integration of care, counseling those in need, creating alliances in the community and with other medical institutions, and meeting social-health needs.

Social workers' experiences in clinical settings serve them as they observe client needs and recommend programs. They test the quality of service with the means available to them, in particular when they do applied studies and draw on their findings to enhance clinical knowledge and improve care. Collaboration is the sine qua non in health settings. The recognition that every health concern has a biopsychosocial component has brought an interdisciplinary view of social-health care, which is attested to by an extensive partnership in practice.

Social workers have a curiosity about their practice that consists of live interactions, in which they seek to learn what is happening, why it is happening, and what will improve services. Observations prompt the questions that lead to exploration and ideas. As social workers "reflect-in-action," they move toward managing their professional selves and their relationships with others and toward a self-directed practice. The complexities of the health care institution and the autonomy of medical practice may well have served as models for social workers to seek their own autonomy and self-directedness. That sense of autonomy, combined with knowledge of the medical organization, has allowed them to advocate successfully on behalf of clients. The complexities of illness and disability have helped them value the tenet of family intercession and the meaning of ethical dilemmas and human values. This knowledge of the environment and community resources has informed individual client counseling and helped the institution recognize the need to share health care planning with local residents.

Competency and skill are governed by knowledge and experience. These are enhanced by professional accountability measures and by quality assurance. Social workers have learned to translate institutional missions and goals into services that benefit patients. Social workers also benefit the institution by providing early intervention and easier access to available resources for patients. Their services have had a value-added marketing effect for the institution and helped reduce the liability of risk.

Social work in the community has created better perceptions of providers and institutions among local residents. As social workers extend their boundaries beyond hospital walls, they see increased interest in their institutions in home care, nursing homes, long-term care, adult day care, schools, special housing, rehabilitation centers, assisted living care, primary care, and in wellness, prevention, and employee assistance programs. Social workers have applied health education in the direct client situation and in addressing the lay public.

With all that has been done to enhance the clinical enterprise, both in performance and in administration, social workers have assumed ongoing responsibility for their own continuing education, for educating tomorrow's social workers, and as key contributors to other health care professional education.

Much has been done, but so much lies ahead. These are critical times. How does social work safeguard its gains, thwart attacks on services, ensure professional survival, and promote programs into the next century? It must "come out of the closet," so to speak. It must be visible, market its services, educate its constituencies, participate in policy deliberation, and, above all, demonstrate the benefits of service to individuals and their families, the communities and its providers, and those who regulate and pay for care.

Beyond its commitment to the profession, social work must join in coalitions with other health care professions to secure and support providing human service. As medical care institutions and providers negotiate with insurers and other payers, commitment to the uninsured and underinsured must enter into the deliberations. As downsizing continues, where will further cuts be made? Safeguarding quality and access must be paramount in commitment to the public. Social work education must move beyond its academic walls and enter into academic-practice partnership with public health professionals, the people, and the business community. Joint planning will help social workers face today's social-health problems, the changing environment, the fiscal crisis, the reengineering of health care delivery, and will determine the realities of social work practice for today and tomorrow.

6

Social Work: Conceptual Frameworks Revisited

Donald Brieland

Wynne S. Korr

This chapter examines the work of those social workers who dedicated themselves to an important indoor sport: a half-century of efforts to develop a unified conceptual framework for the full range of social work. It then raises the question, after more than fifteen years since the last endeavor, what are the prospects for achieving such a framework appropriate for the new century?

The Milford Conference Committee of the American Association of Social Workers recommended a new model of social work training in 1928. The name was chosen because the conferees met first in Milford, Pennsylvania, in 1925. As the English would put it, the group constituted a working party. Twenty sessions totaling thirty days were devoted to the task.

The forty members proposed that a generic casework concept replace the five separate areas of instruction that had been offered: child, family, psychiatric, medical, or school social work. No one educational program had offered all five. The report, including standards for training and for casework practice, was published in 1931.[1] The generic model was to play a key role in legitimating social casework as a university-based field of study.

Defining a profession usually requires a statement of its uniqueness. Consider Helen Witmer's definition of the prime function of social work.[2] It identified social work's uniqueness and also went beyond services to the individual to include functioning of social institutions:

> Not only are individuals aided but the adequate functioning of social institutions is facilitated and human needs are more effectively met.... Social work is an institution that serves other institutions. The interdependence of institutions is characteristic of the total social structure but it is only social work that has the task of rendering the work of other institutions more effective.[3]

Early on, De Schweinitz also offered a brief comprehensive definition: the body of knowledge, skills, and ethics professionally employed in the administration of the social services and in the development of programs for social welfare.[4]

With casework as Milford's sole concern, a unified conceptual approach was much easier to develop than it would be after group work and community work joined casework as generally accepted social work methods.

A conceptual framework appropriate for all of social work would never have been seriously considered in the 1950s if a variety of national organizations, each representing some aspect of social work, had survived. The creation of the National Association of Social Workers, however, brought together organizations from seven fields: casework, community organization, group work, medical social work, psychiatric social work, research, and school social work. It took seven years of negotiation to effect this remarkable merger in 1956.

Meanwhile, while the negotiations were going on to form NASW, the American Association of Schools of Social Work in 1951 published a study of social work education financed by a Carnegie Foundation grant. The association intentionally selected "outsiders" to carry out the project—Ernest V. Hollis, chief of the Division on Colleges of the Federal Security Agency, and Alice L. Taylor, training consultant for the Bureau of Public Assistance.

Chairperson of the association's committee for the project was Harriet M. Bartlett, a leader in medical social work and later a professor at Simmons College School of Social Work. Under the auspices of NASW, Bartlett would seek to define a common base for social work over more than twenty-five years.

The Hollis-Taylor report sought to broaden the scope of social work and to encourage professional development.[5] It recommended that colleges offer content on social welfare to undergraduates but that graduate study be required for professional social work. People with lesser education could serve as technicians or volunteers.

The objectives cited in the report were derived from United Nations pronouncements. Selected statements illustrate how Hollis and Taylor saw social work:

> [Unlike health, education, and religion] the social worker cannot exclude from his consideration any aspect of the life of the person who seeks help in solving problems of social adjustment. . . . The well-trained social worker makes the nearest possible approach to full and constant awareness of the interplay of social, economic, and psychological forces in the lives of the troubled people who come to him for assistance. . . . Consequently, social work seeks to perform an integrating function for which no other provision is made in contemporary society. . . . The well-trained social worker becomes a "social diagnostician" for the community.[6]

The newly organized NASW Commission on Social Work Practice, with Bartlett as chair, lost no time in providing a working definition of social work practice.[7] William Gordon, a professor at Washington University in St. Louis, succeeded Bartlett as chair of a subcommittee that provided a critique of the definition.[8] Gordon considered the first three sentences of the Working Definition as its essence:

> Social work practice, like the practice of all professions, is recognized by a constellation of value, purpose, sanction, knowledge and method. No part alone is characteristic of social work practice, nor is any part described here unique to social work practice. It is the particular content and configuration of this constellation which makes it social work practice and distinguishes it from the practice of other professions.[9]

Unlike most definitions of a profession, the NASW statement did not consider social work to be unique.

Gordon emphasized the focus on "social worker-in-action" rather than the abstraction *social work*. He commented:

> The worker-in-action idea made it possible to begin with a broad enough idea to encompass the different methods formulations (case work, group work, and community organization) rather than the dubious task of trying to extract from each what was common to all.[10]

Gordon also identified the primary and ultimate value of social work: it is good and desirable for man to fulfill his potential, to realize himself, and to balance this with equal effort to help others fulfill their capacities and realize themselves.[11] He offered a definition of social work practice as "interventive action directed to purposes and guided by the values, knowledge, and techniques which are collectively unique, acknowledged by and identified with the social work profession."[12]

The 1958 Working Definition continued to get Gordon's attention. Next, he dealt with the distinction between the components of value and knowledge. For him, *value* meant strongly preferring something to the point of investment of self and goods rather than maintaining what is preferred. *Knowledge* was derived from the most rigorous interpretation to the most objective sense data a person is able to obtain.[13]

Werner Boehm, Director of CSWE's Curriculum Study, provided a definition of social work that others found useful:

> Social work seeks to enhance the social functioning of individuals, singly and in groups, by activities focused upon their social relationships which constitute the interaction between man and his environment. These activities can be grouped into three functions: restoration of impaired capacity, provision of individual and social resources, and prevention of social dysfunction.[14]

He offered the following value statement:

> [T]he human being must be understood the way he is. . . . Man is more than a physical being, he is more than a social and economic being, he is more than a psychic being. He is a unique combination

of coward and hero, troubled and unworried, complicated and simple, magnanimous and petty, creative and pedestrian. He is the utterly unique and precious. And it is our high task as social workers to place ourselves at his service.[15]

Next came the most comprehensive effort to try to integrate a fragmented profession—Bartlett's book, *The Common Base of Social Work Practice,* published in 1970.[16] The volume was written in collaboration with Beatrice Saunders, director of NASW Publications, who was to play a key role in later conferences convened to develop consensus. In Bartlett's view, the young social work profession persisted in asserting its continuous interest in both the person and his environment. To fulfill its purpose as a helping profession, social work must come to grips with the whole person-in-environment phenomenon. However, she contended, earlier attempts at such a conceptualization gave way to psychotherapy as the primary interest. Among the early contributions, she cites Mary Richmond's discussion in *Social Diagnosis* under the topic of social evidence and a statement on capacity and environmental demand from Mary Antoinette Cannon in 1935.[17] Cannon wrote:

No longer in the mind of the social case worker is poverty a sort of moral failure or even a disease of personality; it is a discrepancy between individual capacity and environmental demand upon it. No longer is rehabilitation of the dependent the case worker's concept of cure, but rather the restoration of balance by strengthening environmental support on the one hand and releasing resident energies in the individual on the other.[18]

In the seminal text on social casework, Gordon Hamilton recognized that "the human event consists of person and situation, or subjective and objective reality, which constantly interact."[19]

Bartlett applied Boehm's term *social functioning* as a central concept. She used a medical social work example: "there began to be movement away from concentration on specific diseases (the medical approach) or on unique reactions of individuals (the casework approach) toward identification of common *psychosocial* problems of illness viewed within a social work perspective."[20]

The Common Base drew a distinction between agencies and the social work profession. Agencies and programs come and go, but professions persist for centuries. Of necessity, agencies focus on specific social problems and tend toward rigidity because of their bureaucratic organization, but professions are potentially more flexible and responsive. Social work will grow through its values regarding man's potential and an increasingly scientific body of knowledge about social functioning, seen as the exchange between people and their social environment.[21]

Bartlett described the relationship between the common base and intervention. The first four components of the common base—focus, orientation, knowledge, and value—all underlie intervention. They have priority over techniques, methods, and other forms of action in social work practice. They are followed by a central focus on social functioning and the primary orientation to people.[22]

Social research has a unique contribution to make to the development of conceptions and the testing of generalizations related to the common base. From her interest in integration applied to research, Bartlett, who had a family foundation, gave a grant for a project on metanalysis, which tested research findings in mental health. The project director later offered a definition of metanalysis: a quantitative method for literature reviews that specifies the rules for combining data from original research studies and for analyzing methodological and study features that account for differences in findings.[23]

Metanalysis provided a method to accommodate research in a conceptual framework.

Bartlett's Working Definition and *The Common Base* stimulated the interest of the NASW Publications Committee. In 1974 this diverse group reflected about social work's purposes and activities and questioned whether any consensus could be established that cuts across the profession's specialties.

The concern was sparked by development of a generalist foundation as a base for social work education and a B.S.W. degree approved by NASW and the Council on Social Work Education. As a result, specializations for advanced practice in the M.S.W. degree program were being debated. The editorial board of *Social Work* and the NASW publications committee planned a special issue of the journal to identify major issues facing the profession. They chose a conference as the means to develop the content. Harriet Bartlett was later revealed to be the anonymous donor of the grant for the conference.

Six questions were posed incorporating those of earlier scholars, among them Bartlett and Gordon:

1. What is the mission of social work?
2. What are social work's objectives?
3. What do social workers currently do? What should they do, or not do, to achieve their objectives?
4. What sanctions should social workers have?
5. What knowledge and skills are available that would enable social workers to achieve their objectives?
6. What are the practical and educational implications of the mission in terms of the profession's objectives, interventions, sanctions, and knowledge?[24]

Five social workers with different perspectives were invited to write papers responding to the questions. One innovation, participants received and read the papers in advance of the meeting.

Thirty-six conferees, including four NASW staff, were selected mainly from the publications committee and the journal board. The procedure generally followed the Milford Conference model. The first conference was held at the University of Wisconsin, Madison, in 1976. The special issue, including selected excerpts from the discussion and four response papers, was published in 1977.[25]

Scott Briar's summary recognized the centrality of *mission* and *values*. He highlighted three conclusions from the discussions:

1. The difficulty of devising a statement about mission and purpose. "Most practitioners tend to define the whole profession within the image and limits of their own practice world. . . . Practitioners will adopt with confidence varied definitions of their profession." The unique thing about social work is its diversity. Such a statement as, the purpose of social work is to *"improve the quality of life,"* is too general to differentiate social work from related professions.
2. Concerning values, the continuing controversy between *social change* and *individual change*. No one at the conference would do

away with concern for social change. At the same time, clinical social workers have to help clients adjust to conditions that should be changed.

3. The generalist-specialist issue. A sharp division was clear between those who saw specialization as both inevitable and desirable and conferees like Pincus and Minahan who addressed the problems of fragmentation of social services and the need to bring fragmented resources together to meet the needs of the client as a whole person.[26]

Briar concluded that the profession must continue to raise the questions of purpose and identity. He observed, it is not good when the profession cannot clearly and simply articulate what is common to the activities of all social workers.[27]

Two of the excerpts indicate the spirit of the discussion and treat topics beyond the Briar summary:

On sanction: The business of a profession is expertise. . . . The community gives a particular group sanction if it respects the expertise of that group. How do you operationalize sanction? I think we have to occupy the territory, say it is ours, and then fight for it. . . . In this society, sanction is self-assumed.[28]

On practice and education: Does anyone think that the base can be provided at the baccalaureate level, given the amount of time and space available at that level? Here is what the generalist is supposed to be able to do:

- Hold a broad general view of the whole social situation.
- Analyze the interactions between people and all the resources systems involved.
- Intervene in those interactions.
- Determine what specialists are needed from other disciplines and mobilize their knowledge and skills.[29]

About the time of the conference, another approach to specialization appeared:

Whenever a large number of people is found to be affected by a dysfunctional mismatch between their coping capabilities and one or more of these sectors, an area of specialization may be established—provided a body of knowledge is available that when applied will lead to demonstrably successful corrective interventions. If social work's dual focus is maintained, these interventions may be directed toward effecting change in the individual's coping behaviors, in the impinging environment, or in both.[30]

No clear agreement on the purposes and objectives of social work was reached at the first conference, but the outcomes led the NASW publications committee to convene a second meeting in 1979 in Chicago, again with Bartlett's support.

The purpose was to seek greater agreement and to apply the conferees' formulation to "special areas of practice," that is, specializations—aging, family, health, industrial social work, minority groups, mental health, and schools. That conference used the same format, with papers prepared in advance. The authors selected were identified with the seven special areas.

Social Work published the conference papers and proceedings along with a working statement on purposes of social work.[31] The statement is also reproduced here.

Highlights of reactions to the statement from nine conferees were:[33]

A radical social work conceptualization based on six principles:

1. *Radical practice proceeds from critical analysis.*
2. *Human liberation is the primary goal.*
3. *Social welfare institutions are areas of struggle for liberation.*
4. *Social workers are agents of social reform.*
5. *Private troubles are related to public issues.*
6. *Human liberation necessitates personal change.*

—John F. Longres

Each society, regardless of its form, should function to provide the maximum benefits to all of it members.

—Chauncey Alexander

131

The purpose of social work is to promote mutually beneficial interactions between individuals and society.

—Neil F. Gilbert

(Gilbert and several others rewrote the statement.)
Social work's job is to help people improve, to help restore their social functioning.

—Max Siporin

If the purpose is to improve the quality of life for everyone, how is social work distinguished from any other service profession or organization?

—Robert C. Crouch

The definition of environments should be broadened to include the cultural environment. . . . In a pluralistic society, the cultural and social systems are interactional entities held together by the dynamic of interdependence.

—Federico Souflée, Jr.

I have a sense of the statement being too global and benign. For example, "to improve the quality of life for everyone" is unreal, impossible, out of sight.

—Carol H. Meyer

[Social workers] carry responsibility for a range of services and their delivery including administration that either facilitate person-environment or that ameliorates the transaction or permanent defects in human and environmental conditions.

—Robert Morris

I think the revised statement on the purpose of social work is excellent.
—Carel B. Germain

Summaries of the papers on the special areas of practice were presented in a grid in the conference report.[34] Major cross-cutting issues included whether social workers should be expected to promote quality of life for everybody. The new concept of social support networks had strong support.

Recognition of *case management* was proposed to precede the list of objectives in the conference statement of purpose: The social worker provides direct services. He or she also takes responsibility for obtaining and integrating a range of services from a variety of personnel.

Giving service may change organizations as well as help change clients. The role of the social worker in personal change activities may be that of diagnostician or manager of an array of personnel rather than a direct intervenor.

In any case, as Briar pointed out, defining environment and describing social work as a systems approach have serious difficulties. In his plea for simple definitions, Briar cautioned that we need to use specific terms to describe our activities, terms that the public will understand. He chose examples from Robert Morris, "Social workers provide care," and from Harold Richman, "Social workers provide social supports."[35]

Social Work published several letters to the editor after each conference. After the first one, two articles offered additional ideas.

Charles Levy, a professor at Yeshiva University, emphasized relationships: "Social work connotes how relationships with specific persons can be used to define or prescribe social ends. This is something all social workers are presumed to be able to do."[36]

Robert Crouch, a school social worker, wrote "Social Work Defined," highlighting social work's attempt to assist those who do not command the means for human subsistence to acquire them and to attain the highest possible degree of independence.[37]

After the second conference, A. D. Murdach of the Veterans Administration in Palo Alto identified four elements of social work for "the man in the street" who feels in need of professional service: warmth and sympathy, help with family problems, emergency services, and help to find his way through the system.[38]

Perhaps the most interesting description of social work was reported by Barbara L. Harr of the Greater Kansas City Mental Health Foundation. Her nine-year-old son described social work to another child: "My mother helps people cope when their problems are too hard for them to solve. Usually she just listens, and since hardly anyone listens to them, it really helps."[39]

Members of the leadership of the Conceptual Framework meetings were occasionally asked when there would be a follow-up conference, but no such meeting was proposed.

After the second conference, we reviewed the content to determine whether it had reached a satisfactory consensus, especially on purpose and values. Apparently, it had not. The group accepted the importance of person-in-environment and of values, but considerable disagreement resulted when they tried to define these fundamental terms.

Since the early 1980s, there has been little direct attention to further work on a conceptual framework. From the current *Encyclopedia of Social Work* and CSWE accreditation policies, however, there is evidence of growth and change in the profession. In the preface and introduction to the *Encyclopedia,* its editor, Richard L. Edwards, emphasized a new approach to diversity, providing individual entries for people of different national origins.[40] Terms such as *people of color* or *special populations* replaced the term *minorities.*

Edwards also noted that social work roles continued to evolve in a wider variety of nonprofit and for-profit settings as well as in the public policy arena. Seven social workers, for example, were appointed undersecretaries in the Clinton administration. Managed care came into being and interest in family preservation and other family-based services grew.

The recognition of the need for more research that is also more adequately funded led the major social work organizations to cooperate to form the Institute for the Advancement of Social Work Research in 1992.

Edwards concluded with the observation that many members of the new Congress [1995] believed they had been elected with a mandate to reduce government, decrease services, and increase punitive actions, not only for criminals but for people whose only crime is to be poor and needy. He was correct.

Currently, through accreditation standards, social work education has been responsible for the major changes in social work concepts that in earlier years would have been the product of practitioners. *Social Work* has not covered these changes. Unfortunately, practitioners do not generally read the social work education literature and are not conversant with accreditation requirements.

We will review some of the major developments. The CSWE Curriculum Policy Statements and Accreditation Standards for some years have prescribed a liberal arts foundation and a generalist model at the outset for students in both the B.S.W. and M.S.W. degree programs. The generalist is supposed to concentrate on the commonalities across social work methods and include experience with all size systems. Field instruction for the foundation in both degree programs, however, tends to lack adequate experience with larger systems, namely, groups and communities. The typical setting available limits itself to serving individuals and families.

Classroom content highlights the person-in-environment concept and an emphasis on systems. Both were challenged by some Conceptual Framework conferees as being too vague to be included in a statement of purpose.

Recently, schools of social work have added a variety of major topics including a strengths approach, feminist practice, AIDS, guns and drugs, and managed care.

New abstract curricular concepts make it harder to develop a unitary framework. In 1994, CSWE added Curriculum Policy requirements on diversity, economic and social justice, and populations-at-risk.[41]

Diversity refers to, but is not limited to, the groups distinguished by race, ethnicity, culture, class, gender, sexual orientation, religion, physical or mental ability, age, and national origin.

Social and economic justice coverage requires an understanding of the dynamics and consequences of all forms of human oppression, economic deprivation, and discrimination, as well as related practice experience. As we will see in the chapter on welfare reform, some of the recent legislation suggests that social justice is no longer a major element in public policy.

Populations at risk include people of color, women, and gay and lesbian persons as well as those distinguished by age, ethnicity, culture, class, religion, and physical and mental ability.

On the other hand, CSWE does not require specific concentrations (that is, specializations) for the advanced practice phase of the M.S.W. Agency demand and the size of the enrollment of a school of social work affect the choices. Educational programs must provide clear explication for each concentration they offer.

Only recently did purposes and values get redefined. A statement of mission and core values came in the preamble of the new NASW Code of Ethics that took effect in January, 1996:[42]

The primary mission of the social work profession is to enhance human well-being and help meet basic human needs of all people, with particular attention to the needs and empowerment of people who are vulnerable, oppressed and living in poverty. . . . Fundamental to social work is attention to environmental forces that create, contribute to, and address problems in living. . . . The mission of social work is rooted in a set of core values . . . [that] are the foundation of social work's unique purpose and perspective:

Service
Social Justice
Dignity and worth of the person
Importance of human relationships
Integrity
Competence.

One recent extreme reaction also dealt with the same issues as the conferences. In *Under the Cover of Kindness,* a professor of counselor education at the University of Iowa, Leslie Margolin, challenged social work through a devastating definition, a denial of uniqueness of the profession, and an indictment of social work techniques.[43] For him, home visiting, interviewing, and recording imposed the social worker's power on the poor.

On definition: The meaning of social work has always been incredibly unclear. . . . The effort to define it almost always ends in the greatest muddle. . . . The main functions of social work are not to alleviate poverty or to train useful citizens. . . . social work stabilizes middle-class power by creating an observable, discussable, write-about-able poor.[44]

On uniqueness: . . . things social workers do cannot be restricted to any one profession or group of people. Physicians, psychologists, counselors of all kinds—even nurses, agricultural agents, home economists—can act as social workers because social work is a type of power . . . that traverses every kind of institution or profession. . . . Social work is not a thing that can be possessed by social workers.[45]

Does this hostile view deserve a considered response from members of the profession?

In spite of the increased variety in social work that implies new concerns for the practitioner and policymaker, is it still worthwhile to continue to seek a comprehensive framework of purposes and values? Perhaps the next step should be to test out the Code of Ethics statement as a framework.

We are convinced from this review that no "one fits all" statement can be created to satisfy the profession and also meet the general public's need for a clear understanding of social work (preferably in a hundred words or less). We are still the profession that is least clearly understood by those people upon whom we depend for support.

There is more to do. A critical problem is who will carry on the quest. Most people identified in this historical chapter are now either retired or dead. Who among the younger generation in our profession are interested in a significant challenge and a role in social work history that further work on a conceptual framework can provide?

7

School Reform: A Viable Domain for School Social Work Practice
Wendy G. Winters
Ruby M. Gourdine

A clarion call for school reform transcends the nation. In response to societal conditions such as persistent substandard educational performance, escalating violence, and the promise of technology, numerous reform initiatives are under way. They include national and state incentives ranging from site-based management to school vouchers to locally established charter schools. The rhetoric of education reform conveys the impression that school change is a contemporary phenomenon. Yet throughout history, public schools in America have been subject to transformation. In this chapter, we explore variations of school reform and consider how contemporary social issues and societal changes have spurred school reform. The link between school social work practice and school reform initiatives, both at the macro and micro societal levels, will be examined. It is in this context that the opportunities and challenges in education reform for school social work practice are explored.

Distinguishing Reform in Schools

Reform initiatives have ranged from efforts, in the early twenties and thirties, to release urban school administrations from the control of political bosses to fostering moderation in terms of the demands of the industrial sector that students be prepared to assume positions in the workplace. The seminal *Brown v. Board of Education* decision in 1954, a purveyor of change, laid the groundwork for subsequent legislation pertaining to the education of America's increasing ethnic minority children and the handicapped. Similarly, the Education of All Handicapped Children's Act of 1975 specified the rights of all children to a free and appropriate education, again reflecting the continuum of change occurring in the educational sector. By 1983 the issuance of "A Nation at Risk" by the National Commission of Excellence in Education articulated national educational goals that were to be accomplished by the year 2000, the new millennium. Comprehensive in scope, the goals of this edict transcended the life cycle, targeting both youth and adults, stipulating that young children would enter school ready to learn, high academic standards would prevail, and adult literacy would be the norm. In subsequent years, educational directives at the state and local levels stimulated a variety of reforms. At this juncture in the process, the educational scene, in a most fluid and volatile state, reveals multiple initiatives under the rubric of reform.

Language to accommodate the process of educational revisioning encompasses varied nomenclature. Restructuring, a more generic term, connotes fundamental change in the nature and process of schooling.[1] It accommodates a range of processes resulting in charter schools, magnet schools, internal reorganization within schools resulting in multiple autonomous units, school-based management, and school-community collaboration. Similarly, school reform encompasses a broad range of concerns such as curriculum content, instructional methods, student assessment, school organization, school climate, and involvement of parents and community.[2] The question of whether the nation should have national standardized performance testing has surfaced as a hotly debated political issue.

Restructuring does not occur in an unencumbered vacuum but occurs in the context and matrix of economic, political, and cultural realities. Lipman notes that "if restructuring is to transform the educational experience of marginalized students, it will require both personal and social change, challenging educators' beliefs and assumptions as well as the relation of power in schools and communities."[3] Perhaps driving the impetus for present-day reform are challenges to the overall purposes of education in America. Historically, a primary goal of education was to prepare an informed citizenry capable of assuming responsibilities inherent in a democratic society. This charge looms critical, with shifts in the workplace, spurred by the electronic revolution, the emergence of a global society, and the influx of ethnic and racial minorities to America. Resultantly, the debate is extended beyond issues involving discrimination to the questioning of bilingual and multicultural education.

Social Issues Driving Reform

Restructuring is mediated by myriad social forces, operating in the school, the community, and in the national sphere. The present-day impetus for school reform has been propelled as much by the rapid changes in social behavior and social practices as it has by technological advances. At no point in recent history have schools been asked to respond to such a divergence of social issues. Some critics express concern that contemporary society expects schools to assume the traditional role of parenting, by transferring to schools functions and responsibilities that usually fall within the purview of the family.[4] Expressive functions such as school breakfast and other feeding programs, sex education, and parenting classes now take place in the public educational arena. These practices have changed the role of education, especially in urban and poor communities.

Historically, public education in America provided a base for moral and character development. The school as a homogeneous entity realized practices that were congruent with community values and morals, perpetuated in character education. The heterogeneity of today's school population is a reality not evident a century ago. Schools are now being called upon to provide highly visible curricula in character development in response to some very troubling behaviors being witnessed in society. McLaughlin and Irby highlight the excessive amount of nonprogrammed time available to inner city adolescents as they venture aimlessly on the street when schools are dismissed.[5] After-school programs, both school and community based with adult supervision, are sorely needed to stem the proliferation of alcohol, drugs, sex, and violence among America's school-age children.

TEENAGE PREGNANCY

In many urban areas, programs for pregnant teenage girls and teen parents are now included in public school curricula. In response to high teen pregnancy rates, some school districts have incorporated prevention and counseling programs. School systems that have instituted school-based programs that provide advice and birth control devices for teens find themselves confronting public outrage in some communities. There are those educators, parents, and citizens who believe that the inclusion of such programs sanctions and encourages promiscuous behavior. Yet research documents that supportive systems reduce the incidence of repeat pregnancies and improve educational opportunities.[6]

Consequences of sexual activity among teenagers is not limited to early pregnancies. Ladner and Gourdine assert that in addition to an unwanted pregnancy, "the higher stakes for adolescents are played out in the following scenario. Teen girls are more likely to get sexually transmitted diseases, including AIDS, which is a death sentence; and they are also more likely to be exposed to drugs, which is a life sentence."[7] The responsibilities of parenting place a heavy burden on a population not prepared to carry out this role. Children born to these parents are often caught in a life of poverty and disadvantage, which leaves many of them unprepared for school, thus challenging schools to educate them without their having adequate preparedness for learning.

An interesting phenomenon has developed; both male and female teenagers often express envy of their peers who have babies. For some, pregnancy and birth are anticipated outcomes. Urban racial and ethnic minority males express a desire to impregnate their teenage girlfriends, verbalizing their intent to leave a legacy. These boys, still in their teens, believe they will not reach adulthood. Their fatalistic attitude reflects the reality and imprint of violence in the lives of these young people.

VIOLENCE

In urban areas, gang-related activities have made not only neighborhoods unsafe but schools as well. Children walking to school have had to relinquish jackets, sneakers, and other personal belongings when threatened with physical harm. But violence is not confined to America's urban communities. In suburban and even more remote rural areas, violence has penetrated the sanctity of the school. In the 1997–98 school year, national attention has been drawn to the seemingly unprovoked murders that have occurred in usually tranquil communities. These killings are reportedly prompted by perceived personal affront, adherence to cultlike beliefs, or alleged mental illness. School systems have had to undertake hard-line measures in response to the physical and often fatal violence occurring, not only in close proximity to the school, but in the actual school building. In urban areas, in order to maintain a safe environment, security personnel (and in some cases police officers) are assigned to school duty and search high school students as well as visitors as they enter the school building.[8] Other systems have installed metal detectors. Such drastic measures, reflecting changes in school policies, are in response to the violence occurring in society.

Yet despite the violence that has permeated a number of urban schools and their immediate neighborhoods, Brown and Gourdine document in an exploratory study how even though teenage girls identified a high level of violence in their schools and communities, they view their schools as places of refuge.[9] Based on a national survey of school social workers, Astor, Behre, Fravil, and Wallace highlight how violence is perceived among school social workers. Whether in suburban or rural settings or in urban or inner-city settings, school social workers equally minimized the implications of life-threatening violence. Those in suburban or rural settings tended to minimize violence even more. The authors urge "school social workers and other school personnel to view the school as having a serious violence problem if a potentially lethal form of violence is present at least once during the school year."[10] School social workers are encouraged to embrace this principle and join in the school violence discourse.

These issues alert a citizenry to the changes that challenge the traditional organization, content, character and purpose of public schools. In response, schools have initiated violence prevention programs and peer mediation programs as part of their curricula.[11] Since 1995 Safe Start, an operational component of CRESPAR (Center for Research on the Education of Students Placed at Risk) at Howard University, has implemented a comprehensive school-based violence prevention program in Washington, D.C. The project is designed to have a positive influence on the school climate and to develop protective mechanisms among individual children, families, and communities. The intervention includes the following components: (1) teacher training and development, (2) integrated violence prevention curriculum for the classroom, (3) after-school academic and cultural enrichment programs, and (4) parent/school/community empowerment network.[12]

SUBSTANCE ABUSE

The pervasiveness of drugs in our society has not eluded our youth. Children in elementary schools are used as runners or lookouts. A number of middle and high school students are experimenting with or are addicted to drugs, while they and their peers reap financial gain from engaging in the selling of drugs. Drug sales in and around schools have prompted schools to take more drastic measures than just posting signs stating that the school is a "drug-free zone." Some schools have resorted to periodic searches of lockers and impromptu drug testing for athletes. Assuming a more proactive stance, schools have implemented programs and special courses to warn and educate children of the dangers of drugs and alcohol, offering them other choices.

The proliferation of drugs in our society has resulted in more insidious outcomes, such as children born addicted. These children enter school with a range of serious problems: hyperactivity, low attention span, and physical problems that effect their academic performance and ability to adjust in the classroom.[13] The Individual with Disabilities Act of 1997 requires school systems to provide services for these children. However, school systems with this population of children struggle, first with the diagnosis of their condition and then with the provision of adequate programming.[14] Multiple social stressors, some related to the school experience itself (such as an inability to keep pace academically) are traumatizing children, a number of whom exhibit posttraumatic stress syndrome similar to that experienced by war veterans.[15]

143

HOMELESSNESS

Homelessness among school-age children is a more recent condition that school systems must confront. The advent of homeless families has resulted in the problem of homeless children in the schools. This phenomenon surfaced in the 1980s because of the failure to provide a safety net for growth in the number of single-female-headed households. With increasing numbers of children among the homeless population, the passage of the Stewart B. McKinney Homeless Assistance Amendments Act (1990) required school districts to make adequate provisions to meet the needs of homeless children. Given the disruption, uncertainty, and lack of continuity in their lives, these children endure a multiplicity of problems that are reflected in school. Bassuk, Rubin, and Lauriat report that homeless children have irregular attendance, disproportionate rates of failure and retention, and a high probability of being placed in special education classes.[16] Homeless families suffer poverty, lack of education, inadequate job skills, poor health, and racism.[17] This situation may worsen with implementation of the Personal Responsibility and Work Opportunity Reconciliation Act (PL 104-193), a welfare reform act passed in 1996. Families now living in precarious situations are at risk to become homeless because they cannot meet the criteria required under the welfare reform legislation.[18] Unstable family situations increase the likelihood of poor school performance and dropping out of school. In response to escalating societal problems placing children at risk, a range of initiatives is under way in the educational sector.

School Programs Undergoing Reform

SPECIAL EDUCATION

Special education has been entrenched in public schools since enactment of Public Law 94-142 in 1975 mandating specific programs for children with emotional, social, or other disabling conditions. In response to this legislation, states initiated a range of programs for children with special needs, such as the learning disabled, orthopedically impaired, mentally retarded, seriously mentally ill, deaf and hearing impaired, autistic, and those with other disabling conditions. By and large, children in these programs receive educational services in settings apart from children in regular classrooms. At varying times during a school day, they may join children in the regular classroom, a process referred to as mainstreaming. More recently, there is a national impetus to include children with disabilities in regular classrooms. Advocates believe that inclusion is a more humane way to educate children with disabilities. School districts adhering to the legal mandates in the Individual with Disabilities Act are sometimes confronted by a public opposing this concept.[19] Those who oppose blanket inclusion say that efforts to carry out inclusion of students covered by these acts is sometimes poorly planned and executed. Cited are instances of children with special needs being in classrooms where they are ostracized and without appropriate support services. Others argue that the presence of students with disabilities requiring special services in regular classrooms compromises the education of other students in the classroom.[20] Often teachers are overwhelmed in efforts to manage these children in the classroom.

Since the initiation of the special education laws, special education has been in a transitional state. According to Allen-Meares and colleagues, the current major changes driving special education are (1) "transition programs and the creation of seamless programs from birth to age twenty-one; (2) the never-ending trail of court cases relating to appropriate educational due process and discipline"; and (3) the achievement of assessing, screening, and placing children.[21] Current teaching strategies are considered inappropriate. Training and recruitment of experts in the field of special education will remain a problem for schools in the twenty-first century. Lack of sufficient staff and expertise is overwhelming educators, administrators, and related services staff as well. These issues are compounded by the special needs of poor, urban, rural, and immigrant children.

LANGUAGE PROGRAMS FOR MINORITY CHILDREN

Another emerging issue on the national scene is that of educating children who are limited english proficient (LEP), whether they are legal or illegal immigrants. This is an issue made even more complex by the presence of those who are in this country illegally. Their presence has triggered a sometimes volatile political debate. From new reform initiatives and propositions have come the question of whether specialized services to LEP students are warranted. Precedence for this as an issue dates back to the case of *Lau v. Nicholas,* brought in behalf of Chinese public school students against the San Francisco school district in 1970. Although the results of this court hearing did not specify concrete educational programs, it did serve to showcase the issue of limited english proficiency.[22]

To distinguish ESL programs and bilingual education is difficult, since programs vary from state to state. English as a second language can take the form of children being taught academic subjects, such as reading, math, writing, history, and science in English. They can also receive instruction in English for a varying number of sessions with an ESL specialist. In contrast, in California, for example, approximately, "30% of all LEP students are taught some or all of their academic subjects in their home language," referred to as bilingual education.[23]

The continuing debate on issues related to English as a second language and bilingual education envelopes legal and illegal residents alike. The forum for this debate ranges from the halls of Congress, as legislators debate whether illegal and legal immigrants qualify for services (including education) under the new welfare reform legislation, to the voting booths of California where Proposition 227 abolishing bilingual education was passed.[24] Some critics maintain that ESL programs are too costly and basically ineffective. Others maintain that bilingual education, equally costly, serves to reenforce separatism rather than foster shared language and hence, a shared American culture. Rather, they endorse language immersion programs in which LEP children are placed in regular classrooms. In some urban areas, the competing demands for services to respond to language and cultural needs are stretching already meager resources. The state of California has legislation on ALIENS pending a court ruling by the higher courts.[25] The state argues that if the United States allows immigration, the federal government should foot the bill for these services.[25] The rippling polarization among school personnel and local community members have caused rifts in relationships in the schools.[26]

In some areas with large numbers of legal immigrants, in the minds of some majority citizens they are viewed as marginal—and the problem. Many local school districts are unprepared to respond to the needs of ethnic and immigrant populations, and bilingual personnel are at a premium. Many note that unlike immigrant populations of the past, where assimilation was the expectation, these new immigrants have a high proclivity to maintain their own language and culture. In this context, the basic premise of the democratic process will be tested, and schools will continue to confront the challenge of educating people of diverse cultures.

MULTICULTURAL CURRICULA

A trend toward the immigration of poor people of color has caused a level of discomfort for much of America.[27] The discomfort and current debate do not seem to apply to people from European countries, although they do seem to focus on racial and ethnic minorities who have long histories in the United States but who have yet to achieve equity. The major concern for multiculturalists concerned with education is how to include other racial and culturally diverse groups in the school curricula. The overwhelmingly Eurocentric perspective has left many American citizens feeling left out and their contributions to, and place in, American society minimized. Banks notes that curricular integration, with an outcome of multiculturalism, is no easy task. Accomplishing multicultural education transcends "a reconfiguration of the curriculum." A comprehensive undertaking of multicultural education involves integrating content, constructing knowledge, reducing prejudice, and embracing the total social structure to empower the school culture and achieve pedagogical equity.[28]

Central to school reform is evidence that the educational system is not adequately educating urban and poor children. Education looms as a monumental task in an "urban terrain . . . defined by disadvantage, isolation, and the scourge of drugs, crime, chronic under- and unemployment, teenage pregnancies, violent deaths of the young, deteriorating housing, boarded-up buildings, and homelessness. All of these are visible indications of social disintegration."[29] In its current state, no longer does public education serve the poor and inner-city minority populations.[30] The range of social issues, and societal responses to them, creates a complex situation for education reform. Conversely, education reform weaves a complex terrain for societal planning and implementation. The ramifications for school social work practice and points of intercept suggest an ecological practice approach.

School Social Work in the Context of Reform

Social work has a vital role at the intersect of macro- and microsocietal interaction in the restructuring process. This role can include influencing the educational enterprise itself; negotiating transactions and exchange between diverse role groups in the school community; or urging reconsideration of retention practices or educational curricula that encompasses moral and value issues, as in teen pregnancy programming or violence-prevention initiatives. On the macrosocietal level, where systemwide reform initiatives such as assessment, multicultural education, or magnet schools are under consideration, there are many roles it can play, including advocating and facilitating community representation and participation in the process, as well as bringing social work expertise to the process as members of planning bodies.

Given the complex social context of schools, a reorganization of staffing is necessary. It would seem that a more viable role for school social workers should be crafted. The turbulent social scene dictates a school social work role more integrated in the day-to-day life of the school. Recognizing the need, Fordham University spearheaded an initiative that brought schools of education and schools of social work together to develop training programs that would prepare their respective constituents to work together.[31]

WITNESS TO A LEGACY

The practice of social work in schools has a legacy embodied in intervention on behalf of individual families and in charting social change. The domain of school social work, which encompasses environmental issues, social inequities, and individual functioning, dates back to the turn of the twentieth century. It is a legacy that was borne of a commit-

148

ment to respond to the issues and demanding special circumstances surrounding the arrival of large numbers of European immigrants. By the 1920s social problems had escalated; employment of large numbers of children in sweatshops not only affected the children but had ramifications for the educational sector as well. Malnourished children suffered unmet physical needs. Juvenile delinquency was rampant in urban areas throughout the United States. An initiative emanating from the private sector established school social work programs. The Commonwealth Fund, a national philanthropic foundation, provided funds to support school social work programs in thirty cities throughout the United States.

According to Costin, the goals of school social work encompassed both microsocietal direct services geared to individual families and macrosocietal initiatives to realize social change.[32] A major objective was to have a positive influence on educational outcomes. Winters and Easton, prophetic in their discussion of social work roles, note that, "social workers in schools attend to the transaction between all units in the school and to the intervention with systems in the environment outside of the school to the extent that they affect pupils' learning."[33] With the onslaught of challenging societal issues and subsequent reform efforts, the changing needs of students, their families, and communities must be addressed. Traditionally, school social workers were viewed as the vital link maintaining contact between home, school, and community, in response to poor performance or malfunctioning on the part of the referred child or family. The dimensions of that link have expanded to include initiatives on the part of the school social worker that embrace outreach and advocacy. Yet as noble as these roles are, a complete reconfiguration is needed because the social situations are too grave for pontification and resistance to the need for social change.

The complex social context of public schools today dictates an expanded role for school social work that is more integral to the educational process. As Maslow notes, unless basic needs are met, children will not function at the appropriate academic level.[34] The social work profession brings to the educational process knowledge and skills about human behavior and development, interpersonal relationships, group dynamics and processes, and social policy development and implementation. Schools of social work bear responsibility for redefining and reframing their curricula to meet new demands imposed by changes in society. The social work profession has not taken the lead in defining how social issues emanating in society influence the educational process and the implications for the social work curriculum. Rather, the profession has sought to provide a degree in school social work and has settled for a minor role in transforming public schools into more productive institutions. For too long, social work has relinquished its role as advocate and agent for change, which were the hallmarks of the profession at the beginning of the twentieth century. Recognizing the need to synthesize elements of social work, Martinez-Bradley identifies the leadership potential and role for social work in the context of social change.[35] But the profession has yet to develop clear leadership roles vis-à-vis public education.

School systems do not accept school social work as an integral part of the team needed to effectively change the educational environment of the school. This is particularly disturbing because it is clear that the current learning problems of children do not have as much to do with innate abilities as they do with poor socialization and societal problems. The social work profession must assume a more assertive approach in the context of school reform.

Shared Decision Making: A Critical Component of Reform

An essential element in school restructuring is the issue and process of shared decision making. In the context of school reform, paralleling the focus on higher performance standards and academic content is the focus on social interactions inherent in decision making. Incentives that foster inclusivity (such as site-based management, local school restructuring teams, and governing bodies) engage teachers, parents, and other school-based personnel, including them in decision making. Social workers, have not often been party to decision making.[36] By changing governance structures to encompass site-based management, the intent is to engage the participation of all role groups, but those critical to the fundamental process of education have been excluded from participation. By and large, educational decision making operates within a hierarchical process. In the context of school restructuring, no longer is decision making or strategic planning limited to the purview of a system's or school's chief administrative staff. Site-based management is a process in which "some formal authority to make decisions in the domains of budget, personnel, and program is delegated to and often distributed among site-level actors. Some formal structure (council, committee, board, team) often composed of principals, teachers, parents, and, at times, students and community members is created."[37] Inclusive undertakings such as these perpetuate the involvement of critical participants in the school community in decision making.

The shared decision-making process connotes an exchange of ideas and interaction to which all the stakeholders must become acclimated. As Lipman argues, while the outcome can be beneficial for teachers and enhance their professionalism, it is the ultimate outcomes for students that are paramount.[38] Yet as teachers become empowered stakeholders, this is bound to reap a positive effect on their interaction with students and their families. Lipman further emphasizes that school reform and its inherent promise gather prominence in those areas with disproportionate populations of at-risk students, namely the poor and ethnic/racial minorities. An anticipated outcome of restructured schools is the reduction of bureaucracies that have impinged on educational development and have served as barriers to engagement of diverse role groups in school governance.[39] By virtue of participation in structures that govern and control their lives, it is believed that empowerment can be the outcome for teachers, parents, and students.[40] Whelage and colleagues report that a number of privately funded projects stipulate that community-based individuals and teachers engage equally in tackling school problems.[41] Similarly, governmental request for proposals (RFPs) stipulate that both parents and community be involved in the initial stages of proposal development.[42] The exchange that occurs between role groups in the process of restructuring is influenced by political, ideological, and cultural differences. When multiple groups—teachers, administrative staff, parents, community representatives, and in some instances, students—come together at the local school level to engage in policy determination or allocation of funds, tensions will develop.[43] For both school-based staff and parents the process represents uncharted territory. Literature on parental involvement and collaboration among educators, business leaders, and community members explore ramifications of participation in the shared decision-making process for teachers.[44] Research examining the implications of this challenging role for parents is beginning to appear.[45]

EXPANDING FUNCTIONS OF SCHOOL SOCIAL WORK

No longer can the school social worker operate in a marginally defined sphere. Local businesses and neighborhood organizations view the school as having an essential and vital role in the well-being of the community. Incentives at the federal level target partnerships between the community and the school.[46]

The work of Dryfoos illustrates the extent to which some schools across the nation are embracing and responding to social and health needs that are not being met in the community. As she points out, "In periods of poverty, unrest, and disadvantage, service provision in school has risen."[47] Benefiting from both generalist and specialist training, school social workers have a vital role to play in educational settings in which a variety of health, social, community, and recreational services demanding a range of skills are offered. A collective entity composed of social workers and school administrators would combine the attributes and skills of both disciplines. The outcome would be an administrative structure that develops strategies to encompass the whole child (intellectual, social, and physical) in educational planning.

The province of social workers is expanding to include facilitator, collaborator, educator, mediator, advocate, manager, broker, policy initiator, and developer. Selectively, these functions are summoned to support the traditional role of the individual, group, or family worker.[48] One social work activity being revitalized is that of community organizer, once an accepted practice in the field. In the fifties and sixties, community organization was a viable social work role that enjoyed designation as a practice modality in schools of social work. By the early eighties, with the shift toward clinical practice, community organization as a social work tool was eliminated in a number of schools of social work. More recently, with the onset of community deterioration, we find the resurgence and reconstruction of social work skills common to community organization. While this resurgence is related to the instability that is engulfing the nation's inner cities, these communities are far from dormant and are assuming active reformist postures.

In the area of education, citizens in blighted urban areas are articulating their expectations for the education of their children. Schools are being induced to reach out and include in their deliberations parents, interested citizens, and community participants. As diverse constituencies take their place at the negotiating table, they bring a range of ideas, concerns, and agendas. National professional social work organizations can assist school social work in defining a role to enable communities to organize and prioritize their concerns and gain community endorsement before bringing their agenda to the table. This process presumes facilitating a number of meetings with community representatives and allowing community participants to assume leadership and assert ownership. The social worker continues in the mediating role at the point when school personnel and community representatives come together. In a reform climate, administrative and planning skills are essential. The social worker who has experienced a multitude of functions related to the educational agenda can then assist in shaping the reform agenda in schools. As consensus builder, social workers can facilitate process outcome.

FACILITATING CURRICULUM INITIATIVES

By and large, in the area of curriculum matters and development, school social workers have not usually had a significant role. In our complex contemporary society, however, curriculum issues cannot be considered apart from students' social and developmental needs, and school social workers cannot be separated from those needs. Not all social workers who have a role in public school education are employees of the public school system. In Safe Start, a school-based violence prevention program discussed earlier, a social worker as co-principal investigator provides leadership and training as a primary member of the project's administrative team.[49] There is a need for school social work, particularly in urban and rural schools where academic and behavioral problems abound. Social workers can join with their peers in school psychology and counseling to assist classroom teachers in developing and implementing a comprehensive educational model that targets social and academic skills. Such intervention becomes a necessity as more children with severe disabilities are being mainstreamed into regular school activities.[50] Social workers can be vital participants in planning and executing school-based initiatives and character-building programs in response to teen pregnancy, substance abuse, and violence. At Visitacion Valley Middle School in San Francisco, a social worker meets with students during lunch in a forumlike setting on preventing violence and managing anger.[51]

New alliances with school personnel can be formed at a time in American education when teachers and principals in many parts of the country will be rated on the academic accomplishments and test scores of their student body. Involvement in curriculum is uncharted territory for school social work and awaits initiative. Such an enterprise should be undertaken at the outset, where the school social worker already has an ongoing relationship with the teaching and administrative staff from the very beginning. For example, at Visitacion Valley, a group of eighth-grade teachers "meet weekly with a social worker and sort through the complex problems their students have. . . . teachers shared their observations on a long list of troubled students and discussed ways to help them."[52] Paving the way for school social work input in matters related to curriculum takes planning, patience and perseverance.

FACILITATING COMMUNITY-WIDE COLLABORATION

Across the nation, a variety of reform initiatives seek to engage parents and communities in public education. Focus on the engagement of parents in the educational process is a primary goal of the School Development program, a school-reform initiative originated in 1968 under the leadership of James P. Comer, M.D. Parent involvement was viewed as a vital component of the educational process if children were to experience academic success. In celebrating the thirtieth anniversary of the program, Dr. Comer speaks to expanding the mandate: "Our task is to get more people to recognize that the outcome of schooling is the product of a huge, complex, interactional system that involves students, staff, parents, community. But it also involves making school districts, schools of education, legislators, opinion leaders and the people with the power, both economic and social, to understand, think about and promote child development."[53] Reform initiatives to engage parents and communities in the quest to improve student academic achievement are under way in schools from Texas to Boston to California.[54]

In the present climate of reform, the business community is defining and establishing a role in the process by investing large sums of money in various educational endeavors both at the local and state levels.[55] One example, operating in twenty-five states, is the New American Schools, a national network of teachers, schools administrators, parents, community and business leaders, policymakers, and educational experts committed to improving student achievement nationwide. Since 1992, NAS has fostered the development and implementation of eight comprehensive designs, or blueprints, for improving student performance. NAS spent several years developing and field-testing its designs.[56] Utilizing an inclusive comprehensive methodology, community and parents are essential to whole school and curricula reform as witnessed in the School Development Program, NAS, and local school initiatives.

Governmental agencies and private corporations provide mentorship programs and supplies to schools with which they partner. The Annenberg Institute on Public Engagement for Public Education cites an impressive number of initiatives that engage private corporations, community groups, and public schools working together in the interest of school reform.[57] A driving incentive is to influence educational outcomes, resulting in a population of young people prepared to assume positions in the workforce. Functioning as broker and developer, social workers can mediate the planning process to bring school personnel, community representatives, and business personnel to mutually agreed-upon goals and direction. These community and business leaders have much at stake when they make commitments to schools and students. By investing in education, they seek to develop a workforce capable of competing in the global economy.

The agenda of reform dictates modification in the connection and interaction occurring between school, home, and community. In the role of liaison, one traditional function of the school social worker was to assist teachers in understanding children's developmental needs that influence their readiness for learning. While this need still persists, the role of liaison now includes facilitating the interactions among school personnel, parents, and community. In this context, a collaborative modality involves exchanging information, engaging in a mutual planning process, sharing and refining goals and objectives, participating in the ongoing work to realize goals, and taking stock. An ongoing and continuous process, collaboration requires an unfaltering commitment. Further, it requires the insight of participants to understand that everyone benefits when appropriate comprehensive programs are available to children and families. While collaboration is often embraced eagerly and approached enthusiastically, it is not a simplistic undertaking. Collaborative efforts are complicated, difficult to ensure, and no panacea.[58] School social workers play a key role in facilitating collaboration.[59]

Collaboration is the necessary hallmark of the comprehensive full-service community school concept, which includes the following: school-based physical and mental health services, dental clinics and related personnel, family resource centers, and recreational and cultural enrichment after-school programs.[60] On the leading edge of reform in the educational sector, full-service school-linked services recognize and respond to the multiple needs of children and their families.[61] First, they recognize the needs of the whole child; second, they support and reenforce the family; and third, they focus on early intervention and, ultimately, prevention.[62] An essential aspect of the full-service community school concept is extensive community and parental involvement, but this interaction can become charged and reach high levels of intensity as constituents advocate their positions and vie for limited resources. The training and preparation of school social workers enable them to have a critical role in mediating and reducing these conflicts. Social workers operating in the school must not only have skill, but must be comfortable in negotiating the complex ecological environments.[63]

FACILITATING PARENT INVOLVEMENT

Parent involvement is basic to the ongoing education reform movement, whether in relation to school choice, charter schools, or school-based management, and constitutes a complex but necessary undertaking. The process is time-consuming, absorbing, potentially conflicting, and bound to trample on territory conceived as the province of the educational professional.[64] But a number of school programs, from the East Coast to the West, have demonstrated the viability of parent and community involvement in the process of school reform and improved educational outcomes.[65]

Even with positive examples, many school personnel, particularly in urban and rural communities, continue a cautious if not adversarial view of parents, thus influencing their expectations of parents and the role they see parents as having in the educational process. Conversely, parents who live in at-risk neighborhoods, with marginal resources, income below the poverty line, products of limited or substandard education themselves, keep their distance from the school, viewing the school as a potential threat. This hostile posture can be intensified if their children are experiencing difficulty in school. For the most part, their contact with the school is limited to their being summoned for emergency conferences. Although vulnerable and placed at risk, schools cannot relinquish responsibility for this population. Hopps, Pinderhughes, and Shankar provide a compelling discussion of the intricacies, issues, and incentives in working with clients whom they identify as overwhelmed.[66] Social workers operating in schools can reach out and provide needed service to oppressed and disadvantaged populations.[67] This is a challenging and time-consuming task, and it behooves social workers to keep school personnel, especially administrative staff, apprised of efforts in behalf of these families. Many families living in deteriorated neighborhoods are more receptive than one might expect, and they can be encouraged to participate in school functions and educational activities; some may even influence their reticent neighbors. What's required is repetitive notification, personal outreach, and programmatic undertakings on the part of school personnel, a role appropriate for, and in concert with, the training and preparation of school social workers. Potentially, it is a mutually gratifying enterprise. Winters defines parental involvement as "the structural mechanism, put in place by the school, that governs and orchestrates parent interaction in school organizations, processes, and activities." Through their participation, parents provide resources for the school and, in turn, learn new skills from the system.[68] In essence, this type of involvement reflects a return to the social work mission.[69]

While their involvement is no panacea, parents living in more affluent communities come better equipped and are more likely to be influenced and engaged in the educational process and school reform. Granted, there are challenging issues that have yet to be resolved, but interactions between school personnel and parents in more privileged communities are on a more equal footing, which tends to affect the interaction and outcomes.

The Promise of School Social Work and School Reform

School social work has an essential role in mitigating the interplay of varying ideologies, cultures, and power relations played out in schools or in school districts. Effective educational change depends on change in belief systems and values held by the stakeholders.[70] Restructuring the role school social workers can undertake blends social work legacy with the inherent challenges of school reform. A basic lack of understanding of the value of social work by the community at large behooves the profession to undertake a positive image-building initiative. Unlike business and corporate leaders who enter schools armed with a system of mentorships and financial resources, the legacy of social work is less visible. Central to school social work practice is ecological sensitivity, recognizing that multiple forces impinge on the educational process, such as race and class issues that permeate reform and restructuring efforts. These potentially charged issues require an encompassing perspective fortified with the understanding and skills to orchestrate negotiation. A collective endeavor by parents, the community, and teachers is required to achieve the goal of improved academic performance.[71]

As we enter the new millennium, the challenge faced by school social workers is making the case for equity in education by promoting the objectives of multicultural education. This will require not only promoting the acceptance of differences but also changing the behavior and attitudes of the adults who teach, rear, and otherwise influence school children. Another area in which social work has primacy is attending to the goal of inclusivity, a primary goal underlying school restructuring initiatives. As school social work enters the twenty-first century, the techniques and strategies developed during the emergence of the discipline as a vital helping profession still apply, with reconceptualization and expanding roles and functions. With the knowledge gained through a hundred years of service and research, school social work as a specialty of the discipline can provide the vision to participate in, as well as to help define, change, and implement new strategies for merging the educational and social policy agenda for the next millennium.

8

A Competence-Centered Perspective on Child and Family Welfare

Anthony N. Maluccio

Child and family welfare is an increasingly complex, controversial, and changing area of social work practice, especially as it seeks to confront contemporary challenges and social problems such as oppression and discrimination, family violence, child abuse and neglect, and homelessness in the midst of drastic reductions in funding and other societal supports for human services.

Building on recent research and theoretical developments in social work as well as related fields, this chapter presents a competence-centered perspective on child and family welfare. Such a perspective is not intended as a formal theoretical model, but as a way of integrating ideas from related fields into a point of view that can inform social work practice. The emphasis will be on practice with and for children and adolescents and their families from vulnerable population groups. Following presentation of a competence-centered framework for social work, the chapter will consider a range of principles for policy and practice as well as future directions in child and family welfare.

Sections of this chapter have been adapted from P. Pecora, J. K. Whittaker, A. N. Maluccio, and R. P. Barth. *The Child Welfare Challenge: Policy, Practice and Research,* 2nd ed. (New York: Aldine de Gruyter, in Press).

Competence-Centered Framework

The competence-centered framework draws from four major areas: an ecological orientation, a competence-centered view of practice, developmental thinking about individuals and families, and a permanency planning focus in serving children and families.

ECOLOGICAL ORIENTATION

An ecological orientation draws from such fields as general systems theory, anthropology, organizational theory, and especially ecology. As Germain and Gitterman[1] indicate, "ecology rests on an evolutionary, adaptive view of the development of human beings and the characteristics of the species." As an orientation to practice, ecology helps us appreciate that human beings are engaged in continuous transaction with their environment. By offering a broad conceptual lens for viewing human functioning and needs, it underscores that social work intervention should focus on improving the transactions between people and environments in order to enhance adaptive capacities as well as enrich environments for all who function within them.[2]

For example, many families currently are functioning poorly, at least in part because of multiple stresses in their environment. The economy creates conditions of high unemployment or underemployment; families do not remain in one community long enough to establish adequate support systems; and children demand a great deal of attention. Under these circumstances, it is easy to see how children at times become the targets of their parents' frustrations and anger, especially in light of their own unmet needs. When viewed from the perspective of ecology, the above example suggests various principles useful in child and family welfare practice.

First, practitioners must help mobilize the actual and potential strengths and resources of individuals, families, and groups, while simultaneously seeking to render environments more responsive to the adaptive and coping needs of human organisms.[3] Second, workers must understand the relationships between families and their environments, identify the significant sources of support as well as stress and conflict, and assess the complex personal and environmental factors affecting parents and children. Third, effective practice requires that practitioners appreciate the unique qualities, styles, and needs of different ethnic, racial, and cultural groups and thus facilitate the provision of services that are culturally relevant, particularly for children and families of color, who are not only disproportionately represented in the child welfare system but also may receive differential, racially biased treatment. Fourth, it is useful to conceptualize child welfare as a comprehensive continuum of services with a strong preventive component. In this way, the ecological orientation stimulates a marked shift from a narrow orientation of inadequate parenting to a broad view of child welfare that emphasizes a multifaceted practice approach to children and their families in the context of their life situation and environment.[4]

COMPETENCE-CENTERED VIEW

The ecological view heightens our awareness of the importance of an ecological person-environment perspective in understanding human beings and intervening in human problems.[5] Also crucial is a related perspective about which there is a growing consensus in the human services, namely, a competence-centered or strength-oriented approach to practice that contrasts with the more traditional pathology or deficit model.[6] While the metaphor of ecology provides a way of perceiving and understanding human beings and their functioning within the context of their environment, knowledge about competence development offers specific guidelines for professional practice and service delivery.

The competence perspective draws from ego psychology; psychodynamic psychology; and learning, developmental, and family systems theories. In social work as in other fields, competence is generally defined as the repertoire of skills that enable the person to function effectively. However, a distinction should be made between the notion of discrete competencies or skills and the broader, ecological or transactional concept of competence. The latter may be defined as the outcome of the interplay among the following:

- a person's capacities, skills, potentialities, limitations, and other characteristics;
- a person's motivation, that is, his or her interests, hopes, beliefs, and aspirations;
- the qualities of the person's impinging environment such as social networks, environmental demands, and opportunities.[7]

Building on the above perspective, competence-centered social work practice embodies a set of attitudes, principles, and strategies designed to promote effective functioning in human beings by focusing on their unique coping and adaptive patterns, mobilizing their actual or potential strengths, emphasizing the role of natural helping networks, building on their life experiences in a planned way, and using environmental resources as major instruments of help. In conjunction with the ecological perspective, the competence orientation suggests several interrelated themes useful in guiding social work practice with children and families:

- Parents and children are viewed as engaged in ongoing, dynamic transactions with their environments and in a continuous process of growth and adaption.
- Parents and children are regarded as "open systems" that are spontaneously active and essentially motivated to achieve competence in their coping with life demands and environmental challenges.
- The emphasis shifts away from "treating" clients toward teaching them coping and mastery skills as well as ways of using their life experiences in a planned way.
- Each person's efforts to grow, achieve self-fulfillment, and contribute to others is sustained and promoted by varied environmental opportunities and social supports.
- Appropriate supports are matched to the person's changing qualities and needs in order to maximize the development of her or his competence, identity, autonomy, and self-fulfillment.

DEVELOPMENTAL THINKING

Developmental thinking focuses on understanding the growth and functioning of human beings in the context of their families and their families' transactions with their environments. Going beyond ecology, it brings in other aspects such as the stages and tasks of the family's life cycle; the biopsychosocial principles of individual growth and development; the goals and needs that are common to all human beings and families; and the particular aspirations, needs, and qualities of each person and each family, in light of diversity in such areas as culture, ethnicity, race, class, and sexual orientation.

The developmental view serves to highlight a number of themes for child and family welfare.

- Family-centered services and practice need to take into account the concept of development, through explicitly considering this question: Which interventions are effective, with which specific child/family problems, in which environmental settings, and at what particular developmental stage?
- Policies, services, and practice should reflect current knowledge about the development of women, minorities, and other special populations, rather than rely primarily on traditional models such as those derived from psychoanalysis. For example, Gilligan[8] has questioned Erikson's "ages and stages" model as being unrepresentative of female development.[9] Okun and Devore and Schlesinger,[10] among others, have focused on human diversity and its significance for ethnic-sensitive social work practice.
- Caution should be exercised in applying to human beings or families any developmental scheme said to be normative. Instead, competence-centered practice is guided by an optimistic view of the capacity of children—and adults—to overcome early deprivation and other adverse early life experiences through nurturing and supportive experiences throughout the life cycle. In short, human development is a dynamic process that involves complex and interdependent connections among human beings, their families, and their social and physical environments. Human beings actively shape, and are shaped by, their social contexts.

164

PERMANENCY PLANNING FOCUS

Since most children coming to the attention of the child welfare system are at risk of placement out of their homes, a comprehensive framework for child and family welfare practice must incorporate the values, goals, and principles of permanency planning, whose essence is that all children are entitled to live in permanent families. Permanency planning incorporates a basic idea: every child is entitled to live in a family (preferably her or his own biological family) in order to have the maximum opportunity for growth and development. It is an idea that has ancient origins, and it has been restated over and over throughout the history of child welfare. In essence, it refers to the process of taking prompt, decisive action to maintain children in their own homes or place them permanently with other families. Above all, it addresses a single—but crucial—question: What will be this child's family when he or she grows up? It embodies a family-focused paradigm for child welfare services, with emphasis on ensuring family continuity for children across the life span.[11]

The goal of permanency for each child is also reflected in federal legislation, namely, the Adoption Assistance and Child Welfare Act of 1980 (PL 96-272). This law mandates the states to promote permanency planning for children and youths coming to their attention, through such means as subsidized adoption, procedural reforms, and preventive and supportive services to families. Public Law 96-272 has been supplemented by more recent federal legislation, the Adoption and Safe Families Act of 1997 (PL 105-89), which changes and clarifies a wide range of federal policies. In particular, it seeks to improve the safety of children exposed to abuse and neglect, promote adoption, and support birth families.

As discussed elsewhere,[12] permanency planning embodies a number of key features:

- a *philosophy* highlighting the importance of the biological family and the value of rearing children in a family setting;
- a *theoretical perspective* stressing that stability and continuity of relationships promote a child's growth and functioning;
- a *program* focusing on systematic planning within specified time

frames for children who are in foster care or at risk of placement out of their home;

- a *case management method* emphasizing practice strategies such as case reviews, contracting, and decision making, along with participation of parents in the helping process;
- *active collaboration* among various community agencies, child care personnel, lawyers, judges, and others working with children and their parents.

Despite current questions regarding its relevance or effectiveness, permanency planning is timely as well as forward-looking. It should endure, both as a philosophy and as a method or program; in today's context, it means serving children at risk of out-of-home care and their families through policies and programs that

- balance concern regarding the parents' or children's pathology with attention to the conditions that create or sustain family dysfunctioning;
- emphasize family preservation, through intensive, home-based preventive and supportive services;
- promote collaboration among the various helping systems, particularly child welfare, courts, education, housing, health, and income maintenance;
- provide supports to child welfare workers, foster parents, and other child care personnel and empower them to do their job, rather than burn out in an unrewarding and unsupportive work environment;
- establish a continuum of services, from day care to residential treatment;
- strengthen the roles of mental health practitioners with children and youths in settings such as child guidance clinics, psychiatric programs, and the juvenile justice system;
- address juvenile court and other legal and procedural issues that inhibit the timely decision making required in permanency planning;
- provide aftercare services to maintain the child in the biological or other permanent family following discharge from foster care.

Principles for Policy and Practice

This chapter thus far has presented a competence-centered perspective on child and family welfare, which leads to a range of principles and guidelines for policy and practice.

FOCUS ON THE FAMILY

The developmental approach suggests a shift from a child-centered to a family-centered focus in child welfare. Focus on the family does not imply that the child's needs and interests are of secondary importance. It means that, in most cases, the child can best be helped by regarding the family as the central unit of service or focus of attention, whenever and as much as possible. Human beings can best be understood and helped within their significant environment, and the family is the most intimate environment of all. It is here that the child develops and forms her or his identity and basic competence. The family has the potential for providing resources throughout the life cycle, especially as its members are sustained and supported by various services. The family's own environment can be employed as the arena in which practitioners intervene to help strengthen communication, parenting skills, and parent-child relationships. As Laird has observed, "Family clinicians view the family as the most salient context for understanding and changing many individually defined problems."[13]

In addition, when children must go into out-of-home placement, preserving family ties between them and their families as much as possible is a great challenge. The natural bonds between children in care and their parents continue to be prominent for parents as well as children long after they are physically separated, reflecting the significance of the biological family in human connectedness and identity.

A key means of accomplishing the preservation of family ties is consistent parent visiting of children in substitute care. The findings of various studies have highlighted the crucial role played by parental visiting or other parent-child contact in the outcome of the placement as well as the child's functioning and development. For instance, research has

167

demonstrated the importance of parental visiting of children in foster care as the best single predictor of the outcome of placement. In their longitudinal study of foster care in New York City, Fanshel and Shinn found that children who were visited frequently by their parents during the first year of placement "were almost twice as likely to be discharged eventually as those not visited at all or only minimally."[14] More recently, in an extensive investigation of children leaving out-of-home care, Davis, Landsverk, Newton, and Ganger reported that the majority of children with parental visits at the level recommended by the courts were ultimately reunified.[15]

ESTABLISHING A CONTINUUM OF COMMUNITY-BASED SERVICES

The ecological approach ultimately requires a shift to a society-centered approach to child and family welfare that focuses especially on economics, employment, public health, and education. In the meantime, in response to the multiple needs of families in basic areas of living, there must also be comprehensive as well as intensive services. These include both "soft" services, such as counseling, and "hard" services, such as financial assistance. Various studies have shown that troubled families require a range of services to support overwhelmed parents, prevent out-of-home placement, or reunite children with their families.[16] Emphasis should be on a continuum of services providing both therapeutic help and environmental supports to the family before, during, and after the child's placement in care. Moreover, services should concentrate on strengthening the parents' coping and adaptive capacities. A family often may require services on an ongoing basis, even after the immediate crisis is resolved.

Research has also shown that services are most effective if they are not only comprehensive but also located at the neighborhood or community level. Such services allow for maximum effectiveness and responsiveness to the needs and qualities of each child or family.[17] The community orientation is seen in such approaches as maintaining continuity between group care settings and community-based services, facilitating integration of services for "troubled" and "normal" youths, and establishing family resource centers.

RESTRUCTURING THE FAMILY'S ENVIRONMENT

Through the provision of comprehensive, community-based services, practitioners have an opportunity to help families restructure their environment, that is, to modify or enrich it so that it is more suited to their needs and qualities and more conducive to their positive functioning. Although consensus may exist about the need to improve a family's social and physical environment, it is often difficult to do so. But it is not impossible, and various guidelines are available, as considered below.

First, it is important to develop a close working relationship between professional helpers and informal helpers in a family's social networks. In many cases, much can be accomplished by helping parents to identify and use actual or potential resources in their social networks, for example, relatives, neighbors, friends, volunteers, and other informal helpers. Studies have shown the value of complementing professional help with the services of paraprofessionals such as homemakers or older persons who model effective parental behavior and coping skills. These aides help to meet the basic needs of parents, enrich the family's environment, and prevent placement or replacement. They provide parents with opportunities to learn skills, fulfill needs, and develop competence.[18]

In addition, a major source of help often can be the family's own extended kinship system. For example, Boyd-Franklin notes: "For many Black extended families, reciprocity—or the process of helping each other and exchanging and sharing support as well as goods and services—is a very central part of their lives."[19] Emphasis should be on strengthening and preserving cultural resources for children and their families.

Above all, restructuring the family's environment means that agencies and social workers must become involved in advocacy and social action to help resolve the systemic or societal problems that lead to out-of-home care in the first place. Ample evidence exists of a high correlation between entry into out-of-home care and social problems such as poverty, deprivation, and racism.[20] In particular, attention must be paid to establishing a living wage and decent employment opportunities for all families, with adequate income maintenance and day care services to support families struggling in the workforce. From an ethical standpoint, child welfare staff should at times serve not only as clinical and administrative practitioners but as policy advocates and practitioners as well.[21]

169

FOCUSING ON STRENGTHS OF CHILD AND FAMILY

The competence perspective leads to emphasis on the child's and family's strengths. Such emphasis, in turn, leads to various implications. First, parents and children are regarded as active and striving human organisms who are basically motivated to grow and achieve competence. Pathology is deemphasized, along with acknowledgment that the problems faced by troubled families reflect the societal conditions that limit the power of parents and interfere with their coping efforts. In addition, human problems, needs, and conflicts are translated into adaptive tasks providing the client with opportunities for growth, mastery, and competence development. A parent who is labeled as abusive or neglectful, for instance, can be helped to learn or relearn skills in child care. To accomplish this, the problem has to be redefined or reframed as a condition involving lack of knowledge or inadequate parenting skills, rather than a situation of parental neglect. In short, the focus is on identifying and removing obstacles that interfere with the parents' coping capacities and on practice strategies that help empower children, parents, and families by mobilizing their strengths and potentialities.[22]

The emphasis on human strengths also leads to the view of parents as resources on their own behalf—as partners in the helping process—rather than as carriers of pathology. As we shift from a pathological view of parents to a competence orientation, we are more likely to identify strengths in parents themselves and involve them in growth-producing activities. When they are given adequate opportunities, parents and other family members are better able to mobilize their own potentialities and natural adaptive strivings. They are thus empowered to act on their own behalf.[23] For example, substance-abusing families and their consequent child neglect represent a huge current issue; empowering parents requires that we confront the lack of treatment facilities, housing, and employable skills, to name just a few needs.

To support the efforts of parents to be resources for themselves and their families, agencies need to stress educational approaches, such as teaching skills in social interaction, communication, advocacy, problem solving, and parenting. Practitioners also need to emphasize the participation of parents and children in processes such as case contracting and decision making and in parent training programs. In particular, parent training can be an effective means of helping parents become more competent, especially when it is offered in a nonstigmatizing setting such as a family center, and with due regard to the parents' personal needs, lifestyles, and cultural values.

Adopting a competence perspective also means helping parents to become involved in self-help groups. Indeed, as demonstrated in recent years by the success of self-help groups such as Parents Anonymous, parents can be regarded as resources who can help each other. Practitioners should aim toward encouraging clients to accomplish their purposes and meet their needs through individual and collective efforts, as Solomon argues in her book on empowerment in black communities.[24] For parents of children in foster care, for instance, working together to obtain needed resources for a better life for themselves and their children is an excellent way to counteract feelings of powerlessness and promote competence and self-esteem. By participating as citizens in efforts to influence policies and programs, they "can develop personal, interpersonal, and intergroup knowledge and skills that improve both their self-concepts and their day-to-day functioning."[25]

ROLES OF PRACTITIONERS AND CLIENTS

From the competence-centered perspective also flow various implications regarding the roles of social workers working with families, as well as the roles of biological parents and children, foster parents, and other child care staff members. The primary role of the social worker is that of a catalyst or enabling agent, someone who actively and systematically helps the family to identify or create and use necessary resources. The worker uses flexible approaches and calls on a variety of resources to help provide the conditions necessary for parents to achieve their purposes, meet life's challenges, and engage in their developmental processes. Above all, practitioners should become experts in methods of environmental modification, use of existing community resources and natural helping networks, creation of new resources that may be needed by their clients, and mobilization of family members' own resources.

In line with the emphasis on collaboration that is inherent in permanency planning, efforts should be made to have parents, foster parents, and other child care personnel regard themselves as partners in a shared undertaking, with common goals and mutually supportive and complementary roles. This can lead to new helping systems that are ultimately more effective and rewarding for everyone concerned. For instance, foster parents can be involved as resources for parents through such means as role modeling or serving as parent aides.[26] In various ways, they can become allies of biological parents and be more actively involved in the treatment plan in behalf of each family, as long as their roles are clarified and they are provided with adequate supports and rewards. Further, in many cases the foster family could become an integral part of the overall treatment program and help promote the adaptive functioning of the biological parents.[27]

Engaging children and adolescents is also important. Children and youths themselves can be actively involved in the helping process, including such aspects as reaching decisions regarding the best living arrangements for them. As practitioners become more comfortable in asking about their views, they find that children and youths have a lot to say that should be taken into account in planning services on their behalf. Some older children thus make it clear that they prefer to be in a long-term foster home with continuing contacts with their parents rather than being adopted or placed in an institution.[28] In addition, the contract or written agreement can be profitably used as a means of helping children to make decisions, assume responsibility for their hehavior, and take some control over their lives. In particular, with adolescents in foster care, agreements can be used to clarify the tasks to be performed by the young person, the foster parents, and the social worker so as to facilitate the process of preparation for emancipation and independent living.[29]

Looking to the Future

The perspectives and principles presented above have been enunciated, in one form or another, throughout the history of the profession, but there have been multiple and recurring obstacles to their full and consistent implementation.

At the societal level, these have included such aspects as a history of human oppression and racism; national and state policies that fail to support children and families; and inadequate or inconsistent funding for the human services. At the professional level, social workers have long been hampered by an institutional infrastructure that is characterized by service fragmentation, insufficient interagency and intersystem collaboration, and a consequent inability to respond comprehensively and effectively to the varied needs of families. At the educational level, increasing emphasis in schools of social work on specialization and technical skill development has resulted in social workers not being fully prepared to function as autonomous practitioners in a complex work environment.

As we enter the twenty-first century, however, some examples demonstrate how to implement a competence-centered perspective on child and family welfare in an effective and durable fashion. First is the experience of intensive family preservation services. Although skepticism continues regarding their effectiveness, several studies have shown that these programs can help some families prevent unnecessary or inappropriate placement of children.[30] As the technology of family preservation is refined, expanded and improved, application of its concepts and methods should be planned.

A second example is that of permanency planning, which during the 1980s resulted in a substantial decrease in the numbers of children in foster care; reduction in the length of time in care for many children who needed to be placed; more attention to the rights, roles, and needs of biological families; placement of fewer younger children; reunification of more placed children with their birth families; and more adoption of older children and children with special needs. Permanency planning will be even more crucial in the future, as there will be an expansion of children at risk of out-of-home placement in our increasingly multicultural society.[31]

A third example is that of "participatory management" in child welfare agencies. This approach, which reflects a deliberate commitment to involve workers at all levels in organizational decisions, has been tested in a state child welfare agency with excellent results. The approach included forming an interdisciplinary task force comprising agency staff and administrators, foster parents, court personnel, and community service providers; having the task force conduct an intensive self-assessment of the agency's family reunification services; and developing action plans for change.[32]

Through the process of applying participatory management principles, the task force in the above project developed a comprehensive set of recommendations for strengthening family reunification policies, programs, and practice. The resulting model of self-assessment and planning for system change in family reunification can be adapted to other agency services and programs, especially as administrators see the value of involving staff at all levels in program evaluation and management.

Conclusion

In each of the above examples, social workers were guided by principles that are consonant with the competence-centered perspective considered in this chapter, principles that respect the contributions of all while seeking to mobilize human strengths and render environments more responsive to the needs of children and families. The range of valued participants includes workers who will demand to have a vote in the way they work and in the way the agency operates; administrators and policy makers who will facilitate decision making and case management; foster parents and child care staff who will rise to the challenge of being members of the helping team; parents and children who will feel empowered to act in their own behalf; and practitioners with diverse competencies and backgrounds who will be ready to collaborate within a multidisciplinary framework.

Yet it should be acknowledged that encounters with past nostrums and experiences with PL 96-272 and other recent federal legislation indicate that there are no panaceas. Although the complexity of human interactions precludes simple solutions, it is still essential—and worthwhile—to persevere in the ongoing challenge of working in behalf of children and families.

9

Restoring Communities within the Context of the Metropolis: Neighborhood Revitalization at the Millennium

Claudia J. Coulton

Over the last two decades in the United States there has evolved a renewed appreciation for the role that communities and neighborhoods play in the spread of poverty and a growing consensus that community change is essential to its alleviation. The earlier debate about whether place-based strategies or people-based strategies were the most effective approaches gave way to the recognition that the well-being of individuals could not be divorced from the neighborhoods and communities in which they lived. A new wave of research that transcended the prevailing hostility among structural, cultural, and individual explanations helped to foster this new understanding of urban poverty and neighborhood distress. It effectively linked important macrostructural changes in metropolitan areas to adverse social processes within low-income communities, which were further linked to individual behaviors that undermined success in the mainstream economy.

The eighties and nineties also witnessed a growing skepticism and ideological opposition to large-scale federal solutions to the problems of poverty and distressed neighborhoods. Devolution of many programs to the state and local levels was the result of both this belief and an effort to control federal expenditures. The nation began to look to localities and even neighborhood residents themselves to tackle the growing problems of poverty and deterioration. An important model for local work was community development, a place-based approach to mainly physical restoration. Although the community development movement was expanding and achieving notable success, there was a growing recognition among practitioners and funders that regional economic forces and adverse social conditions within neighborhoods could undermine the success that had been achieved. Restoring poor neighborhoods would require harnessing the energies of residents and outsiders in new ways to reverse negative social processes and metropolitan trends.

Finally, commentators and scholars examining American culture at the end of the century tapped into widespread feelings of disconnectedness and lack of meaning for which community began to be seen as the antidote. The nature of social relationships and participation within communities were seen as key to the effectiveness of democratic institutions and civil society and to the well-being of individuals. Community was increasingly thought to be necessary everywhere even though it was seen as particularly diminished in poor neighborhoods. In fact, metropolitan-wide participation in the restoration of poor neighborhoods was felt to be a vehicle for strengthening community as a whole.

In this chapter I examine the trends that have contributed to the changing awareness and understanding of urban poverty and community in the United States. Next, I describe the recent amalgam of place-based and people-based approaches known as comprehensive community initiatives and community building that have grown up as a result of the new conceptions of urban poverty. Finally, I discuss the promise of, and challenges to, these new initiatives with respect to the complex metropolitan forces that affect distressed neighborhoods.

Communities and Poverty

A NEW UNDERSTANDING OF URBAN POVERTY

In the mid-1980s William Julius Wilson published *The Truly Disadvantaged,* which overcame a silence of several decades regarding the lives of the inner-city poor.[1] Drawing on his studies in Chicago, Wilson argued that the neighborhoods in which many poor families lived had changed rapidly and radically since the 1960s. He attributed the extreme impoverishment and disorder in these neighborhoods to the out-migration of the middle class, the declining employment opportunities for the low-skilled worker, and the deterioration of community infrastructure and institutions. Life in these neighborhoods had begun to create serious disadvantage for the residents, and the neighborhood influences presented formidable barriers to their escape from poverty. Wilson's analysis acknowledged that severe behavioral, attitudinal, and skill deficits had developed in many residents due to the lack of effective role models, information, and social networks that could enable them to succeed in the mainstream economy.

That a scholar of Wilson's prominence would acknowledge the growing amount and severity of disadvantage in U.S. cities was groundbreaking. He had successfully posited an argument that began with macrosocial and economic forces but linked them to individual behavior through the mediating structure of community. Although there was considerable controversy about aspects of the argument, it stimulated a new way of thinking about poverty.[2,3,4,5] The acknowledgment of both structural and behavioral aspects of poverty served to bring together what had been seen as warring camps of liberal and conservative thinkers who either blamed the system or the individual. That communities were the pivotal link between the two served to focus renewed attention on neighborhoods within urban areas. Improving them began to be seen as urgent, not just for the future of the cities but for the life chances of the people within them.

The use of the term *underclass,* which had been reintroduced into the popular media,[6] galvanized attention toward the growing number of distressed people living in distressed communities, even though there were important debates about the meaning and validity of the concept.[7,8,9] Whereas much of the scientific research on poverty had fallen into the province of economists for the previous several decades, Wilson's argument and the subsequent discussions awakened the interest of many disciplines ranging from urban geography to community and developmental psychology. There was a burgeoning of new research and a renewed interest in existing research on urban neighborhoods. The formation of the Social Science Research Council's Committee for Research on the Urban Underclass with support from the Rockefeller and Russell Sage Foundations connected researchers and policy analysts from many disciplines and fostered a comprehensive look at urban poverty and communities. The result was a fairly thorough analysis of the economic and demographic changes in metropolitan areas and the impact on neighborhood life within the inner city.

THE CHANGING METROPOLITAN CONTEXT

Researchers began exploring economic changes within U.S. cities with the release of the detailed data from the 1980 census. They soon discovered that, even though poverty in the nation as a whole had not increased in the previous decade, it was increasing in many metropolitan areas, contributing to a growing awareness of urban problems. These trends were found to continue or worsen between 1980 and 1990. Among the significant metropolitan dynamics in the last quarter of the century were the growing concentration of poverty in the center city, the concentration of affluence at the outskirts of metropolitan areas, the changing mix of jobs and their relocation to the suburbs, and the persistence of racial and ethnic segregation and its role in creating neighborhood disadvantage.

GEOGRAPHIC CONCENTRATION OF POVERTY AND AFFLUENCE

Several important studies traced the growing spatial concentration of poverty in large metropolitan areas between 1970 and 1980.[10, 11] Aided by the advent of computerized mapping techniques, these studies demonstrated that a rising portion of the land area of some big cities had become extremely poor. In part, this happened because the middle class had left these areas, leaving them less populated but more homogeneously poor. Furthermore, a greater portion of the urban poor, especially African American poor, had come to live in these distressed neighborhoods,[12] subjecting the residents to the difficult social conditions that concentrated there as well.[13] Not all parts of the country, though, showed this spatial concentration of the poor. It was worst in the industrial cities of the Northeast and Midwest and in a few cities in the South.

The analysis of the 1990 census revealed that the spatial concentration of poverty had continued to increase in the largest central cities. Whereas 16.5 percent of those big city poor people lived in extreme-poverty neighborhoods with poverty rates above 40 percent in 1970, this had risen to 28 percent of the poor residents of the cities living in extreme-poverty areas by 1990.[14] The concentration was even higher in industrial cities such as Milwaukee, Detroit, Cleveland, and Chicago and for African American poor than members of other ethnic groups.

By 1990 many of the central cities affected by the poverty concentration trends were seeing vast areas of their landscape mired in the deterioration and distress associated with the loss of economic resources. Public and media awareness of these conditions had also been piqued, although these trends were not universal. In the West and South, for example, the poor were more likely to live in nonmetropolitan areas or in nonpoor neighborhoods within the cities,[15] and the number of neighborhoods that suffered extreme poverty were still remarkably few. Nevertheless, reversing the trend of growth in extreme-poverty neighborhoods became a focus of action in many large cities.

Although it received less attention, a growing geographic separation between the poor and the affluent had also occurred.[16, 17] By 1990 new areas of concentrated affluence had emerged at the outskirts of many metropolitan areas.[18] The distance between affluent enclaves and poor neighborhoods was most apparent in the large industrial cities that had extreme income inequality and a history of black-white segregation. By the mid-1990s the trend of outward migration of higher-income households leaving fewer and poorer residents behind had also hit the older, first-ring suburbs.[19]

URBAN SPRAWL

The escape of the affluent to the far distant suburbs raised concerns about the ability of the central city and inner-ring suburbs to deal with the problems of poverty while important resources were moving beyond the city limits. The fortunes of the city dwellers and their institutions seemed to be divorced from the households moving farther and farther away, creating a spatial and social divide.[20] The greatest financial impact of this selective out-migration was for older cities that had relatively small land areas, were hemmed in by suburban municipalities, and whose revenue base was shrinking.[21] The consequences of urban sprawl for the central city also were different, depending on whether the region was growing or not. It was in the low-growth regions that movement outward meant a profound thinning of the center as well as the conversion of farmlands to low-density residential and industrial use.[22]

The forces creating urban sprawl were a significant threat to many central cities and their surrounding older suburbs. In response to this threat, a few forward-looking regions began to use regional partnerships to manage growth, both preventing farmland conversion and promoting denser land use in the urban cores.[23, 24] There were some exceptions to the increasing poverty in city neighborhoods where middle-class housing was build or restored.[24a] Nevertheless, in many cities the chances of attracting higher-income households back to the center had been undermined by the social and physical deterioration created by their movement to the outskirts of the region.[25, 26]

EMPLOYMENT

Employment levels in poor, inner-city neighborhoods by 1980 were well below levels of previous decades. While this low level of labor force participation came to be understood as having a very negative influence on social conditions,[27] there was some debate about the reasons employment had fallen so low. An influential point of view grew out of a series of analyses that documented the loss of manufacturing jobs,[28] the movement of low-skill jobs to the suburbs, and the increasing skill requirements of the service sector jobs remaining in the city.[29] An examination of the inner-city residents' educational attainments suggested that many would be unqualified for the kinds of jobs that were opening up near their neighborhoods. Further, they lived at a growing distance from the suburban jobs for which they could qualify, and this distance made it harder for them to learn about or travel to these jobs.[30, 31] Thus, there was said to be both a skill and spatial mismatch of inner-city residents and jobs, created by the deindustrialization and suburbanization that characterized many metropolitan areas from the 1960s onward.

The idea that there was a spatial mismatch hindering employment of inner-city residents made sense, but there was considerable debate about how important it was as a cause of their unemployment.[32, 33, 34] If employers had moved to the suburbs to avoid hiring minority workers,[35] for example, the barriers to their employment might have more to do with racial preferences and discrimination than distance. The fact that suburban firms with black hiring managers were more likely to hire African American workers than inner-city firms with white hiring managers supported this contention.[36] It was also recognized that employed workers might move to the suburbs because of their jobs, making it seem (in cross-sectional studies) as if proximity had conferred an employment advantage to suburban residents. The debate among researchers, though, did not prevent policy analysts from concluding that connecting inner-city residents to suburban jobs had to be part of any strategy for revitalizing neighborhoods and reducing poverty.[37] At the same time, it was recognized that the distance between city workers and suburban employers was more than spatial and that perceptions, preferences, and social networks were all at work in producing disadvantage for inner-city residents in regional labor markets.

THE SEARCH FOR NEIGHBORHOOD EFFECTS

A key component of the evolving understanding of urban poverty was the realization that living in an extremely poor neighborhood could actually undermine an individual's life chances. In other words, troubled neighborhoods were not just a problem for the city but had negative effects on their residents. This seemed intuitively understandable to anyone who had ever tried to move to a better neighborhood, and it captured the attention of both the neighborhood revitalization and family support movements. The logic suggested that neighborhoods should be improved not just for their own sake but as a way of producing better outcomes for families and children. Indeed, the thinking implied that problems of families and children could not be solved through individual services alone but depended on creating family supportive communities.

For researchers, though, neighborhood effects proved remarkably elusive to prove. An early and important review article tackled the question of whether the socioeconomic status of neighborhoods could be shown to have statistically reliable effects on outcomes for youth, such as educational attainment, employment, criminal behavior, or teenage childbearing.[38] A limiting feature of this article was that most of the studies reviewed were conducted in the 1970s and early 1980s, before poverty concentration had reached its peak. Further, most of the studies represented the neighborhood context by a statistical measure of its socioeconomic composition, which was a very narrow conception of possible influences. Nevertheless, the conclusion of this widely cited review was that the effects of neighborhood context were weak, nowhere near as predictive of outcomes as family characteristics. In addition, the effects that were documented sometimes showed different results, depending on the gender, race, or age of the individuals in the study.

An important problem in establishing the magnitude of neighborhood effects was the fact that neighborhood characteristics were highly correlated with family characteristics, making these two effects difficult to disentangle. Traditional statistical models generally considered contextual effects to be what remained after family factors were controlled.[39] If disadvantaged families brought their personal limitations into troubled neighborhoods, this statistical partialing out of individual characteristics would be valid. However, if prolonged residence in troubled neighborhoods had predisposed families to display certain characteristics, controlling for these would make neighborhood effects look smaller than they really were. The prevailing statistical techniques were unsuccessful in sorting these forces out in meaningful ways, but an important natural experiment served to support the belief that neighborhood effects might be more important than the extant research suggested. As the result of public housing discrimination litigation, the court ordered a lottery process through which some public housing residents were selected to move to the suburbs and others were selected to move to relatively poor, inner-city neighborhoods. A comparison between these two groups showed that the adults in the suburban locations were more likely to become employed than their city counterparts.[40] The children in the families that moved to the suburbs did better in school than the children whose lottery status placed them in the city.[41] These studies did not reveal exactly what conditions in suburban neighborhoods conferred this advantage, be they community resources, social modeling, proximity to jobs, or other processes. The nearly random method of determining who moved and who did not, however, served to disentangle the family characteristics from neighborhood characteristics and provided the most compelling evidence that poor inner-city neighborhoods limit their residents' chances for success.

Subsequently, considerable work was done to try to pinpoint how and for whom neighborhood effects were significant, much of it captured in an important, two-volume compendium on the subject.[42] In a departure from a simple focus on socioeconomic composition, the new wave of neighborhood-effects research began to tackle the formidable task of identifying the social processes that might be responsible for the differences in outcomes between poor and more affluent neighborhoods.[43, 44] For example, parents were found to adapt their parenting practices to stresses and dangers in their surrounding neighborhoods, sometimes with grave results.[45, 46] Also, more impoverished neighborhoods differed from more affluent ones in that residents were afraid to intervene with neighborhood children and exert social controls in their neighborhoods.[47, 48] Finally, resources and services for families and children were often more limited within poor neighborhoods.[49, 50, 51]

It now appears that social resources, social controls, and social solidarity, which are present to varying degrees even in poor neighborhoods, may be the active ingredients of neighborhood effects,[52] but such mediating processes are difficult to model statistically.[53] The research as it stands currently is not refined enough to tell which aspects of neighborhoods need to change and how much families and children would benefit from change in socioeconomic structure or more supportive social processes. The search for these answers goes on, however, and there remains an expectation that the neighborhood effects will emerge once the methodological challenges can be overcome.

THE IMPORTANCE OF SOCIAL CAPITAL

It was recognized that social processes in poor communities were unsupportive of human development and that success in mainstream society came amid a general concern in America about decline in community.[54] The term *social capital* seemed to capture the sense of what had been lost by the end of the twentieth century. Although the term had been used before,[55] it was the publication of Robert Putnam's widely read and discussed book about making democracy work that gave name to the malaise. His analysis of civic, political, and economic institutions in northern Italy served to connect the strength of community to the fabric of democratic society. Its loss was not merely detrimental to people but could threaten American democratic institutions. Social capital was defined as "features of social organization, such as trust, norms and networks, that can improve the efficiency of society by facilitating coordinated actions."[56] It is capital that can be used to accomplish collective aims and is embedded in the social relations among persons and organizations. Social capital is thought to be fostered by social participation and civic engagement, which in turn enable the productivity and success of such efforts. The ability to associate is thought to depend on the degree to which people and organizations within communities share norms and values and are able to subordinate individual interests to those of the larger groups. Out of such shared values comes trust, a key to accomplishment of both individual and group aims.[57]

In another provocative article, "Bowling Alone," Putnam provided empirical evidence that social participation and civic involvement were on the decline in America.[58] This resonated with people in many quarters and was quoted in sermons, civic forums, and living rooms across America. Others, however, countered that participation was taking new forms, which could not be seen, than in the traditional types of participation examined by Putnam.[59]

Low-income communities were thought to have diminished social capital as a result of numerous factors such as a shortage of associations and organizations, the fear and distrust among residents resulting from crime and neighborhood instability, a lack of property or assets to protect, and powerlessness in civic affairs.[60] However, volunteerism and participation in community organizations were not necessarily lower in inner-city areas than elsewhere,[61] although there was considerable variability among low-income communities in this regard.[62] Trust among residents and in institutions did seem to be lower in minority communities[63] and was thought to be particularly problematic in African American communities because of their history of oppression in America.[64]

Sorting out the existence and magnitude of community social capital from its effects has been particularly problematic in low-income communities. Social capital is thought to evidence itself in the ability of the community to take action or in its collective efficacy.[65] But the failure of low-income communities to achieve goals may have more to do with their lack of economic resources than their diminished social capital.[66] Access to communal and institutional resources may, indeed, foster the development of social capital.[67] While more empirical studies of social capital are needed to pinpoint its effects, it has become a key element of current thinking about neighborhood decline and revitalization.

THE DEVOLUTION OF GOVERNMENT PROGRAMS AND THE FAILURE OF SYSTEMS SERVING PEOPLE IN LARGE CITIES

In the last quarter century, many of the systems serving residents of large cities were in crisis.[68] Of considerable relevance to the poor and to distressed neighborhoods were the declining academic performance of city children, the epidemic of violence, the rise in the amount and severity of child abuse and neglect, and other signs that key institutions were failing. Big city school systems, child welfare programs, police departments, the courts, and public health departments were all facing new problems and working in a changing metropolitan context but were unable to transform their complex systems quickly enough. There were occasional demonstrations of successful models of education or services in large cities, but these seldom led to wholesale improvements across the board.[69, 70] The public and many professionals became pessimistic about the ability of big government agencies to serve people effectively.

This lack of confidence in large public systems occurred in the context of a more general disaffection from big government in the United States and concern about government spending. Known as the "devolution revolution,"[71] many federal responsibilities were transferred to state and local authorities. While quite a few federal programs were simply abolished, others were turned into block grants to state or local agencies.

Spending on programs targeted toward the poor and toward disadvantaged communities was reduced.[72, 73]

This devolution of government responsibility called upon states and localities to develop new capacity for financing, planning, and managing major government programs. While it was possible that state and local government would simply cut spending further, it also presented an opportunity to adapt programs to fit local conditions and to give the public greater voice in decisions that were made. An example of both possibilities can be seen in one of the most massive social policy changes in the twentieth century, welfare reform (Personal Responsibility Act of 1996). Cash assistance to poor families was turned from an entitlement to a block grant to the states, which now would have wide latitude regarding benefit levels and eligibility standards. States and localities, however, can use this flexibility as a chance to make major changes in their services, including bringing them much closer to the community.[74]

Despite the increased flexibility and community control that come with block grants, they often represent deep cuts in government funding for the poor and for disadvantaged communities. Thus, while the powerful, interconnected forces creating neighborhood distress and undermining the chances of their residents to better their situation had been recognized, the resources to ameliorate them were shrinking at the end of the twentieth century.

Restoring Opportunity to Urban Communities

The approaches to neighborhood revitalization that have emerged in the last two decades reflect an understanding of many of the forces affecting the metropolis as a whole and low-income communities in particular. To varying degrees, current neighborhood initiatives operate within the context of deindustrialization and suburbanization. Acknowledging the interdependence of people and their communities, they have embraced the neighborhood as both a target of change and a vehicle for enhancing the lives of individuals and families. The latest neighborhood revitalization efforts have moved away from a narrow focus on housing or employment to an understanding of the simultaneous need for building human, economic, and social capital. To achieve sustainability, they recognize that they have to build local infrastructure and know-how rather than rely on government programs or outside experts. Finally, the resources, both financial and human, needed to carry out these efforts are generated through entrepreneurial and collaborative methods from diverse private and public sources.

The idea that low-income individuals and families can be helped by strengthening and enhancing the places they live is not without its critics. Historians have noted that neighborhood initiatives have sometimes been a way of just letting the poor fend for themselves and diverting attention from the structure of inequality in a capitalist society.[75, 76] Furthermore, place-based approaches to reducing poverty are sometimes seen as inconsistent with the principle that geographic mobility is a road to opportunity and necessary for efficient labor markets.[77, 78] Indeed, retaining economically successful residents in their neighborhoods is necessary to reduce the concentration of poverty that has developed in recent years. Retention of working families in central city neighborhoods, though, is contrary to recent trends in which they have followed the jobs to the suburbs and escaped some of the problems of the city.

While the characteristics of the current neighborhood initiatives are responsive to the changed understanding of urban poverty and metropolitan dynamics, they also draw from an American tradition of neighborhood-based approaches to addressing poverty and human need. A short history of these approaches will show the continuity as well as the departures from the past.

A SHORT HISTORY OF NEIGHBORHOOD APPROACHES

The history of efforts to improve low-income neighborhoods in the United States is rich, complicated and reflects ebbs and flows in thinking about the causes of poverty and the role of citizens and government in addressing conditions in poor communities and the barriers to opportunity.[79, 80] To varying degrees, neighborhood programs and actions of the past contained elements of the approaches emerging today. Over time, however, approaches to addressing poor neighborhoods can be seen as reflecting alternative understandings of the problems and what to do about them as well as the social and political movements of the day.

The Settlement House Movement

Early in the twentieth century, settlement houses were started by charities in neighborhoods with immigrant populations. This development
reflected concerns about the societal changes brought by growing industrialization and urbanization. Progressive reformers led the movement
to protect children and better the lives of the poor and the workers in
America's growing industrial labor force.[81] Socializing the immigrants
and others to the American way of life and helping them to adapt to the
demands of industrialization were important features of the settlement
houses' work. Settlement house volunteers and workers focused their attention on both people and the places they lived, with the relative emphasis varying from one settlement house to another. Community
organizing was a widely used strategy to improve neighborhood conditions and as well as to socialize residents. The community organizing
tradition of the settlement house movement has its counterpart in today's neighborhood initiatives.

Urban Renewal and Public Housing

The conditions in poor sections of big cities became the object of concern after World War II. However, urban renewal was not about rebuilding these communities for low-income residents but rather
removing them from visible, central city locations and using the land
for other purposes. During this period, a great deal of low-cost housing was destroyed and residents, largely African American, were forced
to move. Public housing tracts were constructed in less desirable areas
but did not replace much of the housing that was lost. It is now recognized that communities were destroyed in the process of urban renewal and that the most significant toll was taken on African
Americans whose movement was severely constrained by blatant and
pervasive discriminatory housing practices.[82] Federal and local governments supported urban renewal and the construction of public housing. Private developers also played a significant role, establishing
alliances between private market interests and public policy to the disadvantage of the relatively powerless citizenry.[83] Today's efforts to in-

volve residents in public-private partnerships for neighborhood revitalization are sometimes plagued by mistrust born of this era.

Conflict Style Organizing

The powerlessness of unorganized residents to fight urban renewal was an impetus to radical organizing.[84] Residents of poor neighborhoods were polarized because organizers, often from outside the neighborhood, were the ones who selected business or government targets and issues around which to mobilize the community. Drawing on the legacy of the labor movement, conflict was seen as the vehicle for bringing people together and allowing the community to challenge the power of big business and government. New approaches to community revitalization have largely abandoned conflict style organizing in order to emphasize partnerships among residents, businesses, and government. Nevertheless, they encounter some of the same conflict and power differentials that significantly affect their success.

Community Action and the War on Poverty

Although the War on Poverty of the 1960s had many new programs directed at human development, such as Head Start, community action was the primary approach to neighborhoods.[85] Its slogan, "maximum feasible participation," was based on the belief that the poor had been left out of decision making and that involving them would lead to effective action to reduce poverty. The fact that the community action program was designed in Washington and delivered to localities without the involvement of local and state governments is one explanation for the political resistance to it.[86] In some places community action was weak because neighborhoods did not have the social and political infrastructure to quickly engage citizens in a successful planning and action process. Although short-lived, an important legacy of community action was the principle of citizen participation in decisions that affect them. Moreover, some of today's neighborhood leaders also got their start in community action programs. But residents whose hopes were raised by the invitation to participate in community action and who saw few results were greatly disappointed. Current efforts to involve residents in neighborhood revitalization are often challenged to prove that they are about real change rather than participation for participation's sake. This suspicion can, to some degree, be attributed to the failed War on Poverty.

Service Integration and Neighborhood-based services: As the War on Poverty waned in the 1970s, attention turned to more traditional social service approaches to helping low-income individuals and families. However, services were thought to be fragmented and plagued by lack of access and relevance to community. The movement toward neighborhood-based and integrated services was also influenced by European models of personal social services, particularly the Patch system operated by local authorities in parts of Great Britain.[87] The placement of multiple services within one location, or even one team of social workers, was seen as a way to improve access and efficiency and make services an integral part of the community, but the categorical nature of federal and state agencies was seen as a barrier to achieving such integration at the neighborhood level. So states and counties experimented with ways of reorganizing service delivery from the top down or collocating services in one-stop centers.[88] However, the complexities of integrating massive bureaucracies stymied many of the system reform efforts. Limitations on funding by the late 1970s and early 1980s resulted in many agencies moving out into the neighborhoods and pulling back to their more basic and often statutorily regulated functions. While the integrated neighborhood-based approach to service delivery ultimately took hold in only a few places, the need for coordination and reform of service systems and people-serving institutions remains an important theme in current neighborhood initiatives.[89]

Community development: As individual approaches to reducing poverty in neighborhoods were losing favor, the community development movement was emerging. In fact, many in the movement were hostile to social service and welfare programs that they viewed as creating dependency.[90] Community development arose out of the realization that market conditions in poor neighborhoods were unable to produce housing and business development. Community development corporations (CDCs) were created as mechanisms to replace and restore these markets. Their intervention in the markets was largely in the form of putting together public incentives and subsidies with private developers to produce residential and retail development compatible with the needs of the community.

These place-based antipoverty strategies were governed by community boards.[91] They were heavily influenced by government and philanthropic funders and by the financial institutions on which they relied, even though they usually had some community residents on their boards. Although some CDCs emerged out of the tradition of conflict style organizing, this became incompatible with the goals of financing and building housing. Most early CDCs did not so much work directly with community residents but they influenced them through building management and tenant selection.[92]

By 1990 there were more than 2,000 CDCs in the United States.[93] The most visible success of these organizations was in the production and restoration of low-income housing and building management.[94] CDCs and their funders, though, began to become concerned about whether they could maintain what they had built and make it economically viable because of the other forces affecting these communities.[95] It was clear that housing alone could not restore the social fabric of the community or change the opportunity structure for the people who lived there.[96] Some CDCs expanded their role considerably to include community organizing, social services,[97] and business and workforce development.[98] This has largely been accomplished through partnerships that connect organizations within the community and the community to the metropolitan context. In some ways, these CDCs have become partial models or cornerstones for the latest innovation in restoring poor neighborhoods.

The Next Generation of Neighborhood Strategies: The history of approaches to low-income neighborhoods in the United States has been one of shifting emphasis back and forth from the needs of poor people to the desire to improve neighborhood conditions. It has also been one of targeted strategies such as housing, economic investment, or service reforms versus more general efforts to organize and increase citizen participation. Historically, most of the approaches have been focused internally on neighborhoods themselves.

Today's evolving understanding of urban poverty has fostered a merging of concerns about people and places rather than the old dichotomy. It is understood that targeted programs for physical and economic development and human services will not be effective unless they are supported by cohesiveness and collective efficacy within the community.[99] In other words, social capital is necessary to the production and preservation of physical, economic, and human capital.[100] There is also the recognition that neighborhoods have evolved and changed due to the economic and social dynamics of the metropolitan area and cannot be addressed in isolation from the region. Partnerships are thought to be needed within the neighborhood, with people and institutions throughout the city, and between the city and the entire metropolitan area.

Comprehensive Community Initiatives and Community Building: A relatively recent approach to restoring poor communities is known as comprehensive community initiatives and community building. Comprehensive community initiatives (CCIs) are "neighborhood-based efforts that seek to improve the lives of individuals and families, as well as the conditions of the neighborhoods in which they reside. They are defined as much by how the initiative works to promote individual and neighborbood well-being and by who makes the decisions and does the work, as by what actually gets done."[101] The framers of the initiatives generally believe that neighborhood transformation depends on developing capacity, at the neighborhood level, to define and effect responses to local needs on a sustained basis. Community building is, therefore, a defining component of CCIs, which reject traditional approaches to neighborhoods and people that are categorized and narrow, or models that have been imposed from outside. When models have come from the outside in, communities have not always had the capacity or influence to make these traditional methods work, so they have often been short-lived.[102]

Most CCIs are run by neighborhood-based nonprofit organizations and funded, in large part, by foundations. They may also receive government funding for certain specific activities such as housing development and employment programs or services. Some receive private gifts from individuals, engage in profitable activities, or put together deals with businesses and developers.[103] CCIs and community building are just beginning to emerge as a concept and a movement, and although there are many projects under way across the country, most are only in the beginning phases of implementation. Nevertheless, early experience suggests that commonalities and differences among specific initiatives may be seen in their goals and in the principles that guide their work.

GOALS OF CCIs

The goals of most CCIs are inclusive of changes in people, neighborhoods, and systems. The majority want to improve economic opportunities for their residents and support human development so that the people will be better off. They also want to improve the conditions in their neighborhoods so that the neighborhood can be sustained and attract and retain prosperous residents and businesses that, in turn, are likely to make the people better off. Systems that serve people and benefit neighborhoods are of CCI goals because these systems have become ineffective in low-income communities or present barriers to CCIs achieving their goals for resident and neighborhood change.

While these are the long-term outcomes that CCIs generally embrace, they may focus more or less on one or another of these. Some CCIs emphasize creating family and child supportive communities and effective services for them. Others have an important objective of demonstrating more effective systems, which can influence institutions on a larger scale.[104, 105] Still others focus mainly on improving those aspects of the neighborhood and its opportunities that residents feel are strategically important.[106]

The initial goals of CCIs may be affected by whether they have grown out of an existing community-based organization, a foundation initiative, a government program, or a community process. Quite a few CCIs have begun through expanding the role of a community development corporation,[107] a family resource center,[108] or a settlement house. As such, their goals tend to relate to the original organization, although they become more comprehensive and participatory. Some of the best-known CCIs, though, have resulted from national foundations' programs that are implemented in multiple locations.[109] Usually, some expectations regarding goals and outcomes are built into foundations' grants to lead agencies and neighborhoods. When the government launches community initiatives, they typically have even more explicit goals and predetermined outcomes in mind, even though the individual communities eventually shape them. Hope VI and the Empowerment Zones are examples of federal programs that support community building along with comprehensive physical and economic development.[110]

Because CCIs are partnerships among foundations and/or government, neighborhood-based organizations, and residents, there is often some ambiguity about goals.[111] All parties typically agree that neighborhood residents must establish the goals relevant to their own communities. However, funders also have implicit ideas about the kinds of community changes that are needed. This situation can result in tension on both sides. Funders struggle with setting some expectations and holding grantees accountable while trying not to impose too much direction from outside. Simultaneously, residents and local organizations search for consensus on their own objectives while wondering whether certain things must be accomplished to sustain the interest and support of the funder.

CORE PRINCIPLES OF CCIs

There are several principles that are generally espoused by the architects of CCIs.[112, 113, 114, 115] CCIs are said to be:

Resident driven: Residents guide the agenda and carry out much of the work of the initiative.

Comprehensive: They address all aspects of neighborhood life or conditions affecting the people there.

Collaborative: The initiatives work through and with existing organizations and leaders inside and outside the neighborhood, increasing the synergy of their work.

Asset oriented: The initiatives focus on strengths, drawing upon the talents and potential of the residents, their organizations, and their leaders, as well as incorporating assets or resources from the outside.

Sustainable: The community becomes able to achieve its goals and act in its own interest over the long term, adapting to the ever-changing metropolitan and global context.

While these principles are widely endorsed, CCIs differ in whether and how these principles are implemented. Also, there seems to be a range of ideas in the field about how and why these characteristics of CCIs are likely to create change. CCIs, which are a relatively new phenomenon, have not yet had much experience with some of the principles, but the realization of these principles is the major vehicle that CCIs are relying upon to revitalize communities.

Resident Driven: Virtually all CCIs strive for high levels of resident participation and control, a principle that has been very important in the formation stages of CCIs. They seem to hold a range of expectations, though, about what is to come of this involvement. Some CCIs emphasize that such involvement will benefit the individuals and community because residents will gain skills, knowledge, and a sense of being empowered as a result of engaging in community planning and action. With other CCIs, resident involvement is seen as a way of creating networks and relationships, which will raise the level of social support for residents and trust within the community. Still other CCIs expect residents who are involved to set clear standards for behavior in the community and to hold each other more accountable for behaviors that affect everyone. Finally, the purpose of resident involvement in some CCIs is to guarantee that the actions taken by the initiative are compatible with and supported by residents and to ensure that residents will help to make changes occur. In other words, the anticipated outcome of resident involvement in CCIs may be empowerment, networking, normative consensus, or accountability.

These varying expectations for resident involvement produce somewhat different activities, structures, and arrangements. For example, if widespread networking and trust is the expected outcome, CCIs tend to emphasize involving large numbers of people in all parts and sectors of the community and connecting previously unconnected individuals. On

the other hand, if the purpose is shaping actions that are more responsive to resident perceptions and have high resident support, a smaller
group of opinion leaders and persons with direct knowledge of the community needs to be involved. When empowerment is a key objective, resident involvement must allow for opportunities to learn new leadership
skills and to directly feel the results of one's own part in collective action.
If residents are to enforce shared norms and expectations within the
community, involvement needs to produce consensus and mechanisms
for enforcement.[116]

In many CCIs, though, resident involvement may be an end in itself as
well as a means to an end. Promoting social change through democratic,
participatory means has ethical and practical purposes. Participation is
seen as ethical in that it promotes a citizen's right to be heard and influences what happens in the community. It is also practical because it is
seen as the only way to sustain things and to have them work and be accepted. Some people describe resident involvement as creating a changed
way of thinking about their neighborhood—a growing sense of ownership. To quote one resident in a Detroit initiative:

> The community is all of ours . . . the schools, the stores, the
> parks. . . . if you don't treat them right, you hurt yourself. It's not so
> much about meetings and process and planning . . . It's a way of
> thinking in terms of day-to-day neighborhood life.[117]

Comprehensiveness: Comprehensiveness had become a hallmark of
CCIs, partly as a reaction to piecemeal solutions that have not worked
and the recognition that poor neighborhoods are beset by a number of
interrelated challenges that are economic, social, physical, and cultural.[118]
Thus, most CCIs pay attention to economic opportunity, physical conditions, social and health services, and safety concerns. Comprehensiveness has been approached in many ways.[119] Some initiatives have
attempted to implement this principle by engaging in comprehensive vi-
sioning or planning, taking all aspects of neighborhood life into account.
Others have started with a focal concern, such as youth, and gained comprehensiveness by examining all of the features of the community that
affect this group of residents.[120]

Regardless of the starting point, comprehensiveness is based on the assumption that what is holding back low-income people and their neighborhoods are a number of complicated, interrelated factors and that many of these must be overcome simultaneously in order for people and places to move forward. Removing barriers one at a time is not sufficient to achieve the desired outcomes because they are synergistic or mutually reinforcing. The expected result of comprehensiveness is that action will occur along many fronts, and these actions will be more successful than they would otherwise be due to their synergy.

Working at cross-purposes to some degree, with the notion of comprehensiveness is the desire to achieve high levels of resident involvement. Comprehensiveness tends to require an elaborate planning process and a very far-reaching vision for a future community, but this is difficult to achieve and very time-consuming. To mobilize residents, many CCIs feel that it is essential for the initiative to show early signs of success through action. They must therefore be ready to seize opportunities and produce visible results at the outset rather than tackling large and comprehensive strategies.[121] Further, residents may become impatient with a comprehensive planning process and may be interested in only their issue.[122] The diverging interests of residents that undermine comprehensiveness are most likely to occur in diverse neighborhoods where needs of groups are markedly different. For example, in a neighborhood with both extreme poverty and middle-class home owners, there will be a divergence of opinion about the importance of working on a comprehensive agenda versus one that is more narrowly focused.

Even when the planning process has led to a comprehensive vision, CCIs struggle with how to take action in a comprehensive way. Sequential, parallel, or truly integrated actions are all possibilities.[123] Although an agenda that tackles multiple concerns in one integrated process has been the ideal, practicality often dictates that issues be worked on one or two at a time. This may, in part, be due to the limited resources of CCIs relative to the myriad issues of concern in the communities. The problem of achieving adequate scale to implement the comprehensiveness principle continues to face CCIs.[124]

Collaboration: Collaboration is also a cornerstone of virtually all CCIs and is seen as contributing to multifaceted solutions because the collaborators bring varying perspectives and resources to the table. It can also contribute to strengthening and deepening social networks through organizations, associations, and individuals working together on common agendas. An anticipated by-product is growing trust and shared expectations among residents and the community's formal and informal organizations.

An additional outcome of collaboration is that organizations and individuals working together can amass significant amounts of resources and target them toward selected strategies. This is seen as ensuring change of greater magnitude and visibility than that which could be achieved working alone. Early success by CCIs with collaboration is seen as producing know-how and skills among residents and community organizations to take on additional and larger collaborative efforts.

CCIs differ in how they implement collaboration. Many CCIs have begun with a defined entity called a collaborative, with key partners from inside and outside the neighborhood represented in the structure and governance of the initiative.[125] Other CCIs with resident governance structures have sought collaboration with organizations around specific action projects or issues.[126] The question of when and how to involve collaborators is related to perceived power differentials. While CCIs will eventually need partners from the government and business sectors outside the neighborhood to achieve their aims, some choose to focus initially on strengthening partnerships internally.

Although collaboration is an important principle for CCIs, it can mean many things ranging from providing advice and comment on what another group or organization is planning to full integration of the human and financial resources of several organizations toward a common agenda. The predominant mode of collaboration in CCIs at present seems to be collaborative planning and joint ventures around new action projects.

Competition for scarce resources among existing organizations, however, can often serve as barriers to collaboration within neighborhoods. Clear and long-term commitments to these partnerships need to be made by private and public funders to overcome the survival needs of organizations, which can prevent them from sharing resources and power.[127] The potential collaborators should understand that their own mission is furthered, rather than undermined, by working together toward a comprehensive set of neighborhood concerns.

Assets Orientation: Community building raises the capacity of the community to achieve its goals by drawing upon the talents, information, and resources, both realized and potential, within the community. The term community builders use is *assets,* and they mean this in stark contrast to the problem or deficit orientation of many service and neighborhood programs of the past.[128, 129] These assets need to be identified and incorporated into the planning and action process of CCIs.

An asset is something of value owned or influenced by residents or institutions. Low-income communities may not have recognized and appreciated their assets in the past, but this is addressed through community building. An assets inventory is often a starting point for identifying human, financial, and physical assets that might be harnessed in the process of achieving community change.[130] Something that was once seen as a problem, such as vacant land, can be converted to an asset, such as a place for the development of businesses or housing. It becomes an asset when it becomes part of the community's vision for itself.

Institutional arrangements to build and support assets have often been missing in low-income communities.[131, 132] Community building needs to go beyond inventories to creating the structures necessary to support asset development. For example, individual development accounts and other programs that enable the accumulation of capital in the neighborhood have become an important part of some CCIs.[133]

An assets orientation is not a turning away from problems and issues of concern to the community; rather, it is intended to uncover the power and resources available to the community to address these issues and to diminish their dependence on outside solutions and programs. It also serves to highlight the features of the community that can support development, attract investment, and contribute to community identity and pride.

Sustainability: The disillusionment with quick fixes and government interventions has led to the recognition that communities must have the permanent capacity to plan and act in their own behalf. This is true for all communities, not just low-income ones; however, years of disinvestment and lack of power and control have diminished this capacity in some neighborhoods. Community building seeks to restore the traditions, structures, and skills that a community needs to maintain itself.

The concept of social capital is key to the notion of sustainability. Social capital is there to be used when needed and resides in the relationships and trust among people and their local associations and organizations. CCIs tend to believe that this capital will rise as residents and local organizations gain experience acting together and achieving success.[134] Social capital is renewed and expanded through this process.

Achieving this sustainability is a challenge, though, because many CCIs now depend on temporary foundation or government funding, and the knowledge of how to succeed is just beginning to emerge. Although CCIs seek to create a permanent capacity within their communities, this requires sustenance internally as well as externally.[135] Thus, to be sustained, CCIs have to connect themselves to the resources and traditions of the larger society, not just special purpose, temporary funding. They also need to contribute to the knowledge base of effective community change so that the capacity can spread throughout the society.

Metropolitan Context Challenges Community Initiatives

I began this chapter with a description of the metropolitan dynamics and changed understanding of poverty and poor communities that have produced today's concerns about low-income communities in the United States. At the millennium, CCIs and community building have emerged as the prevailing response to these challenges. The question now is, to what degree are the goals and principles of CCIs adequate to stem the devastating effects of these forces: urban sprawl and concentrated poverty, the negative effects of poor neighborhoods on their residents, the loss of social capital, the devolution of government, and the failure of large systems serving people.

ADDRESSING URBAN SPRAWL AND POVERTY CONCENTRATION

The movement of people and jobs to the suburbs, along with the out-migration of the middle class from many central cities, has isolated the poor in the most distressed neighborhoods of the region. These selective migration processes are powerful and have the potential to undermine the efforts of CCIs and community building in these neighborhoods unless they become linked to metropolitan solutions.[136] Distressed communities cannot simply work internally to the neighborhood or even to the central city. They have to connect to the entire metropolitan region, which, in many places, is spreading rapidly into the countryside. The spread takes in more and more political jurisdictions, complicating these connections. CCIs need many partnerships beyond their neighborhoods to address these metropolitan issues.

One area that depends vitally on metropolitan connections is employment, both connecting neighborhood residents to job growth in the suburbs and linking urban business development with the region.[137] CCIs must address trust, information, access, and skill gaps between their residents and the growth industries of their regions. Collaboration and partnerships within and outside the community are key to reducing these barriers to employment, but the partnerships have to stretch across many miles and overcome social as well as physical distance. Without addressing these challenging employment barriers on a metropolitan scale, CCIs are unlikely to stop the flow of employed families from their neighborhoods, and the opportunities for their neighborhood residents will continue to worsen.

Some CCIs have begun to implement programs for connecting inner-city workers to suburban jobs.[138] One model is for neighborhood organizations to recruit and assess the local labor force and to coach them through the process of finding and keeping work. They link residents to several job training or placement programs depending on their needs and skills. The programs are usually geared toward training or preparing workers for specific sectors with labor needs in the suburbs. Many cities with a manufacturing sector, for example, have advanced manufacturing programs to prepare the new kinds of workers that can make this sector more competitive. These activities reduce the companies' cost of finding the needed workers, and they build on the informal networks and relationships that exist in the community, providing that information link and bridge to suburban employment.

Many metropolitan areas have found that there is a labor shortage in the suburbs, and that there are many people in the city needing jobs. This is fertile ground for the building of neighborhood and suburban coalitions to reduce the city-suburban barriers. Regional councils or networks, made up of industry, government, training and placement providers, vocational educators, and representatives of community development and community-building initiatives, are often the initial step in linking workers with employers throughout the region.

Housing markets are additional metropolitan factors that CCIs must influence to achieve their goals.[139] It is not surprising that low-income families congregate in particular parts of a city because that is the location for the majority of affordable housing in the region.[140] Although CCIs often work to create better or more low-income housing within their neighborhoods, this does little to reverse the growing concentration of poverty in these areas. Unless affordable housing can be created throughout the region and a middle-income housing market can be reestablished in city neighborhoods, the process of concentration and isolation of poor neighborhoods is likely to continue.

Finally, CCIs need to join partners throughout the region to begin to control urban sprawl. Otherwise, the central city on which CCI neighborhoods depend will continue to lose its hold on the population and resources that it needs. The inner-ring suburbs are often natural allies in this regard because they have begun to experience some in-migration of poorer families from the central city and are beginning to face many of the challenges of the central cities.[141] In several places, city and suburban churches also have become partners in the effort to curb the movement to the hinterlands and the resulting disassociation of the affluent from the poor.[142] Metropolitan-wide coalitions have been successful in changing public policy to facilitate controls on regional growth and are key ingredients of CCIs' ability to overcome the concentration of poverty in their neighborhoods.[143, 144]

HARNESSING POSITIVE NEIGHBORHOOD EFFECTS

The neighborhood imbeddedness of CCIs suggests that they have much greater potential to reverse detrimental neighborhood effects on residents than programs that originate outside the neighborhood. The fact that they are comprehensive, tackling many conditions that have been of concern, also promises to result in better outcomes for families and children. An important question, though, is how and to what degree must the neighborhood change in order to foster these positive outcomes for the people who live there. There is some evidence, for example, that there may be a threshold that must be reached on levels of employment or the number of middle-class residents before poor residents are likely to experience benefits in terms of their own economic success.[145, 146] This would suggest that positive neighborhood effects are unlikely to emerge until the barriers to employment and housing are substantially reduced. Crime and violence are another example of neighborhood conditions that are thought to negatively affect residents, particularly children.[147] If CCIs produce a great reduction in these incidents, positive benefits for residents should follow, but little is known about how long it takes to achieve a sufficient magnitude of change.

Earlier benefits from positive neighborhood effects may be achieved, however, if resident participation leads to better social control and collective efficacy or to more elaborated social networks and social support.[148] Although at this point there is no scientific evidence that participation alone can accomplish these things, it has seldom been tried in such targeted and intensive ways as CCIs are now doing. But unless CCIs gear their residents' participation toward changing those aspects of neighborhood life that have become harmful to residents, such as poverty and instability, positive neighborhood effects may be a long way off.

SOCIAL CAPITAL IS ELUSIVE AND PERVASIVE

For many CCIs, the creation of social capital is an important feature of everything they do; it is the glue that ties the community together. CCIs see social capital as both a process and a product. It enables them to achieve community change but is also expected to result from their efforts to engage people and organizations in collaborative action. Participation and collaboration alone, however, do not have all of the ingredients to create social capital. In order to build social capital for a community, the participatory and collaborative efforts need to engender widespread trust, reciprocity, and a common set of norms. Further, it would seem that for social capital to foster the kind of action envisioned by CCIs, the social networks of individuals and organizations must be sufficiently interconnected and dense both within the community and with external networks throughout the metropolitan region.

Participation in organizations and civic affairs is not synonymous with trust at the individual level,[149] although participation does seem to be a necessary precondition. Yet fostering trust and a sense of obligation to one another in the community, especially among people who are having economic and other difficulties themselves, may require particular kinds of experiences in collective action. The action must be effective but also give something back to the participants, making them trust the process and willing to give back in turn. In diverse communities or between city and suburban communities, there is also the challenge of fostering trust among people who see themselves as different from one another and have a history of ethnic or class conflict. Interaction among people of good will who are involved with a CCI is a first step but needs to be accompanied by massive and widespread efforts to change hearts and minds throughout the metropolitan area.

Given the complexities, CCIs cannot assume that social capital will follow from their principles of resident involvement and collaboration but must examine this carefully along the way. They need to be deliberate about the social capital building potential of the actions they take and the relationships they establish. In particular, they must foster the building of trustful and reciprocal relationships among residents and their own institutions and among residents and institutions outside their neighborhood boundaries. Social capital that goes beyond the neighborhood would seem to be vital to the success of CCIs and necessary for their sustainability, especially after their initial funding support declines.

DEVOLUTION OF GOVERNMENT AND SYSTEMS CHANGE

The lives of residents of CCI communities are affected by the large public systems that have often floundered in urban America, such as public schools, public welfare, children's services, and the justice system. These systems alone vastly outspend CCIs and their collaborators within these neighborhoods, and their functions cannot be replaced by collective action or the kind of innovative programs that result from the work of CCIs. Yet, for the community to achieve its aspirations, these systems have to become more effective with the people in the neighborhoods they serve. Unfortunately, communities are usually too small to have much of an influence on large systems when operating on their own; they need to engage in building coalitions of multiple communities and cross-community interest groups. Another model for influencing large systems is for CCIs to demonstrate effective changes in school buildings or neighborhood offices, and then work toward spreading the demonstration throughout. Perhaps the most promising role for CCIs in affecting system change, though, may be in readying the community to work with those who have already committed to becoming more community based.[150]

Devolution may present opportunities for communities to have greater influence over policies and practices in these systems than they have had before. Federal programs and decisions have been devolved to the states, and many states are allowing great latitude and decision making at the county or regional level. Within counties, many agencies are seeing the need to move their planning and decision making further down into communities. CCIs must build the capacity of the community to effectively shape these decisions in ways that will increase program effectiveness. Key to this success will be the ability to monitor program outcomes at the community level so programs can be modified and changed over time. Devolution, without capacity building at the community level, is unlikely to repair the systems and, in fact, could undermine them even further.

GOING TO SCALE WITH COMMUNITY BUILDING

The need for comprehensive community change and community building has now been widely recognized. It is based on a number of convictions: that categorical initiatives shaped in Washington do not work; that market forces are not strong enough in these neighborhoods to be relied upon alone; that volunteerism is not enough; that organizing residents to confront systems does not go far enough; that the fate of the metropolis will be affected by the fortunes of these growing numbers of distressed areas; and that within the most distressed areas there are assets on which to build.[151]

The expansion of the CCI and community building movement is occurring through concept replication.[152] The basic principles and theories of these initiatives are being shaped and tailored to each community and metropolitan context. Indeed, the structures and activities put in place to operationalize the principles or concepts vary markedly from place to place. Concept replication, as a way of increasing the scale of these efforts, is in marked contrast to traditional replication of model programs in which an effort is made to copy, to the degree possible, the actual practices and methods developed in the model.[153]

The prevailing approach, starting these initiatives from the bottom up but using common concepts to guide them, promises that the initiatives will be tailored to the uniqueness of each situation. However, any effort to institutionalize and expand such a movement encounters the question from policymakers and funders of whether and how such initiatives are working. In other words, they want to know what is their impact on the barriers and problems affecting urban communities. While this question can, in part, be answered for particular initiatives, the lack of common operational methods will make this difficult to answer for the movement as a whole using traditional evaluation methods. Innovative methods of providing meaningful evaluation of this diverse group of initiatives will be necessary if a compelling argument is to be made for their expansion and sustainability.[154]

Although many communities are moving forward on building their capacity to sustain change, the movement is vulnerable. Current efforts to restore poor communities through CCIs are not nearly large enough to address the problems of the cities and their residents today.[155] A national agenda to rebuild inner-city communities must bring substantially more resources to bear on the problems to overcome the metropolitan forces that have come to be well-documented at the millennium.

Social workers can play an important role in building communities by drawing upon their historic roots in the settlement house and service integration movements, but this role must be expanded and strengthened. Community social work practice in the twenty-first century needs to be directed at the dynamic forces that devastated poor and inner-city communities in the last half of the twentieth century. Community practitioners will need the skills and knowledge that can enable poor communities to overcome their social and economic isolation within the region while building their internal capacity to achieve their own goals.

10

State Social Welfare: Global Perspectives

Demetrius S. Iatridis

The old, liberal, social democratic state social welfare is under restructuring in the United States[1] and in most parts of the world,[2] notably in technologically advanced countries in both eastern and western Europe, but also in developing regions. Restructuring is defined differentially among authors, but fundamentally it denotes the need to rearrange and reform the structure of state social welfare so that it can respond more effectively to drastically changing economic, social, political, technological, and cultural worldwide forces.

In eastern European countries the universal, central command planning state welfare system is now atrophic, dysfunctioning, and in transition. It has been undermined by the collapse of state socialist regimes; the discrediting of statist socialist philosophy, policies, and programs; and the rapid socioeconomic and cultural transition from communism to capitalism. The rapid transformation from central command planning to market economy, and the radical changes in public ownership, law, and means of production and distribution, necessitated in these countries the reduction or replacement of state social welfare universal and comprehensive benefits by low-cost, residual forms of social welfare benefits.[3]

Throughout the West, governments are restructuring the tenets of postwar Beveridge-inspired state social welfare systems with neoconservative individualism, which promotes economic globalization, reduced taxation, market competitiveness, and minimal residual public services. Neoconservatism questioned the ever-expanding Titmussian state social welfare approach and rationale, and rejected fundamental liberal citizenship principles, including the canons of empowerment and emancipation based on social justice and equality.

Social welfare as a function of the western state, and its discourse in eastern and western Europe, is now under political and socioeconomic pressures to drastically reduce public welfare programs and services as well as state investments in social capital formation. Notably in technologically advanced countries, restructuring is fundamentally based on policies to replace welfare by work.[4]

In several developing countries the restructuring takes the form of transforming at least part of state social welfare so that it can contribute to economic and social development rather than impede it.[5] In this "developmental approach" context, priority is given to state social welfare policies and programs, which contribute to economic and community development in the context of social capital formation and self-employment.

The global restructuring discourse in advanced capitalism raised a fundamental question about the harmonious coexistence of state social welfare and sustained economic growth. Four major postwar-related developments are thought to be the parameters of the state social welfare discourse.

- First, post–Second World War changes in the worldwide social economy, supported for several decades a consensus about the coexistence and complementarity of a globalized competitive economy with state social welfare. Then the shift to the new political Right and developments in the 1970s and thereafter challenged the consensus and the coexistence principle.
- Second, globalization as a socioeconomic stabilization tool in advanced capitalist economies enhanced the shift of emphasis from national to regional socioeconomic communities.
- Third, privatization has reduced the responsibilities of governments and increased the role of private sectors and local communities.

- Fourth, the emergence of social science perspectives, which emphasized postpositivist rather than positivist approaches in the analyses of societal phenomena, and social policy planning, generated a new critique of state social welfare from the Left.

The Post–Second World War Era

THE CONSENSUS: THE 1940S, 1950S, AND 1960S

The post–Second World War consensus, notably between the 1940s and 1960s, enhanced the role of the state in providing social welfare while enhancing economic growth in western and eastern European countries. Fundamentally, the consensus supported the state as a provider of social progress, policies, programs, and services within capitalist and socialist frames.

The democracies of the West, chastened by the brutalities of pure capitalism, the two world wars, a depression, and a worldwide post–Second World War commitment to democratic global reconstruction to provide better living standards for all, accepted the necessity of a mixed economy for socioeconomic reconstruction. They concluded that a global market economy needed to be tamed and domesticated to coexist with ever-expanding capitalist state welfare systems and a decent, stable, and just market economy. The economic and sociopolitical consensus was designed to meet human and social needs within advanced capitalism. In this context, Western societies, including the United States, Britain, and Scandinavian countries, expanded social reforms on the wave of worldwide reconstruction and a long economic boom. This development is associated with distinct social policy and social work approaches based on social justice and equality.[6]

The former USSR and its allies in eastern Europe were committed to rapid post–Second World War reconstruction of their social economy in the context of central command planning, democratic centralism, social justice, and equality. Hence, they established extensive universal state social welfare policies and programs for all citizens, with emphasis on full employment, broad citizenship rights, and comprehensive public services, including recreation, culture, and vacation for all workers.[7]

THE DISINTEGRATION OF THE CONSENSUS: THE 1970S, 1980S, AND 1990S

The changes in advanced capitalism undermined the global consensus about state responsibility for social welfare.

The ungluing of the postwar consensus in western Europe, occurring in the middle of the 1970s, marked the end of the expansion of labor demand, labor movements, and the welfare state. The economic stagnation and declining rates of economic growth of the 1970s, massive restructuring of capital and labor, new forces of production, mass communication, technology, globalization, and the resurgence of organized business as a political force undermined the social coalition of elite political forces.[8]

The revived credulity in pure markets and a shift to radical Right ideologies in the 1980s, brought about by new, worldwide socioeconomic developments, moved social policy planning away from the state to local governments, and to residual, low-cost social programs. In this context, Keynesianism was attacked because it favored increased central government spending and expanding public social welfare programs in economic crisis.[9]

The fall of the USSR and the radical shift from communism to unfettered economic markets in late 1980s and early 1990s undermined the state social welfare system in eastern Europe[10] and countries in central Asia.

Globalization and Regionalism

The new forces of globalization swept the world enhanced by increasingly closer and interdependent global links. Worldwide interdependence and socioeconomic integration have been forged by new global realities, including communication technology, high technology and space innovations, mass media, migration, and urbanization. The demands of the new world era of social economy have direct impacts on government socioeconomic policies, programs, and projects, including deflation, unemployment, state social welfare, and social work. Globalization, which entails not simply the opening of economic markets but also societies, is as much a social and political construct as it is economic.

As economics and technology reigned supreme, countries moved furiously into a postindustrial, information age with explosions of new industries and wealth. The old world of international policies, protection, and security seems obsolete. Even thinking in terms of national boundaries rather than treating the world as a single system seems old-fashioned. What occurs in one part of the world has direct worldwide impacts.

In 1997 the Thai economy suffered a financial meltdown when the currency lost 40 percent of its value vis-à-vis the dollar. The Thai stock market crashed, off 70 percent from its peak in 1994. By the end of the year the crisis had spread throughout Southeast Asia and even affected the richer economies to the north, especially South Korea. The value of currencies across the region collapsed, including Indonesia and Malaysia. Southeast Asian financial markets crashed as well. In Thailand the steep downturn cost over two million jobs by the end of 1998, while in Indonesia stagflation pushed nearly one half of the population into poverty.[11]

Because the Southeast Asian financial crisis triggered a deflationary spiral likely to suck all of East Asia, and many parts of the world, into a depression, Thailand and Indonesia are in receivership, undergoing austerity measures administered by the International Monetary Fund in return for emergency loans to help repay foreign lenders. The East Asian bailout package is so far over $100 billion. Latin American, European, and Russian currencies all have come under attack. Even the booming U.S. economy slowed in 1998 under the ballooning trade deficit caused by fewer exports to East Asia.[12]

The aftermath of the Asiatic financial and political flu continues in the global economy. The United States is preparing to commit American taxpayer funds as part of a lending program (expected to total several billion dollars in direct aid) to try to insulate Brazil, and with it the rest of Latin America, from the worst effects of the financial turmoil circling the globe.[13] Emphasizing the globalization of the economy and its impact worldwide, the International Monetary Fund, the World Bank, and the Inter-American Development Bank, among others, participated in the rescue program by contributing approximately $25 billion.

Globalization and regionalization at the end of the century have fundamentally transformed governmental policies and responsibilities and the rules of the game for capital, production, distribution, protection, and state social welfare. The emergence of "Euroland" and the European conversion to a shared currency in 1999 will also affect more than just money and currency. The European Union creates a whole new social economy landscape that shifts to regionalization and transcends national boundaries. Euroland already encompasses a block of shoppers, producers, consumers, and capital that may quickly rival other countries, including the United States, as an economic and social colossus. The trend toward even more globalization appears to be distinct and unmistakable.

PRIVATIZATION: A GLOBAL STABILIZATION TOOL

Global privatization, on the other hand, has further enhanced the shift from state responsibility for social welfare to free market profit and the reduction of national public social welfare services in favor of local community responsibility.

Global sales of major public enterprises have been impressive. Worldwide sales increased from $39.2 billion in 1988 to $52.4 billion in 1993. Sales in developing countries increased from $2.4 billion in 1988 to $18.3 billion in 1993.[14] In 1995 worldwide privatization again increased some $50 billion, matching the pace set in 1993 and 1994. From 1982 to 1992 more than 7,000 enterprises were privatized around the world, of which roughly 2,000 were in developing countries.[15] In the fury to balance national budgets, governments resorted to selling their assets.[16]

Whether countries are capitalist or socialist, developed or developing, in the Northern or Southern Hemisphere, privatization has emerged as an economic tool to balance budgets and reduce state bureaucracy—a buzzword at the epicenter of global development. It involves a shift from public interests to market profits, and from publicly to privately produced goods and services; the development of public-private partnerships; and changes in the collective institutional interests of society, including social justice, power relations, and equality. As privatization alters the institution of property and ownership, and distributive outcomes among individuals, groups, and classes, it has generated controversies about justice, fairness, and equality.[17]

At the heart of the controversies are what are thought to be the competing and conflicting functions of state responsibility and market freedom. This includes public social welfare services. In eastern European countries, mass privatization is being used to transform central command planning into mixed economies.[18]

In Great Britain, Margaret Thatcher's government made privatization the cornerstone of its social welfare and economic policy, and to some extent so did France under François Mitterand and Sweden under its conservative government.

In the United States privatization was promoted aggressively during the Reagan administration and the Republican Contract With America. In Boston, Massachusetts, privatization has shifted the responsibility for thousands of acutely mentally ill patients from the state to a private for-profit company.[19] The program ran into political opposition and was the subject of widespread protests by social service providers. The conflict was further fueled by an increase in the death rate among these patients, which some opponents attributed to privatization.

Privatization was promoted in American public services ranging from education to prisons. Private firms promised to boost students' performance in failing urban schools, eliminate waste, and manage schools for a profit—at no additional cost to the taxpayers. But the largest firm of its kind, Educational Alternatives, Inc. (EAI), has failed dismally so far. Its projects in Dade County, Florida; Baltimore, Maryland; and Hartford, Connecticut, have ended with EAI ousted for disappointing performance.[20]

With more than one million people behind bars, the United States imprisons a larger share of its population than any other country. Facing serious overcrowding problems with federal and state prisons currently operating well beyond capacity, governments turned to the private sector for solutions. Proponents of prison privatization claim that privately run prisons have shown significant cost savings while still being profitable. Opponents argue that historically, prisons for profit may abuse inmates and violate their citizenship rights. They point out that governments must protect inmates and should not move prisoners to other states far away from their families.[21]

Giant companies are entering the race to overhaul and run state and local social welfare programs. As state governments are increasingly handing over to private companies some functions that were previously handled by government workers, a rich new business is created by the privatization of poverty. Corporate America is attracted to the poverty business, which has a potential U.S. market of more than $30 billion a year.[22] State and local governments face tighter welfare budgets and new welfare reform regulations as the Personal Responsibility Act of 1996 has turned cash assistance to poor families from an entitlement to block grants to the states, which now have wide latitude and responsibility for benefit levels and eligibility standards. The act also calls for financial penalties if states fail to move most recipients into jobs in two years. Hence, state and local authorities turn to the for-profit sector to help them save some money and improve efficiency.

Big corporations, including Lockheed Martin, Electronic Data Systems, Curtis and Associates, and Andersen Consulting, bid for multimillion dollar contracts to place welfare recipients in private sector jobs, determine welfare eligibility, pursue parents for child support payments, find foster homes for abused children, and act as brokers in the Medicaid managed-care field. In Texas, Governor George W. Bush encourages companies to run the welfare, Medicaid, and food stamp operations— $563 million in welfare functions.[23] Modern contracting-out of complete management for specific welfare services is a new rich source for profit making in the poverty field. It is also a serious concern of many that the profit imperative can violate the rights, protection, and dignity of welfare recipients.

Privatization plans for state social welfare, which shift the responsibility from government to the private sector, may not only decrease state protection of social welfare recipients, but also the protection of women and gender equality in Social Security proposals. Plans to replace some of the existing Social Security program with a new system of personal retirement accounts would undermine the financial security of older women. Notably, it will undermine protections provided under the current Social Security system and protected as a right by law, including progressive benefits formula, dependent's benefits, lifetime benefits, and inflation adjustments. Poverty among American women over sixty-five is already twice as much as among men over sixty-five.[24]

Postpositivism's Critique of State Social Welfare

The emergence of postpositivism enhanced pressures to restructure state social welfare from the left of the political spectrum. Typically, postpositivist practitioners challenged the dominant power structures of society. Based on radical analyses of community structure and institutions, they support social welfare changes to enhance just and equal social relations, democratic social liberation, empowerment, and emancipation of social welfare recipients. Rejecting the traditional positivist mantra of value-neutral, apolitical, asocial, status quo, technical analyses, and research practice—postpositivists propose to restructure those state social welfare policies and programs that, in their view, tend to incorporate class, race, and gender divisions and inequalities of society. In this context, they reject unfair economic interests imposed by the ruling class on social welfare recipients, and they oppose residual, paternalistic, and sexist social welfare policies and programs. The postpositivist agenda for restructuring social welfare supports working-class interest, including fair and just treatment of powerless welfare recipients, and adequate benefits standard, which promote social solidarity and citizenship rights.[25]

The emerging postpositivism is thought to introduce "new" dimensions in social welfare analyses and practice, including the notion that all practice knowledge is constructed (constructivism) and consists of what individuals create and express. It also introduces phenomenology that links knowledge to action in the welfare field, and to subjective meanings of the social welfare problem to actors (decision makers and welfare recipients). Both modes suggest that knowledge is created in a community context rather than having an independent existence. Hence, postpositivism suggests community-based social welfare restructuring.[26]

Those who do not subscribe to postpositivist perspectives propose social welfare restructuring based on positivist views, including traditional, incremental, empirical-rational, technical, asocial, apolitical, or peripheral approaches.

Issues for the Year 2000 and Beyond

State social welfare is fundamentally a political issue, and politics in the first decades of the new millennium are thought to be at least as unpredictable as in the past, particularly in the global perspective context.

215

There are, however, some basic parametric issues that are interdisciplinary in nature. They have played in the past—and are likely to play in the future—a critical role in the discourse. The major contextual concerns of the second half of the twentieth century will probably count heavily on state social welfare discourses and restructuring in the early part of the twenty-first century. Hence, revisiting these concerns may lead to the patterns of restructuring likely to occur in the future state social welfare.

Figure 10-1 depicts the institutional, interdisciplinary parameters of state social welfare that provide the structuring of social welfare. In this context, three related concerns are typically fundamental:

- First, the role of government and state (arrows 1, political institutions) in providing public services and protecting the consumer. Public responsibility is related to societal objectives and the philos-

Figure 10–1
Institutional Parameters of Social Welfare

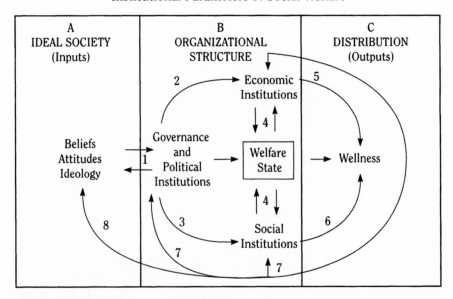

Source: Adapted from Iatridis, D. *Social Policy: Institutional Context of Social Development and Human Services.* (Pacific Grove, CA: Brooks/Cole, 1994), 153.

216

ophy of state and government (section A). These inputs are linked to prevailing canons of power, liberalism, political parties, interventions in the economic market, and the forging of a political consensus about regional social economy and state welfare.

- Second, the concern about the link between economic efficiency and equality rights in the context of social justice and citizenship rights (arrows 2, 4). This discourse includes the economic institutions, privatization, and increasing prerequisites of advanced social economies for growth and development.
- Third, the concern for systematic and adequate investments in communities in the context of social institutions and particularly social capital and social capital formation. This includes the social institutions and the well-being of communities as a target of social welfare policies as well as a vehicle of individual and family socioeconomic development.

As in the recent past, these three related interdisciplinary concerns (the role of government and state, economic efficiency as it relates to social justice, and community social capital formation) are likely to influence synergically the restructuring of state social welfare around the world in the decades to come. They are highlighted in the following sections.

THE ROLE OF GOVERNMENT AND STATE

While a political consensus can be ephemeral, it also typically reflects longer political trends. Political perspective that demolishes state social welfare and those that favor an ever-expanding state social welfare are likely to shift in the future toward a broad political consensus in the context of the political center. A consensus of the center is thought to be forged by competing commitments to enlighten self-interest, community interdependence, compassion, and innovative partnerships of public and private domains.

Currently, it is thought that government should serve the ordinary, hard-working individual and family by providing safety, protection of people from unfair or excessive aspects of the marketplace, physical public goods (communication networks, public amenities, roads and parks) and social infrastructure public goods (social and human capital investments, including health care, education, and employment) necessary for individuals and families to seek opportunity for growth and development. In this context, governments in the future will emphasize policies that provide people with resources to solve their own problems rather than isolated relief programs. New public-private and intracommunity-based partnerships will play a considerable role of integrated policies and programs.

PRIVATIZATION AND THE LINK BETWEEN ECONOMIC EFFICIENCY AND SOCIAL JUSTICE

Even eastern European countries committed to rapidly selling public assets to private sectors, are now keenly aware that governments have (and will have in the decade to come) a fundamental role to play in restricting excessive economic market demands toward privatization and unrestricted economic efficiency at the expense of fairness, social justice, and equity. In several parts of the world it is now thought that economic efficiency and social justice are complementary rather than antithetical. The typical economic perspective, which calls for reduction of public social spending because it hinders economic growth, is now challenged by new distributive research data in developing countries. It is thought that fairness and equality in the marketplace enhance rather than hinder economic growth and development. This includes policies to make sure people with power do not exercise it in an irresponsible way, or in ways that prevent growth and development opportunities for the powerless. In brief, and in the context of restructuring state social welfare, economic growth and development are thought to be enhanced by increased state social welfare programs that encourage fairness and social justice.

Until recently the dominant view among most economists and governments emphasized the negative connection between income equality (social market concern) and economic growth (economic market concern). The view that fairness and equality are a drag on economic growth reflected tensions between social and economic markets and represented conflicts between equality and efficiency—an antithesis between social accountability and economic planning. Consequently, income inequality in the marketplace had rarely been considered a problem by the business world. After all, some successful societies in history have existed for millennia with enormous inequalities of wealth and income.

Recently, however, modern economies and democracies have a problem with this "old" view and with rising economic inequality around the world. There is now increasing evidence that income inequality is a drag on economic growth. For example, countries, including South Korea, that have less income inequality have more economic growth.[27]

This was surprising news for the business world, not so much because inequality undermines the democratic political canon of one person one vote and defies the moral principle that the economically strong should drive the economically weak into extinction, but rather because this introduced a new dimension in the discourse about efficiency and inequality. It suggests that income inequality can play a significantly negative role in directing countries on the path toward stable growth.[28] Far from being a tradeoff or a follower of economic growth, reduced income inequality is seen now as having a positive connection with economic growth. Countries with more income equality also have higher growth rates.[29] By the same token, countries with less income equality also have lower growth rates.

Traditional economists are less likely in the future to promote social spending cuts for the poor, and tax cuts for the wealthy, if such policies impede economic growth rather than promote it.

COMMUNITY SOCIAL CAPITAL INVESTMENTS

As poverty is increasingly concentrated in urban communities of large cities around the world, state social welfare investments in communities where the poor live is now thought to be a fundamental concern of restructuring. Both in eastern European countries that move away from statism and national centralization, and western European countries where both decentralization and regionalization become increasingly fundamental, there is a new awareness based on research findings that the socioeconomic development of individuals and families cannot be divorced from the resources of communities in which they live.[30]

Moreover, local communities are increasingly the focus of state social welfare because many national governments, including the United States, are transferring social welfare and protection responsibilities to local authorities (decentralization), which now develop new capacity for planning, financing, and managing. The lack of confidence in large public systems and government bureaucracy, and the general disaffection with big government, enhances this trend toward local community social capital investments. The shift from statism to local communities reflects a distinct trend at this time. The restructuring of state social welfare is thought to be based also on the perspective that the local community is both a target of social welfare interventions as well as a vehicle to reduce poverty and enhance the lives of individuals and families.

In this context, current social welfare strategies based on replacing welfare with work are also linked to community-based approaches in restructuring social welfare. Vital to the success of policies and programs to replace welfare with work in technologically advanced countries is the availability of jobs in general, and notably in communities with a high concentration of poverty. The crucial policy question is whether or not there are enough jobs in labor markets for welfare recipients, and where the jobs will come from that recipients are to find and occupy.

If labor demand (aggregate or locally based) is inadequately elastic (which means that a small reduction in going wage rates will not generate a substantial expansion of job openings in the community), jobs will not be there for welfare recipients, and they will not be absorbed in labor markets. If new jobs are not available, forcing welfare beneficiaries into the labor market would only increase unemployment. Some former welfare recipients can find jobs, but only by displacing formerly employed members of the assiduously working poor. Moreover, the effort to increase the demand for unskilled and unqualified labor (welfare beneficiaries) will be not only difficult in a globalized economy but also expensive—notably more so than traditional welfare benefits. It is thought that to replace welfare with work it is necessary to create new, preferably community-based jobs, through some version of public service employment (something like the WPA of the New Deal years.)[31] The need to improve infrastructure in poor communities with intensive use of unskilled labor is directly related to the need to create jobs in communities for welfare recipients.[32]

These three basic concerns and trends are thought to be fundamental in restructuring state social welfare in the decades to come.

Part III

Conceptual and Scientific Critiques

11

Eclecticism Is Not a Free Good: Barriers to Knowledge Development in Social Work

David J. Tucker

Over the past thirty years, numerous researchers have used the paradigm concept as a structure for systematically examining how various fields of study function overall, as well as how they differ from one another. One consistent finding from this research is that the degree of consensus a given field has regarding its theories, methods, and approaches (that is, its level of paradigm development) has very important consequences for that field. Fields with more highly developed paradigms do much better in acquiring resources and in keeping the resources they have. They develop and diffuse knowledge more quickly, have more power and autonomy, and are much more likely to engage in collaborative forms of research. Moreover, because of these and other consequences, fields with more highly developed paradigms are likely to maintain and even improve their relative position of advantage vis-à-vis other fields.[1]

In this chapter I examine the implications of these arguments and observations for social work. I argue that available evidence shows social work as highly fragmented in its approaches to knowledge development and application. This limits its potential to develop paradigmatically and magnifies the advantages that other fields have in the contest for resources and legitimacy. Illustrating one possible way to overcome these disadvantages, I propose a problematic, or central organizing question

This is a shortened version of a paper previously published in *Social Service Review* 70 (September 1996): 400–434.

for social work, and show how such a problematic could be used to construct a social ecology of caring.

Where Does Social Work Stand?

Most observers would readily agree that social work is characterized by a low level of paradigm development, particularly when compared to the social sciences with which it has historical connections: psychology, sociology, and to a lesser degree, economics and political science.[2] This is not to deny that social work has expended considerable effort investigating its paradigmatic status over the past decade. The literature contains numerous books and articles examining the propriety of its central mission,[3] appropriate standards for the appointment of its gatekeepers,[4] how it conducts and how it can improve its research,[5] and what is or should be its epistemology.[6] Although these efforts demonstrate concern for improving the cognitive organization of social work, the fact of their articulation, and continuing, unresolved debates about them, are themselves evidence of dissensus among scholars, educators, and practitioners about the basic tenets of social work.

In addition to these persistent internal disagreements about philosophy, theory, and methods, other factors point to a state of low paradigm development in social work. Donald Baker used citation data and network analytic techniques to investigate the structure of interrelationships among twenty social work journals.[7] The rationale came from theoretical arguments and empirical findings associating the structure of a discipline's journal network with its level of paradigm development.[8] The findings showed that the social work journal network exhibited a core-peripheral structure, that is, a few general journals form a diffuse center, surrounded by subspecialty areas such as health and child welfare that operate in relative isolation from one another. Because this type of structure reflects fragmentation in citation patterns, it implies a low level of paradigm development.[9] In a similar vein, Kam-fong Monit Cheung used citation data to investigate the relationship between social work and other disciplines, finding that social work journals cited other disciplines' journals much more frequently than the reverse.[10] Based on the structural argument noted earlier that citations in low paradigm fields tend to come from more paradigmatically developed fields,[11] the cross-citation pattern observed by Cheung is consistent with an interpretation of low paradigm development in social work.

Other studies focusing on questions about how social work develops knowledge and educates its new members have also produced evidence of a low level of paradigm development in social work. Mark Fraser and his colleagues analyzed over 1,800 articles published in ten social work journals over four years.[12] Their purpose was to characterize social work literature in terms of its use of scientific methods. They found diverse approaches to knowledge generation, leading them to conclude that systematic research methods find only limited use in social work and that, consistent with its historical pattern, "no single way of knowing dominates the profession."[13] In related research, Charles Glisson studied how research reported in five core social work journals changed over a twelve-year period.[14] He noted that research articles covered at least thirty-two different problem areas and issues, appearing to include "the complete list of problems and issues facing contemporary society, as well as a comprehensive list of issues which affect their solution."[15] Viewed within the framework of this paper, one implication of this finding is that there appears to be little consensus in the field about what are the most significant research issues.[16] Finally, Glenn Haworth, in a discussion of new forms of paradigm research and its implications for knowledge development, noted that materials in social work textbooks, although organized to give an outward appearance of wholeness, in fact show a low level of underlying philosophical compatibility and interdependence, an indication of a low level of paradigm development.[17]

Another facet of paradigm development pertinent to social work is journal rejection rates and manuscript evaluation time lags.[18] It will be recalled that current arguments construe acceptance rates as higher, and evaluation time lags as shorter, in more paradigmatically developed fields. Because available comparative studies do not include social work, I conducted my own exploratory investigation. Using data from a variety of sources, I compared acceptance rates and manuscript evaluation time lags across selected journals from social work, sociology, and psychology.[19] The journals studied were included because earlier investigators considered them relevant and important to both comparative as well as intradisciplinary analyses involving social work.[20]

Table 1 presents an overview of my findings. Social work and psychology journals are shown as consistently having higher acceptance rates

Table 1
Average Annual Acceptance Rates, Submissions, and Time Lags (in Weeks)
for 16 Journals During the Early 1980s and the Early 1990s.

Journal	Average Acceptance Rates		Average Annual Submissions		Measure of Change[b]	Average Editorial Time lags[a]	
	Time 1	Time 2	Time 1	Time 2		Time 1	Time 2
Sociology							
American Sociological Review	.11	.12	445	348	.78	8.6	13.0
J. Health & Social Behavior	.15	.19	233	143[c]	.61	6.8	11.5
Sociology of Education	.12	.17	149	129	.87	7.4	12.5
Social Forces	.18	.18	312	265	.85	8.6	9.5
Social Problems	.11	.10	343	319	.93	10.4	11.6
Overall	.13	.15	246	241	.81	8.4	11.6
Psychology							
J. Abnormal Psychology[d]	.17	.26	303	294	.97	10.0	15.0
J. Applied Psychology	.19	.19	424	457	1.08	12.0	8.5
J. Counseling Psychology	.19	.28	291	219	.75	6.5	7.0
J. Education Psychology	.21	.25	290	237	.82	8.5	8.0
J. Personality & Social Psychology	.25	.21	876	788	.90	11.2	15.0
Overall	.20	.24	437	399	.91	9.6	10.7

	Social Work						
Families in Society[e]	.39	.31	171	157	.92	16.0	16.0
J. Social Service Research	.50	.47	40	35	.88	18.0	18.0
J. Social Work Education[f]	.22	.21	122	133	1.09	18.0	14.5[g]
Social Service Review	.23	.25	152	102	.67	16.0	21.0
Social Work Research & Abstracts[h]	.15	.31	52	48	.92	14.0	14.0
Social Work[i]	.14	.22	484	291	.60	20.0	14.0
Overall	.27	.30	180	127	.70	17.0	16.25

Note: Unless otherwise specified, the years used in calculations were 1983–1985 and 1991–1993.

a. This is the length of the time lag between the submission of a manuscript and the editorial decision to accept or reject it.
b. The measure of change refers to changes in the number of submissions Time 1 to Time 2. It is computed by dividing Time 2 submissions by Time 1 submissions.
c. This figure was calculated using data for three years, 1991–1993; 1992 was a transition year, with only 47 new submissions reported. Hence, using reporter submissions for only 1992 and 1993 in calculating the measure of change gave an underestimate of the trend. For psychology journals for Time 1 submissions, the years used for calculations are 1986 and 1987. The reason for this is that prior to 1986, the number of new submissions included revised manuscripts.
e. Formerly known as *Social Casework*. Data used for acceptance rates, submissions, and change are for the period 1986–1994.
f. Data for Time 1 acceptance rates were available only from 1989–1994. Acceptance rates and the change measure were calculated using these data. However, they were not used in the regression analysis because of the limited number of observations. Mendelsohn reported an acceptance rate of .17 for 1983 and 1987, and an average editorial time lag of 18 weeks. See Mendelsohn (n. 19).
g. This is an estimate based on information provided by the journal. This information implied that evaluation time lags ranged from 7 to 22 weeks, with very few decisions being made in the 7-week range (i.e., 90% of eventually accepted manuscripts initially receive a reject/revise designation). The figure of 14.5 weeks is the midpoint between 7 and 22 weeks.
h. The Time 1 acceptance rate was calculated using data for 1987-1988. The acceptance rate for 1983 was .25. See Mendelsohn (n. 19).
i. The Time 1 acceptance rate was calculated using data for 1987-1988. The acceptance rate for 1983 was .16. See Mendelsohn (n. 19).

than sociology journals, with social work journals having the highest acceptance rates.[21] Also, while acceptance rates increased marginally for all three disciplines, social work's relative ranking did not change, and it continues to have, on average, a higher acceptance rate than either psychology or sociology. One-way analyses of variance on Time 1 and Time 2 data show these differences as statistically significant for social work and sociology in Time 2 but not in Time 1. The differences are not significant for social work and psychology, or for psychology and sociology.[22] Because higher acceptance rates are taken to indicate higher consensus and technical certainty about a field's knowledge development processes, these findings appear to qualify the claim presented earlier that social work is more underdeveloped paradigmatically than closely aligned social sciences.[23] Instead, they suggest that social work is aligned with psychology in its level of paradigmatic development and currently is superior to sociology.

An alternative explanation of higher acceptance rates considers processes that characterize the overall journal population. Over the past fifteen years, the number of journals in social work, as well as in closely aligned fields, has increased substantially, giving authors broader submission choices. One possible effect of this change may be the substantial decrease in the number of submissions to the journals noted in Table 1.[24] Because there seems to be no agreement that, even though less numerous, new submissions are higher in quality, the question raised is what ameliorative actions editors are likely to take?[25] One possibility is to reduce the number of articles published. This approach does not seem to have been adopted as a general strategy by most journals, since the number of articles published annually by individual journals has remained quite stable since 1983.[26]

A second possibility is that increased competition among journals for publishable manuscripts results in heightened pressure on editors to increase acceptance rates to help ensure their own journal's viability as well as to keep manuscripts from competitors.[27] Because of data limitations and small numbers, establishing clear empirical proof of this hypothesis is beyond the scope of this paper. However, it is possible to begin to explore its validity by regressing Time 2 acceptance rates on Time 1 acceptance rates and the measure of change in sub-

Table 2
Regressions of Time 2 Acceptance Rates on Change in Submissions,
Time 1 Acceptance Rates, and Journal Status for 16 U.S. Scholarly Journals

Variable	Unstandardized Coefficient	Standardized Coefficient	t
Change in submissions	−.062	−.078	−.509
Time 1 acceptance rates	.849	.862	5.616
Constant	.116		1.134

$$R^2 = .73$$
$$\text{Adjusted } R^2 = .68, F_{2.12} = 15.88$$

Change in submissions	−.004	−.005	−.030
Time 1 acceptance rates	.716	.727	3.977
Dummy variable for journal status	.051	.236	1.278
Constant	.078		.747

$$R^2 = .76$$
$$\text{Adjusted } R^2 = .70, F_{3.11} = 11.69$$

Correlation	2	3	4
1. Time 1 acceptance rate	.848	.171	−.517
2. Time 2 acceptance rate	—	.069	−.613
3. Change in submissions		—	.213
4. Journal status			—

missions. The results, reported in Table 2, suggest that the independent effect of change in submissions on Time 2 rejection rates is minimal. In contrast, the independent effect of Time 1 rejection rates is very strong, implying considerable stability in rejection rates. Separating the effects of being either a sociology or psychology journal does not significantly change these findings. Overall, therefore, this analysis does not support a claim that acceptance rates have been affected by changes in numbers of submissions.[28] Hence, a claim of a higher level of paradigm development for social work is not contradicted.

Although this inference of a higher level of paradigm development is in line with arguments made by some social work scholars, examination of another aspect of the review process affected by consensus, that is, the length of the time lag between the submission of a manuscript and the editorial decision to accept or reject it, questions its validity.[29] Assuming all other things to be equal, fields with higher levels of consensus are likely to have shorter editorial time lags than fields with lower levels of consensus.[30] The theory behind this is that in higher consensus fields, there will be fewer disagreements between referees and authors about appropriate research problems, theoretical approaches, or research techniques. Hence, fewer manuscripts will be subject to conflicting recommendations from referees, resulting in a quicker manuscript evaluation process because editors will find it less necessary to seek further opinions or extensive revisions.

The data in Table 1 show that, on average, editorial time lags in social work decreased slightly from 17.0 weeks to 16.25 weeks. Regardless, they are still longer on average than the editorial time lags for either psychology, which increased from 9.6 to 10.7 weeks, or sociology, which increased from 8.4 to 11.6 weeks. One-way analyses of variance on Time 1 and Time 2 data show the differences in editorial time lags between social work and sociology, and social work and psychology, as statistically significant for both time periods, with both sociology and psychology having significantly shorter editorial time lags than social work.[31] By the same token, neither sociology nor psychology differs significantly from each other in their editorial time lags. Based on the theoretical argument in the preceding paragraph, the implication of these findings is that the manuscript evaluation process for social work journals reflects more dissensus than the evaluation processes in sociology and psychology. Thus, contrary to the implication of the earlier finding on acceptance rates of higher consensus in social work, the findings on editorial time lags support the more dominant view of social work as comparatively more underdeveloped paradigmatically.

Zimbalist's historical account of the growth of social work's research tradition documented its discontinuous and diverse nature.[32] Now, nearly twenty years after the publication of that work, it seems reasonable to suppose that progress would have been made on this front. There is substantial evidence, however, to suggest this is not the case. Recent studies show social work as fragmented structurally and highly dependent on other disciplines for its knowledge. They also present evidence showing its scholarship as diverse and frequently unsystematic and limited in its agreements about central research problems, themes, and standards. At a more general level, proponents of different philosophical, ideological, theoretical, and methodological approaches currently advocate vigorously for a preferred position for their respective approach. Regardless of what one thinks of this state of affairs in substantive terms, it is, by definition, a state that signifies social work as fragmented and as not sharing the consensus characterizing more paradigmatically developed fields.

Path Dependence and Knowledge Development

Path dependence is a concept used to describe how increasing returns, or positive feedback loops, cause certain patterns to become self-reinforcing.[33] Initially, it was used to explain why technological solutions to particular problems persisted even though more efficient alternatives were available.[34] More recently, it has been used to help explain the developmental patterns of various economic institutions as well as selected academic disciplines.[35] Here, I invoke path dependence to argue that because of self-reinforcing processes generated by their existing character, different fields of inquiry, including social work, will be inclined to maintain the same relative level of paradigm development that exists. Hence, paradigmatically developed fields will persist in their existing paths, generally not losing and perhaps improving their relative position of advantage vis-à-vis other fields. By the same token, less developed fields are likely to continue in their particular paths, remaining comparatively underdeveloped and therefore unlikely to adjust out of their existing paths.

This is illustrated by considering how the outcomes affected by the level of paradigm development themselves work to reinforce constancy in the existing level of paradigm development. From Table 1, we see that more paradigmatically developed fields obtain a greater share of available resources. Also, they show different patterns of organization; academic talent is less dispersed, and collaboration and coordination are more likely. Because these conditions interact positively in more paradigmatically developed fields, the results tend to be more extensive and more sophisticated research efforts, producing a quicker and more visible pace of knowledge development and, thus, enhanced prospects for further development.)[36] This is a positive feedback loop: the more resources a field gets, the more it is likely to improve its capacity and contributions and the more attractive it is likely to be for the commitment of additional resources.[37]

Social work has been concerned for some time with its comparatively disadvantaged scientific status and capability compared with other disciplines and has argued in various ways and in various forums for resources to improve the quality of its scholarship and research.[38] However, other more fully developed fields, having a historical advantage over social work in the contest for resources, have not been inclined to cede that advantage and, in fact, have probably made gains. For example, the National Science Board, in a 1969 report examining the use of social science knowledge in the solution of social problems, noted approvingly that social work was increasingly incorporating social science knowledge and methods into its curricula and knowledge development efforts.[39] However, it did not propose to help social work advance this trend by increasing social work's own scientific capability. Instead, the report recommended increased support for locating social scientists in schools of social work, providing that they had a continuing association "with their particular discipline to ensure continued competence in that discipline."[40] Thus, social work was to be treated as a potential beneficiary of social science knowledge and methods but was not itself to be supported in developing its own scientific competence and knowledge base. This perspective has persisted, with social work essentially making no gains compared to other disciplines in claims of support and recognition from the National Science Foundation. Indeed, on a broader basis, social work continues to struggle with how to advance in its scientific competence, as reflected, for example, in recent research findings indicating that authors with training in social work employ empirical methods significantly less often than authors with training in other disciplines, and that doctoral social work education is limited in its emphasis on training research scholars.[41] At the same time, disciplines such as psychology and sociology have, after a shaky start, consolidated their claims for a share of the National Science Foundation's resources and are regarded as legitimate contributors to the knowledge explosion that has taken place over the past twenty-five years.[42]

Besides funding and patterns of organization, journal acceptance rates and editorial time lags also likely have self-reinforcing consequences for the relative advancement of a given field. Low journal acceptance rates means undertaking work for which there is a high risk of failure and hence, for many potential authors, the possibility of wasted effort. Similarly, longer time lags imply higher levels of unproductive activity because, reflecting the effects of disagreements among referees and the requirements of revisions and resubmissions, they involve committing time and resources mainly to getting one's work into the public realm as opposed to advancing knowledge. Overall, therefore, low acceptance rates and longer time lags seem not to be positive inducements for enhanced commitments to research and writing, particularly in fields like social work, where there has been, and continues to be, ambiguity about the value of such work.[43]

That fields with less developed paradigms import knowledge from fields with more highly developed paradigms has implications for the rate of development of the field. First, it means staying abreast of, and working to understand, a body of literature that is relatively unintegrated, given the propensity for different fields to develop their own jargon and construct their central arguments on tacit assumptions as opposed to clearly explicated ones. This can be a daunting task and one not conducive to developing a strong commitment to research and knowledge development, particularly in a field like social work where there are also heavy professional expectations.[44] Second, it means that the boundaries and domain of less developed fields are more often in dispute and subject to negotiation, resulting in proportionately higher levels of effort and resource being directed at boundary maintenance and definitional activities.[45] Finally, although borrowing knowledge has certain advantages, including the efficient acquisition of relevant facts and insights, it does have the important drawback of diminishing the cognitive authority of the borrowing field, since the prime experts are not members of that field. To the extent that this is known by policymakers, funding bodies, and other significant organizations and groups, the question becomes why support or seek advice from secondary experts when there is always the option of going directly to the source?[46] This devaluation is a disincentive for the leading scholars from less paradigmatically developed fields to contribute only under that field's auspices, which, based on the Matthew principle that in science credit flows to higher status, is likely to help perpetuate the view of a body of knowledge that has limited value in its own right.[47]

It is significant that less paradigmatically developed fields have fewer social connections and specific criteria in such key activities as journal publications and editorial board appointments has self-reinforcing consequences for their further development. Because such decisions are influenced to some degree by considerations of who one is and the position one holds as opposed to the quality of what one is actually saying through publication, there is less reinforcement for quality scholarship, and more reinforcement for engaging in political strategies of career advancement.[48] For social work, indications of this are found not only in the anecdotal evidence but also in various pieces of research: Lindsey's earlier finding that administrators comprised over one-third of social work editorial boards but had the lowest average citation rates of any group represented, as well as the fact that he had difficulty publishing these and other findings about social work in social work journals; Pardeck and associates' replication of Lindsey's finding that social work editorial board members are comparatively less accomplished as scholars; Epstein's arguments about the comparatively higher level of confirmational bias shown by social work reviewers; and Klein and Bloom's observation that the low citation rates they found for social work deans and directors could be interpreted as questioning their status as role models for aspiring authors.[49] Looked at from the perspective of advancing a field through knowledge development, this pattern of differential reinforcement is likely to cast doubt regarding whether productive scholarship is the surest way to achieve status and recognition and, relatedly, to divert effort from scholarship into making contacts, developing strategies, and acquiring influence.[50]

Finding a Pathway to Consensus

The preceding discussion illustrates several of the various ways in which social work's level of paradigm development reinforces its persistence in a less than optimal developmental path. Positive feedback loops magnify the advantages that other, more paradigmatically developed fields have over social work in the contest for resources and scientific legitimacy. The self-reinforcing effects of social work's dependence on other disciplines for theory and methods, the diffuseness of its cognitive authority, and the presence of disincentives for developing field-specific knowledge limit potential for change. This brings me to the central concern of this chapter, namely, professions are differentiated from other occupational groups by reason of their being based on specialized, abstract bodies of knowledge.[51] It hardly seems viable to expect that social work will be able to satisfy this requirement by putting in place a cumulative approach to knowledge development without first achieving a reasonable level of consensus about its central problems, theoretical perspectives, and methodological approaches.

How is this consensus to be achieved? Or, more precisely, why do some fields have more consensus than others, and can facilitating conditions be generalized to fields with less consensus? One common answer is that differences in the level of consensus reflect inherent differences in the nature of the phenomena studied. For example, because the social sciences study human behavior, which is more intangible than the subject matter of the natural sciences, and almost limitless in its complexity and unpredictability, it is inevitable that, compared to the natural sciences, the social sciences will have a higher level of dissensus. Although this argument clearly is valid, it does not explain differences in the level of paradigm development among the various social sciences, or between the social sciences (or subspecialties) and social work.

A second answer is more structural and organizational in nature. It proposes that consensus is created and maintained by vesting authority in elites.[52] The initial assumption is that, for the most part, we derive our opinions of what good work is and who has done it based not on our own direct assessments but on the judgments of those who occupy significant gatekeeper roles.[53] Generally, these roles are occupied by the "stars" of a particular discipline, who, in their evaluations, determine what work is good and what work is unimportant. To establish consensus, gatekeepers must have legitimate authority, which is granted based on one's status as a star. "It is only when the scientific community sees those exercising authority as deserving it that authority will be accepted."[54] Less developed fields without "natural" stars will create them. These will be persons "producing the best examples of the most fashionable style of work in the field at the time,"even though overall their contribution may not be comparable to those made by stars in other more cognitively developed fields, or to earlier stars in their own field.[55]

In constituting its evaluation systems, social work appears to place its highest value on representativeness. Elitism is viewed with skepticism, if not outright hostility, particularly if it is associated with academe. Recall here previously mentioned studies of the composition of social work editorial boards that found little change over a fifteen-year time period in a propensity to appoint members whose contributions to scholarship are comparatively limited.[56] Moreover, exchanges in the literature about this finding reveal strong views from significant constituents that change in this area is not necessarily desirable, and that attributes such as political involvement and acumen, long and distinguished service to the field, and connections to the practice world and local service communities should carry equal weight to scholarly publishing.[57] I suspect that an examination of other organizations in social work that discharge gatekeeper functions would reveal a similar orientation: representativeness and egalitarianism would be stressed over elitism, and professional relevance and experience would receive at least equal billing with scholarly achievement. While there are clearly beneficial effects associated with such an orientation, building a consensus about a paradigm through the development and enforcement of methodological standards and the specification of key theoretical questions is not one of them.

The general implication of this structural view of the origin of consensus is that, because the level of consensus that exists in a field is strongly influenced by how that field is organized and the procedures it uses to regulate its knowledge development practices, increasing a field's level of consensus requires changing the way that field is structured and how it operates.[58] That is to say, the problem becomes one of determining how to achieve field-level, or macro-organizational, change. This is not an easy task, given the earlier discussion of self-reinforcing feedback loops, as well as the inherent pressures toward structural inertia in most forms of organization. At the same time, change is not impossible, since it has occurred in other areas of social science as evidenced by their increased consensus about appropriate theoretical and methodological approaches.[59] Moreover, there is the serious issue of whether change can be avoided, given increasing pressures on academic social work to improve its competitive capability in order to acquire the resources necessary to ensure its continued viability as a distinct entity in university settings. In the remainder of this article, I focus on where I believe change and reorganization should begin, namely, with something that to date seems to have eluded the knowledge development enterprise in social work: an integrated purpose or, in more scientific terms, an organizing problematic.

Conceptualizing a Problematic for Social Work

A problematic is an integrated framework of concepts, propositions, and practices that together define the central intellectual problems of a field.[60] Hence, economics' problematic is defined in terms of how scholars investigate questions about the ways in which human beings acquire and use scarce material resources. Psychology's problematic is defined in terms of how scholars investigate questions about why human beings act, think, and feel as they do. Historically, social work has searched for its problematic in the area of individual-environment interactions, aiming to discover knowledge appropriate for ameliorating problems created at that interface. The persistent difficulty, however, has been in understanding how to interpret the problematic. Which aspect of the problematic is to be emphasized in determining acceptable courses of inquiry and action—the person or the environment? Does one take as the primary basis for practice the behavior of individuals, adducing the nature of interventions from an understanding of how their particular characteristics and behaviors can be changed to "fit" the requirements of the context? Or does one take as a point of departure the environment itself, adducing the nature of individuals' characteristics and behaviors from it, and then formulating strategies aimed at improving the quality of individuals' lives by restructuring the environment?

Social work has attempted to address this issue on theoretical and practical grounds in recent years by adopting an ecological approach to practice. Based loosely on ideas drawn from human ecology and evolutionary theory, the central tenet of this approach is that because people shape environments and, reciprocally, environments shape people, all behavior must be viewed in terms of person-environment interactions.[61] Considered in these terms, social work's ecological perspective is based on a truism since, accepting the individual as the basic unit of analysis, what else might behavior be a function of if not the individual and the environment? In and of itself, this is not a problem. The crunch comes when we ask, What use has been made of this truism? In social work it has mainly been used to derive practice principles and treatment approaches that apply at the level of the individual, not to develop abstract, formal knowledge about the dynamics of individual-environment relationships.[62] Hence, despite the apparent connection of ecological ideas with social work's historical emphasis on individual-environment interactions, the manner of their interpretation has not provided a central organizing question and, concomitantly, the basis on which social work might build a specialized, abstract body of knowledge.

This is not to say that an ecological perspective is unable to give to social work its central organizing question. In my view, it can, as I will show below. But first it must expand the manner of its interpretation, from one that mainly asks how ecological reasoning can be used to develop prescriptions for action, to one that also examines its implications for knowledge development in social work's domain of concern. I begin by briefly reviewing the emergence of organizational ecology in organization theory. My purpose is to illustrate how ecological ideas can be used to define a central organizing question in a manner that gives rise to a specialized, abstract body of knowledge.

ORGANIZATIONAL ECOLOGY: A VERY BRIEF HISTORY

Organizational ecology originated in questions about organizational change and at what levels of analyses it could properly be studied. Historically, the dominant view of organizational change is that it is adaptive, meaning it is an organization-level process resulting from leaders or dominant coalitions in organizations altering selected organizational features to realign their fit with changing environmental demands.[63] This view was challenged in 1977 with the publication of Michael Hannan and John Freeman's classic, "The Population Ecology of Organizations."[64] In this paper, the authors argued that, for various reasons, organizations evolve fairly quickly to a state of structural inertia. Thus, they can be viewed not only as changing infrequently, but also as resistant to change.[65] In order to extend the adaptation perspective of organization-environment relations to accommodate inertial components in organizations, Hannan and Freeman proposed supplementing it with a selection perspective. One important implication of this proposal was that instead of studying organization-environment relations only at the level of the individual organization, they should also be studied at a population level of analysis. This led to the proposition that the central focus of an ecological approach to the study of organizations should be organizational diversity and that, more generally, emphasis should be on answering the question, Why are there so many kinds of organizations, and why aren't there more?

Inspired by this question, students of organization began to explore how social, economic, and political conditions affected the diversity of organizations and the changes in their composition over time. Initially, questions about diversity focused on rates of organizational foundings and disbandings. Subsequently, the scope expanded to include other types of dynamic-change processes, including rates of change in organizational features, the effects of such changes on disbanding rates, and the rates at which new organizational forms are created, change, and die out.[66] More recently, ecological investigations have also focused on internal change processes, and, consistent with the applied tradition of organization studies, scholars and practitioners are starting to derive insights for action from organization ecology's abundant theoretical insights and empirical findings.[67] Overall, Hannan and Freeman's question about why there are so many kinds of organizations has proved very influential, attracting significant research attention and generating an approach to the study of organizational life that is theoretically and methodologically consistent as well as cumulative—important indications of a well-developed paradigm.

TOWARD A SOCIAL ECOLOGY OF CARING

Similar to organization theory, the emergence of ecological reasoning in social work reflected an underlying disquiet with the adequacy of its dominant perspective, the medical-disease model of human behavior.[68] However, unlike organization theory, ecological ideas were not used to define a central organizing question, or to deal with the theoretical and methodological requirements of selecting proper units of analysis. Instead, as noted previously, the emphasis mainly has been on deriving practice principles and techniques, with the most common focus being individuals in their immediate, particular environments.

I argue for an adjustment in social work's ecological perspective to one paralleling the approach to theory and research used in organizational ecology. On the basis of what has been said previously, this means using ecological ideas to articulate a central organizing question. It also means paying closer attention to questions about proper units of analysis and allowing that, in social work's domain of concern, relevant and dynamic change processes occur not only at the level of individuals.

To develop a central organizing question, the first step is to identify an essential property of context that is significant to social work, as well as being amenable to ecological forms of study and analyses. Consideration of historical and contemporaneous writings suggests different points of view on what this essential property might be. For my purposes, I focus on the property of *caring*, particularly as it pertains to disadvantaged and oppressed populations. I define caring as acts of tending as well as acts of development, which occur under formal communal sponsorship. Tending is work undertaken in support of those who, temporarily or permanently, cannot do for themselves.[69] Development is work undertaken to advance the fulfillment of people's potential as well as to enhance their state of material and socioemotional well-being, or to promote the recovery of such a state of well-being. Formal communal sponsorship refers to the publicly acknowledged institutional frameworks and organizational structures within which the work of tending and development takes place.

The next step is to determine the proper unit of analysis. This is important, as the choice of unit has significant implications for research, determining, among other things, which literature is relevant for addressing the task at hand. It is also a complex issue because there are at least five levels of analysis from which to choose, as well as different objects of observation or intervention at most levels. The five levels are (1) individuals; (2) groups, families, and organizational subunits; (3) organizations; (4) populations of individuals, families, and organizations; and (5) communities (populations) of individuals, families, and organizations.

Social work has a strong tradition of empirical investigation at levels 1 and 2. Although there seems to have been some decline in emphasis in recent years, level 4 has in the past received a fair amount of attention through policy analysis studies of disadvantaged human populations. At the same time, instances in social work literature of theory and research directed at understanding organizational life at a population-level of analysis are difficult to find.[70] Level 3, where the individual organization replaces the individual person as the unit of analysis, has received some attention over the years, although the majority of the empirical work has tended to be at the individual level (1) and the subunit level (2), concentrating on such topics as leadership, teams, or program evaluation. Finally, for level 5—communities—social work's focus there has been less on theoretical and empirical investigations than on learning the strategies and tactics of social activism, with community most frequently conceptualized as resulting from people working as groups under a code of authority set largely by themselves to obtain their objectives. There are very few studies that deal with the community in ecological terms as a set of interacting populations of people as well as a set of interacting populations of organizations.[71]

I argue for a parallel emphasis on the development of theory and research at each level of analysis. In some respects, this is not a novel argument, since instances of empirical research that take account of context, at least to some degree, can be found at all five levels, as the preceding paragraph suggests. However, the dominant focus in social work is the person and his or her immediate context, suggesting a general, albeit tacit, acceptance of the individual as the appropriate unit of observation for studying dynamic change processes. Adopting an ecological perspective implies moving beyond this view to one that recognizes the theoretical and empirical importance of paying attention to the hierarchically-nested nature of multiple levels of analysis in the study of the dynamics of human behavior and human organization.[72]

Having defined an essential property of context and outlined a case for studying it at different levels of analysis, I can now more precisely identify a central organizing question for social work research. Just as a researcher in any field must choose a unit of analysis, so must a researcher adopting an ecological approach choose a system of study. In this regard, it is plausible to suppose that systems relevant to the study of interrelationships between caring and context can be defined as analysts in other fields have defined them: by geography, political jurisdiction, function, population served, and so forth. Given a definition of system, and taking my lead from ecologists generally—and organizational ecologists in particular—I suggest that the central task of a social ecology of caring is to seek to understand the distribution of different forms of caring arrangements across environments and at different levels of analysis, and the limitations to efficacy these arrangements confront under different conditions and circumstances. That is to say, a social ecology of caring should seek to answer the question, Why are there so many kinds of caring, and why aren't there more?

Reclaiming the Paradigm Concept

Earlier in this chapter I pointed out that the paradigm concept has been controversial. One important reason for this is the variable meanings given it by Kuhn in his original formulations, as well as his later expansion of the concept.[73] More recently, however, Kuhn himself, as well as students of his work, has returned to the original meaning of paradigm as referring to an *exemplar,* or concrete solution to a scientific problem that a field accepts, and which subsequently provides a pattern of problems and methods that guide further lines of inquiry.[74] In social work, it is this concept of paradigm that would seem to underlie Zimbalist's emphasis on tracing the history of social welfare research by focusing on research themes defined by the appearance at particular times of landmark, pattern-setting studies.[75] It would also seem to be the concept of paradigm underlying Gordon's argument that the development of an empirical tradition in social work should not be equated with a paradigmatic revolution as claimed by Fischer, since, according to Kuhn, cognitive consensus comes not from rules and method but from finding concrete solutions to substantively interesting conceptual and empirical problems.[76]

It is this concept of paradigm as exemplar that I propose as a useful starting point for developing a social ecology of caring in social work. Specifically, I proposed as a problematic an emphasis on understanding the dynamics of caring. How does change at different levels of analysis affect the mix of caring arrangements in a given system, and vice versa? Various ingredients and foci can be invoked in looking for answers to this question. One example concerns the fact that how children are cared for in modern society is characterized by increasing diversity. Recent ecological studies have started to explore the dynamics of this diversity by examining changes over time in rates of founding and disbanding in a population of day care centers.[77] Other ecological studies have examined the rates at which families enter and leave a population of families that care for others' children.[78] It is by moving to refine and extend the theory, methods, and foci of these types of studies that social work could increase understanding of, and generate valid inferences about, the meaning and consequences of diversity in caring arrangements for children.

A second, useful example can be found in changes over the past decade or so in the social organization of caring, as expressed through the traditional human services. Examining these services from a macroperspective reveals the persistence of the traditional voluntary, nonprofit human service organization but, at the same time, reveals numerous changes such as the proliferation of private practitioners and for-profit providers; the emergence of gender, race, and ethnicity as a basis for organization; and changes in the role of governments and the workplace in service provision. Clearly, diversity of form and auspice is now a strong property of the human services sector. Yet, there are few if any studies in any field of the dynamics and effects of this diversity. We do not know, for example, whether increasing numbers of private practitioners and for-profit organizations have depressed the founding rates and increased the disbanding rates of traditional nonprofit human service organizations, or have had an effect on their downsizing. Nor do we know much about the effects of such dynamic change on various social outcomes. Have merger rates increased? Do we now have more or fewer innovations? Have there been changes in the patterns of executive succession? What are the implications for vulnerable clients of fluctuations in the rates of formation and disbanding of different forms of organizationally based caring arrangements? By using ecological ideas and models to examine these questions, as well as to develop other similar questions about the meaning and consequences of dynamic change in organizationally based forms of caring, academic social work would clearly position itself as not only advancing theoretical understanding of a social ecology of caring but also as offering specialized knowledge relevant to policymakers, managers, and individual practitioners.

My final example deals with microlevel processes and concerns an issue of long-standing interest to social work, namely, the creation and maintenance of helping relationships among people. Its relevance in this context is established by the emphasis an ecological framework places on choosing proper units of analysis and on recognizing these units as nested one within the other. Hence, in organizational ecology, the most fundamental unit is the routine, a specific pattern of organized knowledge and skill. Interactions among routines create jobs; interactions among jobs bind groups together, which in turn bind organizations together; interactions among organizations form populations; and, finally, interactions among populations form a community, which interacts with other communities to form an ecosystem.[79] Transposing this thinking into understanding the requirements of developing a social ecology of caring at least in part from the "bottom up" leads to recent research on how knowledge workers such as software specialists interact with consumers to solve problems.[80] Based on analyses of the routines invoked by specialist practitioners in "getting the job done," this research showed how important aspects of individual performance were embedded in larger organizational structures, thus establishing an empirical basis for developing a dynamic and situated theory of practice. Accepting that routines occur in all types of service encounters and in all kinds of organizations, the implication is that social work, by focusing on this elemental component in studying supportive as well as problem-solving helping relationships, could develop its own situated theory of practice.[81] In addition, the consistency associated with the fact that such a theory of practice would have been developed within a framework that explicitly links together hierarchically nested levels of analysis means there would be clear theoretical and methodological grounds for approaching the significant topic of how micro- and macro-level processes interrelate in the overall functioning of a given system of caring.

CONCLUSION

Currently, social work follows an "open-field" model of knowledge development.[82] According to this model, what counts most is the realism of concepts and propositions as reflected in their connection to the perceptions and meanings of participants. Because of the limitless complexities of human behavior, as well as an unbounded supply of social and personal problems, there is little value in general, cross-cutting theoretical frameworks. They are too abstract and involve too many simplifying assumptions to be relevant or useful. As opposed to a theory-based, deductive approach to knowledge development, social work prefers research that is "data driven" and problem-specific, or that is characterized by the direct involvement of participants in the complexities of the phenomenon under study. If theory is to be developed, it should be "grounded" in empirical observations that pertain to the phenomenon at hand. Overall, therefore, and at a metalevel of analysis, knowledge development in social work is properly eclectic, and should stay that way.

As I have shown, however, social work pays for this eclecticism in a variety of ways. Moreover, social work has focused more on craft knowledge, or the kind of knowledge that is required for expert action. Traditionally, it has been much less concerned with developing abstract theoretical knowledge. But as Andrew Abbott points out in his brilliant study of how some professions come to occupy more dominant and controlling positions than others in an overall system of professions, abstract knowledge is the foundation of an effective definition of a profession.[83] It is the basis of a profession's cognitive authority, as well as its main currency of exchange in competition with other professions, disciplines, and organizations over what problems it will deal with, how they can be explained, and what unique treatments will be invoked.

The circumstances and conditions of social work's survival and growth are changing. It is clear that higher education is facing difficult times, which has concrete implications for social work's autonomy, status, and even existence in university settings.[84] Political and legislative actions, in combination with various other economic and social pressures, are changing the institutions and organizations within which social work developed and prospered. Clearly change is inevitable. The question is, What kind of change should it be? The view offered here is that in one way or another, change requires striking a more appropriate balance between abstract knowledge and craft knowledge, as well as between the current "anything goes" view of knowledge development and one that prescribes a single, correct perspective. In brief, discussions of social work's future survival and growth must be centered not only on concerns about its mission, its methods, and the nature of the populations it serves. They must also be firmly centered on the equally important issue of whether it has a question.

12

Social Efficiency and Social Work Research

William M. Epstein

The quality of social work's contemporary research undercuts its professional ambitions for a scientifically credible practice of helping as well as its claims to serve noble social ends on behalf of the disadvantaged. The technical sophistication of the field's research has improved since the anecdotal proofs of practice prior to the 1960s. Nevertheless, the field has failed to produce credible accounts of social problems and of its own interventions. Without scientifically disciplined evidence of effectiveness, social work is restricted to its political meaning—the ceremonies it performs in support of dominant cultural values, summed up in the insistence that social efficiency is possible.

In contrast with any notion of justice, equality, fairness, or wisdom, social efficiency dictates that in order to be politically acceptable, interventions must be both inexpensive and compatible with current social arrangements. Evaluated against standards of scientific credibility, even the best of social work's contemporary research distorts evidence of the field's social efficiency. These standards—randomized controlled trials—while difficult to employ and costly are nevertheless the necessary conditions of credible social research.[1] Yet if the United States is to seriously address its social problems, it needs to reject social efficiency in deference to greater public generosity toward a variety of social services and income supplementation programs.

Social preferences obtrude on even the most rigorously designed and well-intentioned studies. Although postmodernism takes social nihilism a step too far into passive inevitability, Nietzsche's legacy is the standard insight of contemporary social criticism. Predictably, social work enters its assigned and obedient service through the archway virtues of principled independence and high purpose. Nevertheless, the stubborn pitfalls of its research and the defiant misrepresentation of indeterminate findings suggest that academic social work has yet to achieve a "community of the competent" in fulfilling its defining task to evaluate practice, that is, the range of services that it provides to an enormous variety of recipient groups.

Scholarly competence is the compelling justification both for academic freedom and for the seating of an autonomous professional education within the academy.[2] Clearly, Haskell considers science to be the quintessential discipline for the community of inquiry in any field that asserts its objective understanding of "reality."[3] Except for the postmodern squirm of "antireality" to get out from under the weight of objectivity and coherence, social work accepts, at least formally, the necessity of objective social science. Unfortunately, with only tenuous evidence of its scholarly competence, the standing of social work has deteriorated in the academy while the basis of practice—assertions that interventions predictably achieve valuable social ends—remains scientifically immature.

The Early Modern Period: Skepticism in a Period of Doubt

Fischer's 1973 review of social work research concluded that "at present, lack of evidence of the effectiveness of professional casework is the rule rather than the exception."[4] His exhaustive search of the literature from the 1930s through the early 1970s, including dissertations and agency reports as well as journals, identified only seventy studies that addressed the effectiveness of casework. A scant eleven of these met his very minimal inclusion criteria: services in the United States, some sort of comparison group, and a focus on professional practice, that is, evaluation of social workers with a master's degree. In almost half the studies, service recipients in the experimental groups actually deteriorated or improved at slower rates than members of the control groups.

Somewhat earlier, Wootton and Segal had reached similar conclusions, emphasizing the field's preoccupation with personal deviance and socially efficient solutions.[5] Wootton commented on the futility of providing services to treat "the infected individual rather than to eliminate the infection from the environment."[6] Wootton included the vast literature of the social sciences in her review, since social work's efforts were even then at the margins of research competence. Segal noted both the "token attempts" at research as well as the apparent ineffectiveness of psychotherapeutics. "The evidence with respect to the effectiveness of social work therapeutic interventions remains equivocal . . . [but points] strongly in the negative direction."[7]

Wood added weight to the skeptics even while overstating the positive effects of practice and the quality of the research.[8] Anticipating a common bias of later research and research reviews, she conveniently accepted the findings of weak research that confirmed her preferences. Wood's review covered 1956 to 1975 and identified twenty-two studies (all of Fischer's and many included by Segal) that contained at least a comparison group. Only six of the twenty-two studies reported positive outcomes. Yet many of these six studies were methodologically weak. Schwartz and Sample actually reported mixed results while their positive findings were tiny.[9] Moreover, their outcome assessments were derived from unverified self-reports of service recipients as well as the global ratings of "highly experienced social workers" who were not blind to the research conditions of participants. Wood also graduated the standing of Wilson's findings, which were actually far more modest and ambiguous than she contends; Wilson reported a small and relatively unimportant 12 percent difference between experimental and control groups in the number of clients who were free from welfare dependence after two years, but he reported no differences in family functioning and other social indicators.[10] Moreover, Wilson only employed an "approximated" control group.

The literature of the early modern period was in fact largely anecdotal and the result of both deductive thought experiments and blind moralizing. Only one of Fischer's eleven studies appeared before 1961. No scientifically credible tests of practice were conducted; in fact, it was not apparent that the field had accepted empiricism. Experiments were not replicated, and the research tromped into every imaginable pitfall of research: small convenience samples, biased measurement and the lack of blinding, the absence of randomization and frequently even the failure to incorporate any comparison group, short follow-up periods if any at all, and so forth.

The centrality to social work of psychotherapeutics and often Freudian psychoanalysis itself may well explain the field's antagonism to science and its isolation from the more structural theories of social failure.[11] The nature of that literature itself located the constituency of social work practice among the successful and complacent who accept America's social and economic stratification as the outward expression of moral character. In this context, the decisive role of social work was motivation, not care, largely rejecting the lessons of the Great Depression and World War II that collective, structural solutions were needed to address the impersonal problems of mass society. Then as now, social dialectics were largely theological and implicit, demanding conformity and belief. As a result, research was rarely taxed to credibly validate social work's propositions.

These political imperatives faded in the 1960s with the emergence of broad pressure for social reform, particularly the challenge to address American poverty. Fischer's fashionable skepticism was not without cunning. The otherworldly style of his analysis, performed with a seemingly naive disinterest in secular currents and with a hectoring lack of politesse, played to the mood of the times and its emergent constituency for social change—a traditional ploy to capture power within a field whose value is largely determined by social preferences.[12] Along with the other skeptics, Fischer's doubts about the effectiveness of practice refocused the field's professional ambitions through science and on the presumably objective determination of its value. Following Ravetz's argument that science is paired with benevolence, the political kernel in Fischer's seemingly technical argument assumed that objective reality would carry the flag for a practice of social work based on structural assumptions of social failure.[13]

However, the objectification of need and intervention only succeeded in form. The substance of practice remains the same (service to dominant political tastes) and the research, in spite of its opera of rationality and Fischer's own epiphany of social work's conversion to science, continues to avoid any truly credible estimate of social work's effectiveness.

The Modern Period: Faith Restored

Poverty won the War on Poverty, and the conservative agenda dominates American social policy choices. Social work obediently muted self-doubt and its pretenses for social reform as its intellectuals found new grounds for optimism that the field's casework interventions actually were successful, albeit modestly so. Drawing on impressions of "material presented at social work conferences, from the literature and from less concrete sources of evidence such as the new 'spirit' or 'world view' that seems to be emerging among many social workers," Fischer, whose reputation was mellowing from notoriety into fame, christened a new mood in social work:

> In essence the practice of social work appears to be moving away from the use of vaguely defined, invalidated and haphazardly or uncritically derived knowledge for practice. In its most salient characteristics, the paradigm shift appears to involve a movement toward more systematic, rational, empirically oriented development and use of knowledge for practice. For want of a better phrase, this could be termed a movement toward scientifically based practice in social work. . . . [S]ocial workers are increasingly explicating new approaches that are systematic, clear, and oriented to both the rigors of research evidence and the realities of practice.[14]

Fischer's "new approaches" were largely behavioral interventions, and by the "rigors of research" he was referring to single-subject designs.[15] However, single-subject designs, lacking the advantages of randomized controls, are tatters of science, whereas the evidence for behavioral methods is more suspect than profound.[16] Indeed, the research that has tested the effectiveness of all forms of behavior modification, including the token economy, is highly suspect, containing a far greater amount of disconfirmation and ambiguity than Fischer acknowledged.[17] Perversely, in moving from operant experiments with animals to interventions with human beings, the scientific quality of the research actually deteriorated. Had Fischer applied his 1973 skepticism to his 1978 and 1981 research he would have published scorching commentary on failed methodologies, questionable results, and tendentious interpretations.

A field that advertises an inability to handle its defining problems courts a grim destiny. Apparently heeding this caution, an increasing tempo of research, collected in a few notable review articles, came to strengthen Fisher's growing optimism. Reid and Hanrahan identified twenty-two studies between 1973 and 1979 that met their inclusion criteria: randomization between control and experimental groups that received social work services.[18] They reported happy findings:

> All but two or three of the twenty-two studies yielded findings that could on balance be regarded as positive ... less than a third of the [Wood] studies produced findings that could on the whole be regarded as positive. ... Also in marked contrast to the earlier experiments, no recent study that involved a comparison between treated and untreated groups failed to yield at least some evidence of the positive effects of social work intervention. The findings of the recent experiments are grounds for optimism.[19]

Rubin found more grounds for optimism in thirteen studies out of perhaps 6,500 journal articles that appeared between 1978 and 1983.[20] His inclusion criteria were similar to those of Reid and Hanrahan.

Unfortunately, a reanalysis of the base of studies in both Reid and Hanrahan and Rubin contradicts all of their findings. Fifteen of Reid and Hanrahan's twenty-two studies employed samples of twenty-five or less (four studies had samples under ten). All of the studies were open to a variety of expectancy biases, such as the lack of blinding and reactive measures. Furthermore, the authors of the studies themselves often reported more mixed findings than Reid and Hanrahan acknowledged.[21]

Only one of Rubin's studies, by Stein and Test, approximated credible science.[22] Yet even this gem contains debilitating flaws—for example, nonrepresentative samples and a demonstration situation not easily transferrable to routinized program situations—that should have muted enthusiasm for its findings. This study has been repeatedly offered as evidence to deinstitutionalize the long-hospitalized, chronic mentally ill and therefore to cut public budgets for their care. Ironically, Stein and Test actually found that community care, while programmatically feasible, cost *more* than hospital care. The remainder of Rubin's studies are frankly inadequate, and again he mauls their actual findings.

> [O]f the seven papers that Rubin held up as sound demonstrations of positive social work outcomes: one did not meet his own inclusion criteria; two others did not really show positive outcomes; one other did not have comparable control and experimental groups due to high and differential attribution; none, except Stein and Test and Linn et al. (and even these are questionable), established credibly independent outcome judges; and all but two used very small samples. Positive outcomes, when they occurred, were not technically credible.[23]

Similarly, both Thomlison and Sheldon continued to misread research by way of endorsing the professionally convenient conclusions of Reid and Hanrahan, Fischer, and Rubin.[24] Similar to Fischer, Thomlison takes comfort in the ability of behavior therapies to handle "anxiety disorders, sexual problems, psychosis, obesity, alcohol and drug problems" and others.[25] Yet the authors of his cited support are far less sanguine, conceding "a paucity of design altogether"[26] in the research, questionably credible methodologies,[27] dubious clinical relevance,[28] and indeterminate outcomes.[29] Sheldon's base of research, including contributions from Britain that would not be methodologically sufficient for the American summaries, testifies to hope but adds no greater proof.[30] Moreover, both Sheldon and Thomlison drew upon summaries of psychotherapy's effectiveness—notably the Bergin summaries[31] and Smith, Glass, and Miller[32]—that rely more upon professional belief than rigorous analysis.[33]

Videka-Sherman conducted two metanalyses (a technique to compare the results of disparate studies) to identify the determinants of successful outpatient social work practice.[34] Her metanalysis of research on practice with the chronic mentally ill documented a 12 percent gain for the social work patients; the second metanalysis produced a 19 percent gain for less severely disabled patients. The value of metanalysis is obviously limited by the quality of its base of studies, while the analyzed studies were routinely weak. Few of them randomly selected subjects from the under-lying patient population, relying instead on self-selection and recruit-ment from acute settings; less than half randomly assigned subjects to control and experimental groups; treatments were routinely undefined, and treatment integrity could not be ensured; few studies carefully pro-tected against researcher bias, while nearly all of them relied upon pa-tient self-report. In the end, the small reported positive gains become invisible against a backdrop of weak, distorted methodologies, while the question of patient deterioration in treatment stands out.

The randomized experiments of social work practice conducted in the years shortly after the summaries belie methodological sophistication as well as Fischer's revolution of science in social work. Rather, the poor quality of even the best of the research continued to indict the compe-tence of the field.[35] These studies are uniformly trivial and methodologi-cally porous, seemingly oblivious of a communal obligation to achieve objective coherence. Indeed, the literature since the 1970s seems bent on contriving evidence for the field's clinical effectiveness without concern for the actual benefit to patients. This distortion of objectivity through the professional ambitious of social work ritualistically justifies domi-nant social values, belying a true clinical production function.

The most recent summary of the literature, and certainly the rosiest, by Gorey, reports a metanalysis of fully eighty-eight outcome studies of social work interventions that appeared in thirteen "prestigious" social work journals between 1990 and 1994—a remarkable apparent increase in the rate of acceptable outcome research.[36] Yet Gorey's procedures sabotage his conclusions about the rate of research, its quality, and its findings.

Gorey accepted any research that allowed him to compute effect sizes; that is, he included any research that reported means and standard devi-ations.[37] He did not screen for randomized controls but accepted any comparison group. In direct defiance of standard scientific logic, he re-jected statistical significance in favor of "clinical significance," an amor-phous concept but one that conveniently accepts the size of a research finding without adjusting for the size of samples. Gorey defended this decision on grounds that "most social workers want more information about the magnitude of the intervention's effects or its effect size, which is more directly related to its clinical or policy significance . . . and more useful for grappling with cost-benefit concerns."[38] It is also more compliant than rigorous science in contriving proofs of effectiveness.

The failures of the studies themselves climbed into Gorey's metanalysis. In accepting studies for inclusion, Gorey simply ignored the requirements of credible science for reliable and valid measures, for protections against research bias (notably blinding), for random selection and assignment, for large samples, for placebo controls, for follow-up periods, for adjustments or protections against demonstration effects, and so forth. Moreover, Gorey's estimate of client benefit would have probably been reduced by more than two-thirds with any adjustment for placebo effects.[39] With further adjustments for probable researcher and report biases, the issue of patient deterioration would have likely been reprised once more.

Child Welfare and Psychotherapy

Child welfare services may well be social work's emblematic responsibility. Because children are presumably innocent of moral culpability, the adequacy of child welfare services and the scientific quality of the evaluation of adequacy reflect on the humanity of the society and the professional competency and commitments of academic social work. In turn, psychotherapy (including the so-called behavioral therapies) has long been the field's preferred intervention, if not actually its most common application.

CHILD WELFARE SERVICES

Legislation and administrative policy affecting adoption, family foster care, congregate and therapeutic group care, kinship care, family preservation services, and family reunification services have been influenced by empirical studies, notably attempts to measure the quality of care and the outcomes of care. Yet not one study has actually produced a scientifically credible statement. Nevertheless, and with rare exceptions, the literature endorses the effectiveness of minimal interventions in achieving important social ends, notably the socialization of dependent children.

Four of five social experiments—Comprehensive Emergency Services,[40] A Second Chance for Families,[41] the Oregon Project,[42] and the Alameda experiment[43]—suggested that permanency planning was programmatically feasible, thereby encouraging passage of the landmark Adoption Assistance and Child Welfare Act of 1980. The fifth experiment actually provided disconfirming data, but the literature largely ignores it.[44] Yet its many design imperfections do not distinguish it methodologically from the other four experiments. All five of the experiments are beset by a variety of invalidating flaws: convenience samples, biased measures, limited follow-up, distorted reports, demonstration effects, misreporting, attrition, censoring, lack of treatment integrity, inappropriate analyses, and so forth. All claimed to provide some sort of intensive social work intervention—concrete services, counseling, or some combination of the two—and four of the five make great claims for success. Yet these studies never established that permanency planning was either desirable or feasible, while their obvious methodological faults failed to caution legislation or social work. On their face, the experiments were improbable, offering relatively superficial services—services were "intense" only relative to neglect, not need—for severely disrupted and disabled families.

With a single exception, subsequent research evaluating family preservation and family reunification has been similarly flawed and distorted. Putting Families First (PFF) has distinguished itself by conducting a randomized trial on a methodological par with the famous social experiments of the 1960s and 1970s, notably the Negative Income Tax experiment in Seattle and Denver.[45] Yet even PFF, arguably the best single study ever conducted in social work, suffers from too many pitfalls to establish credible outcomes. PFF reported that family preservation was unsuccessful. Unfortunately, the experiment breached its randomization procedures, mistargeted services, employed unreliable measures (the self-report of patients and instruments with low reliability scores) and unreliable measurement procedures, and may not have been able to ensure treatment integrity.[46] The rest of the family preservation literature has been a methodological wash.[47]

Rossi has pointed to the field's curiously intense attachment to family preservation in spite of its flawed research and its occasionally disconfirming findings:

Given what the research has shown, why is it that the child welfare establishment still enthusiastically advocates family preservation? Analogously, why do otherwise competent and surely intelligent persons publish . . . flawed data in order to advance the "family preservation" movement? Are we witnessing yet another triumph of faith over data?[48]

Social work's commitments also express the triumph of the field's political accommodations over the objective needs of its service population. In expressing reigning conservative dogma, family preservation services offer very minimal and inexpensive services for deep social problems. Acknowledged failure would impel a search for more effective, and probably far more expensive, solutions.

The research that evaluates foster care and other public child welfare placements has been similarly flawed and heartless for its failure to measure the actual conditions of the children. The overwhelming proportion of research on placement outcomes simply accepts dispositions as a proxy for quality under the assumption that preservation, reunification, and adoption are preferable (in fact and not just in principle) to foster care. This assumption endangers the child, especially in consideration of the prevalence of maltreating parents and an adoption disruption rate that probably exceeds 20 percent. Fanshel and Shinn conducted one of the few studies to actually measure the conditions of children.[49] The remaining literature seems content to simply measure the degree to which mandated administrative goals—placements prevented, reunifications, and consequently budgetary savings—are being met.

In addition to ignoring the child's actual living conditions, the child welfare literature routinely fails in other critical areas of scientific research. It neither randomly selects children from underlying populations of concern nor randomly assigns a portion of study subjects to standard treatment, nontreatment, or placebo treatment conditions (under various conditions, each choice is both legal and ethical); an enormous amount of the research is simply conducted without any external comparison group. Research samples are routinely small. Outcome measures are reactive to the researcher, the research situation, or the irrelevant motives of subjects. Follow-up assessment periods are typically short. Attrition and censoring are high. Retrospective analyses of records are common, and those records are notoriously unreliable.[50] The range of interventions assessed has been relatively narrow; customary care is usually compared with somewhat enhanced social work services and not truly intensive services. The lead-in period to experiments is short, and results probably reflect the unsustainable efforts of highly motivated workers in demonstration situations. Many studies cannot ensure treatment integrity, and it is unclear whether they actually deliver the level and kinds of care they report. As a consequence, even the best studies can neither establish their reported findings nor dispel alternative explanations for the outcomes, such as unique properties of the sample, maturation, seasonality, demonstration effects, confirmation biases, reactive measures, and so forth. In short, the effects of public child welfare services have still not been identified. More problematical, the quality of that care, even measured against standard criteria of health and safety or of customary conditions for American children, is still not known.[51]

PSYCHOTHERAPY

Social work's commitment to psychotherapeutic interventions in all of its fields of practice has intensified through the years. Psychotherapy is the apotheosis of social efficiency, promising to change deviant individual behavior with only a few hours of professional, office-bound attention. Moreover, the private practice of psychotherapy is often reported as the ultimate professional goal of many, if not most, entering graduate students.

If psychotherapy is not effective, then social work faces a crisis of professional meaning and, more important, society is stuck with three choices: alternative techniques at comparable levels of expenditure, neglect, or greater allocations for need. The minimal provision of concrete care, partially explored in many of the family preservation and family reunification experiments, in Headstart programs, in the pregnancy prevention experiments, in MDRC's training studies, and in many others, has not proven to be effective.[52] Neglect—simply dropping the programmatic failures out of the public budget—while a favored conservative strategy is nonetheless repugnant. Increased public expenditures are probably defensible, at least to achieve social equality and possibly also

260

to realize specific programmatic goals; however, they are politically infeasible, at least at this time. Therefore, the political and professional stake in the effectiveness of psychotherapy is considerable, so large in fact that it probably accounts for the falsification of the research both in social work and, more generally, in the social sciences, notably clinical psychology.

Smith, Glass, and Miller (SGM), employing one of the earliest metanalyses, published a "citation classic" for the effectiveness of psychotherapy.[53] They identified 475 studies of psychotherapy that conformed with "the acknowledged canons of experimental science," that is, they incorporated some sort of comparison group, and their measures of outcomes allowed for the computation of effect sizes. In addition to effect sizes, SGM described the studies along eighteen criteria relating to their methods, the personnel conducting therapy, characteristics of patients, and so forth. When possible, they drew comparisons between treated groups and placebo control groups and concluded that psychotherapy was highly effective.

> the average person who would score at the 50th percentile of the untreated control population could expect to rise to the 80th percentile with respect to that population after receiving psychotherapy. . . . [L]ittle evidence was found for the alleged existence of negative effects of psychotherapy. . . . Nor was there convincing evidence in the dispersion of the treated groups that some members became better and some worse as a result of psychotherapy.[54]

Cognitive therapies in particular appeared to be highly effective, with patients receiving it better off than 99 percent of those in the control groups. The SGM findings were often corroborated in other focused metanalyses.[55]

Unfortunately, the methodological pitfalls committed by SGM and by the subsequent metanalyses that uncritically copied their procedures undercut all of their rosy conclusions. Even more common in the base of outcome research itself, these errors provide prominent testimony to the triumph of professional ambition over rational interpretation. SGM should have subtracted placebo effects from experimental effects, reducing the reported benefit of psychotherapy from about 30 percent to

261

about 10 percent; the Prioleau et al. metanalysis reduced the difference to 7 percent.[56]

SGM's other methodological peccadillos diminish the value of psychotherapy even further. First, the reactivity of measurement (that is, measures that were influenced by the research situation itself) in the base of studies was the only variable that showed a sizable correlation with effect sizes, implying a consistent bias toward effectiveness in the base of their studies. Second, when patients were evaluated at follow-up, therapeutic gains fell by as much as 50 percent. Third, contrary to their boast of rigor, SGM's base of studies also contained analog studies and studies that did not reach statistical significance. In an outburst that questions their commitment to science itself, SGM scolded prior summaries that questioned effectiveness for relying only upon research that met

> "textbook" standards; these methodological rules, learned as dicta in graduate school and regarded as the touchstone of publishable articles in prestigious journals, were applied arbitrarily; for example, note again Rachman's high-handed dismissal on methodological grounds of study after study of psychotherapy outcome.[57]

Rachman had simply insisted upon randomized assignment as a control for the "spontaneous remission" of symptoms.[58] Fourth, a reanalysis of the SGM data suggests a Wild West of outcomes and not the tightly clustered effects that they report;[59] an enormous percentage of patients seem to deteriorate in therapy, although perhaps fewer than in control groups (but even here the problem of bias persists).

Finally, many of the studies that SGM included were conducted under optimal conditions of practice with presumably the best therapists (often university faculty in hospital or clinical settings) under close supervision in short-term demonstration situations with dedicated ancillary staffs. General outcomes in the field—largely populated by entrepreneurial solo practitioners—in comparison with the outcomes published in professional journals are probably far worse, abiding a much greater amount of practitioner irresponsibility and depravity.[60] With adjustments for setting, bias, placebo effects, "spontaneous remission," and demonstration effects, psychotherapy is probably at best ineffective, while the true outcomes of its general practice may well be routinely pernicious.

A case-by-case scientific critique of the literature is more convincing than a summary, even a metanalysis, of uncertain research. The most scientifically credible of the literature, such as it is, fails to offer a single study that substantiates clinical effectiveness on reasonable methodological grounds, let alone on the basis of a sound randomized trial. The NIMH's Treatment of Depression Collaborative Research Program, exemplifying perhaps the best of the field's clinical trials, was so manifestly compromised in design at the outset that it should have been abandoned before data were collected.[61] In operation, its attrition rates by themselves, but also its many other flaws, undercut all of its conclusions. The recent clinical studies of psychotherapeutic outcomes evidences no maturation of the community of inquiry.[62] Moreover, recent attempts to estimate the general effects of psychotherapy from the reports of its patients mark points of methodological regression.[63]

The Demise of Science in Social Services

Child welfare services research may well be the driest area in the desert of social work scholarship, and the evaluation of psychotherapeutic outcomes one of the most intensely distorted. Yet their inadequacies are repeated in other fields of practice with similar effects: improbable claims for the effectiveness of underfunded, superficial, and short-term services. In comparison with social work's efforts, social science research, particularly in economics and sociology, is more sophisticated in technique and methodology; yet social science generally has also failed to conduct credible tests of social service outcomes.

The most prominent social policy experiments in the social sciences have produced more controversy than rational agreement. The best of the negative income tax experiments, in Seattle and Denver, suffered from truncated samples and unreliable outcome estimates of income. The large number of welfare and work training programs were inadequately evaluated by the Manpower Demonstration Research Corporation, a private, blue-ribbon Ford Foundation creation that was organized to produce neutral research (that is, to incorporate random controlled trials into field evaluations). MDRC's findings are crippled by faulty sampling procedures and mismeasurements, while their conclusions are forcibly pitched to their matronizing perceptions of what is best for the nation.

The improbability of social work's effectiveness and the weakness of its research are characteristic of all of the social services. Martinson's conclusion that "nothing works" in corrections appears also to characterize other social services—substance addiction, remedial education, and the immense range of services focused on the welfare caseload and other impoverished groups.[64]

The social sciences have, however, produced impressive longitudinal panel surveys, such as the Survey of Income and Program Participation and the Panel Study of Income Dynamics. Yet even while they probably provide an accurate demography of the United States, the descriptions cannot be converted into explanations of social conditions, that is, they cannot identify cause. The panel surveys did not randomly assign experimental subjects to different conditions, and adjustments for selection bias remain highly speculative. Moreover, attrition has been a problem in the Panel Study of Income Dynamics, while income estimates may be unreliable in all of the large surveys.[65]

Although the most cautious general conclusion of many decades of social service evaluation should be one of indeterminacy, the manifest biases of the research—a déjà vu connivance of professionalism and political preference for social efficiency—suggest that services are most likely ineffective and perhaps often abusive.[66] As noted, the issue of harm, notably of psychotherapy, recurs consistently in the literature and in reanalyses of published findings. Privateering psychotherapy may indeed hint at the problems created by atomizing responsibility for social services in a soulless marketplace of profit. The recurring public impulse to contract out social services—corrections, day care, education, foster care, home care, welfare services, and the rest—has been largely unchecked by accurate estimates of service quality. Science in the social services has given way to "practical" research and other postmodern concessions to advocacy, if not for marginalized populations then at least for the researchers themselves.

Psychotherapy remains a nineteenth century water cure, while the misrepresentation of child welfare services is professionally self-absorbed and socially irresponsible. Skepticism in a period of belief is far more valuable and heroic than skepticism in a period of doubt, especially when the literature of neither period can establish the objective reality of social services. Professional success through bogus research is a Faustian bargain, and although competence is possible, it is not without political risk.

The Primacy of the Political

Social work has not won its place in the academy through a true scholarly production function by establishing a community of the competent. The notable achievement of social work has been to sustain the tension of fulfilling a role markedly antagonistic to its self-professed goals. Still, creative hypocrisy is a poor justification for university standing.

In particular, the quality of its research in child welfare services and psychotherapy measures the field's distance from competence. With few exceptions, the child welfare literature is biased, inaccurate, incomplete, and, most problematic, generally accepted within social work.[67] To be sure, society has skimped on research funds for child welfare. Nevertheless, the moneys that have been available for research, notably to evaluate family preservation and for the studies that ran up to the act of 1980, have been applied with a purposeful disregard for the rules of science and with a quickness to acquiesce political imperatives with compatible—if not actually flattering—results.

Still and all, while the conditions of scholarship are deplorable in social work, they are seemingly not much different in the other semiprofessions, especially as regards social welfare interventions. The skeptics, notably Martinson, have never been adequately answered. Even the core social sciences, in spite of their theoretical and methodological elegance, have failed to achieve their Enlightenment promise of neutral and accurate policy information.

Yet while the social sciences have bent to politics, they have still achieved a competence in research that social work lacks, principally because they have more frequently rejected the substitution of belief for knowledge.[68] Social work remains a form of religious experience, while the better practice of social science pursues an objective albeit maddeningly elusive truth.

It is tempting to play Isaiah—repent, repent, repent—and ignore the absence of a sheltering constituency for the needs of the poor and working America and therefore for professional and academic voices on their behalf.[69] Yet even within the safety of political accommodation, academic social work still lacks any special understanding or intellectual skill that dictates the autonomous preparation of its researchers. In the same way that the laws of physics apply equally on the Earth, Mars, and Pluto, rigorous empirical training applies equally well to the evaluation of any social service whether inspired by economics, sociology, or social work. Indeed, those with the largest stake in outcomes should have the smallest role in evaluation.

The social worker as researcher has been no more effective or socially compelling than the social worker as revolutionary, intellectual, social critic, change agent, psychic healer, surrogate, coordinator, manager, soul guide, or counselor. The lack of adequate resources—the superficiality and frank inadequacy of social services—runs through all of the field's failures. The literature is nearly mute on this theme, however, and without a clearer sense of its role, social work will not mature intellectually and its academic practitioners at least will not achieve competence.

Postmodern and other "practical" alternatives to social science are concessions to narcissism and, more problematical, to prevailing political orthodoxies. Sectarian research has failed; even the best attempts at definitive tests seem to have been hopelessly botched. Independent research is rarely independent, and a scientifically sound application of limited rationality has not been realized. Moreover, the possibility for routinizing the courage and brilliance of a lone researcher, infused with the noble calling to inform the intelligence of democracy through a scrupulous commitment to objectivity, falls to the reality of marriage, family, and mortgage payments. There is, in the end, the need for white-knuckled prayer and devotion to credible social science.

Notes

Chapter 1: Social Work: A Contextual Profession

1. M. Potocky, "Multicultural Social Work in the United States: A Review and Critique," *International Social Work* 40(3) (1997): 315–326.
2. S. Kahn, "Community Organization," in *Encyclopedia of Social Work*, 19th ed., Vol. 1, (Washington, DC: National Association of Social Workers, 1995), 569–576.
3. B. W. Austin and A. J. Young, "The Community of the Future," *Twenty-First Century Leadership in the African American Community* (1998) 199–212; F. Hesselbein et al., "The Community of the Future," Volume 3, *The Druker Foundation: The Community of the Future* (San Francisco: Jossey-Bass, 1998).

    J. H. Schultz, *The Economics of Aging*, 5th ed. (New York: Auburn House, 1992), 42-43; M. Harrington, *The Other America: Poverty in the United States* (New York: Macmillan, 1962).
4. U.S. Bureau of the Census abstract on poverty not being eradicated (Washington, DC, 1977).
5. W. J. Wilson, *The Truly Disadvantaged: The Inner City, the Underclass and Public Policy* (Chicago: University of Chicago Press, 1987); J. G. Hopps, E. Pinderhughes, and R. Shakar, *The Power to Care: Clinical Practice Effectiveness with Overwhelmed Clients* (New York: Free Press, 1995).
6. J. Bernstein, "Growing Poverty in a Growing Economy," *Poverty and Race: Research Action Council* 5, no. 6 (November/December, 1996.)
7. W .E. B. DuBois, *The Souls of Black Folk* (New York: Fawcett, 1961), p.13.
8. "The Status on Blacks in College," *The Boston Globe,* 5 February 1998, sec. A, p. 22.

Notes

9. A. Etzioni, *The Spirit of Community* (New York: Free Press, 1993), p. 55.
10. D. E. Hertz and B. H. Wootton, "Women in the Work Force: An Overview," in Costello, C., et al, *Women and work,* (New York: W. W. Norton, 1996).
11. *The Boston Globe,* 27 July 1998, p. 1.
12. U.S. Bureau of the Census (Washington, DC, 1994).
13. Hertz and Wootton, op. cit. (see n. 10).
14. L. Davis and E. Proctor, *Gender, Race, and Class* (Englewood Cliffs, NJ: Prentice-Hall, 1989).
15. D. E. Hertz and B. H. Wootton, "Women in the Workforce, an Overview," in C. Costello and B. K. Kringold, *"The American Women 1996–1997, Women and Work"* (New York: W. W. Norton, 1996).
16. S. Holmes, "Birth Rate Falls to 40-Year Low Among Unwed Black Women," *The New York Times,* 1 July 1998, sec. A, p. 1.
17. J. G. Hopps and P. Collins, "Social Work Profession Overview," in *Encyclopedia of Social Work,* 19th ed., Vol. 3 (Washington, DC: National Association of Social Workers, 1995): 2266–82.
18. G. Mantsios, "Rewards and Opportunities: The Politics and Economics of Class in the U.S.," in *Race, Class and Gender in the United States,* ed. P. S. Rothenberg (New York: St. Martin's Press, 1992).
19. J. Weiss, "Violence Motivated by Bigotry: Ethnoviolence," in *Encyclopedia of Social Work,* 18th ed., suppl. (Silver Spring, MD: National Association of Social Workers, 1990): 307–19.
20. The Center for Immigration Studies: "Three legislative acts contributed to a combined growth and shift in this population: the Immigration and Nationality Act of 1965 (PL 89-236), which facilitated the change from predominantly European to largely Third World Populations; the Refugee Act of 1980 (PL 96-212), which identified a quota for refugees who could not return to their own countries because of potential persecution; and the Immigration Reform and Control Act of 1986 (PL 99-603), which gave legal status to formerly undocumented aliens," 1988.
21. Potocky, op.cit. (see n. 1).
22. S. Martin, *Refugee Women* (London and New Jersey: Zed Books, 1991).
23. F. Ross-Sheriff, "Displaced Populations," in *Encyclopedia of Social Work,* 18th ed., suppl. (Silver Spring, MD: National Association of Social Workers, 1990)
24. Hopps and Collins, op.cit. (see n. 17).
25. M. Krononwetter, "Violent Crime," and "Violent Crime Control and Law Enforcement Act," in *Encyclopedia of Modern American Social Issues* (Santa Barbara: A.B.C. C/10, pp. 280–281, 1997).
26. A. J. Reiss and J. A. Roth, *Understanding and Preventing Violence* (Washington, DC: National Academy Press, 1993), ix–25.
27. Ibid.
28. J. Ridgeway, *Blood in the Face* (New York: Thunder's Mouth Press, 1995), 35–41.
29. M. W. Fraser, "Violence Overview," in *Encyclopedia of Social Work,* 19th ed.,

Vol.3 (Washington, DC: National Association of Social Workers, 1995): 2453–60.

30. A. Toufexis, "Workers Who Fight Fire With Fire," *Time,* 25 April 1994, 34–37.

31. Reiss and Roth, op.cit. (see n. 26).

32. C. Shew, "More Guns, Less Crime: A Scholar's Thesis Inflames Debate Over Control," *Chronicle of Higher Education,* 5 June 1998, A 14.

33. Ibid.

34. Austin and Young, op.cit. (see n. 3).

35. K. M. Baber and K. R. Allen, *Women And Families: Feminist Reconstructions* (New York: Guilford Press, 1992).

36. J. A. Jones, *American Work: Four Generations of Black and White Labor* (New York: W. W. Norton, 1998).

37. Baber and Allen, op.cit. (see n. 35); K. S. Markides and C. H. Mindel, *Aging and Ethnicity* (Beverly Hills, CA: Sage, 1987).

38. Markides and Mindel, op. cit. (see n. 37).

39. Baber and Allen, op. cit. (see n. 35).

40. Hopps, Pinderhughes, and Shankar, op. cit. (see n. 5).

41. Schultz, op. cit. (see n. 3).

42. Markides and Mindel, op. cit. (see n. 37)

43. op. cit. (see n. 3).

44. C. O'Rourke, "Listening to the Sacred: Addressing Spiritual Issues in the Group Treatment of Adults with Mental Illness," *Smith College Studies in Social Work* 67, no.2, (1997): 177–96.

45. E. D. Smith, "Addressing the Psychospiritual Distress of Death as Reality: A Transpersonal Approach," *Social Work* 40, no. 3 (1995): 402–13.

46. Ibid.

47. Ibid.

48. Ibid.

49. W. F. Tolliver, "Invoking the Spirit: A Model for Incorporating the Spiritual Dimension of Human Functioning into Social Work Practice," *Smith College Studies in Social Work,* 67, no. 3, (1997): pp. 477–486.

50. W. DeVore and E. G. Schlesinger, *Ethnic-Sensitive Social Work Practice,* 3d ed. (New York: Macmillan, 1991).

51. Etzioni, op cit. (see n. 9).

Chapter 2: Greeting the Second Century

1. A. Smith, *An Inquiry into the Nature and Causes of the Wealth of Nations.* (1776).

2. R. Lubove, *The Progressives and the Slums* (Pittsburgh: University of Pittsburgh Press, 1962); J. Leiby, *A History of Social Welfare and Social Work in the United States* (New York: Columbia University Press, 1978).

3. L. Gordon, *Pitied But Not Entitled: Single Mothers and the History of Social Welfare* (Cambridge: Harvard University Press, 1994); T. Skocpol, *Social Policy in*

Notes

the United States: Future Possibilities in Historical Perspective (Princeton, NJ: Princeton University Press, 1995).

4. Leiby, op. cit. (see n. 2).
5. F. J. Bruno, *Trends in Social Work 1874–1956* (New York: Columbia University Press, 1948); B. P. Broadhurst, "Social Thought, Social Practice, and Social Work Education: Sanborn, Ely, Warner, Richmond" (doctoral dissertation, Columbia University, 1972). *Dissertation Abstracts International* 32(9):5342A.
6. Broadhurst, op. cit. (see n. 5).
7. Ibid.
8. M. Newcomer, *A Century of Higher Education for Women* (New York: Harper, 1959).
9. D. M. Austin, "The Institutional Development of Social Work Education: The First 100 years—and Beyond," *Journal of Social Work Education* 33, no. 3 (1997): 599–614.
10. A. Small, "Fifty Years of Sociology in the United States," *American Journal of Sociology* 21 (1916): 779.
11. J. J. R. Everett, *Religion in Economics: A Study of John Bates Clark, Richard T. Ely, Simon N. Pattern* (New York: King's Crown Press, 1946).
12. Gordon, op cit. (see n. 3).
13. M. Olasky, *The Tragedy of American Compassion* (Washington, DC: Regnery Gateway, 1992).
14. E. Devine, "Education for Social Work," *Proceedings of the National Conference of Charities and Correction, 1915* (Chicago: Hildmann Printing), 608.
15. M. J. Carson, *Settlement Folks: Social Thought in the American Settlement Movement* (Chicago: University of Chicago Press, 1992).
16. A. F. Davis, *Spearheads for Reform: The Social Settlements and the Progressive Movement 1890–1914* (New York: Oxford University Press, 1967).
17. Gordon, op. cit. (see n. 3); K. M. Macdonald, *The Sociology of the Professions.* (London: Sage, 1995).
18. A. Flexner, "Is Social Work a Profession?" *Proceedings of the National Conference of Charities and Correction, 1915* (Chicago: Hildmann Printing), 576–90.
19. D. M. Austin, "The Flexner Myth and the History of Social Work" *Social Service Review* 57, no. 3 (1983): 357–77.
20. Devine, op. cit. (see n. 14), 606–9; P. Lee, "Committee Report: The Professional Basis of Social Work," *Proceedings of the National Conference of Charities and Correction, 1915* (Chicago: Hildmann Printing), 596–605.
21. D. S. Kirschner, *The Paradox of Professionalism: Reform and Public Service in Urban America, 1900–1940* (Westport, CT: Greenwood Press, 1986).
22. S. Taylor-Owen, "The History of the Profession of Social Work: A Second Look" (doctoral dissertation, Brandeis University, 1986). *Dissertation Abstracts International,* 47(07): 2742A.
23. Austin, op. cit. (see n. 9).
24. Gordon, op. cit. (see n. 3).

25. Broadhurst, op. cit. (see n. 5).

26. Austin, op. cit. (see n. 9).

27. Broadhurst, op. cit. (see n. 5).

28. Ibid.

29. L. M. Shoemaker, "Early Conflicts in Social Work Education," *Social Service Review* 72, no. 2 (1998): 182–91.

30. E. G. Meier, *A History of the New York School of Social Work* (New York: Columbia University Press, 1954), 28.

31. Broadhurst, op. cit. (see n. 5).

32. Meier, op. cit. (see n. 30), 42.

33. Shoemaker, op. cit. (see n. 29).

34. K. M. Macdonald, The *Sociology of the professions* (London: Sage, 1995) 168.

35. L. Leighninger, *Social Work: Search for Identity* Westport, CT: Greenwood Press, 1987).

36. J. E. Schwartz, *America's Hidden Success: A Reassessment of Twenty Years of Public Policy* (New York: W.W. Norton, 1983).

37. H. Specht and M. Courtney, *Unfaithful Angels: How Social Work Has Abandoned Its Mission* (New York: Free Press, 1994).

38. Skocpol, op. cit. (see n. 3).

39. Gordon, op. cit. (see n. 3).

40. E. Taylor, "The Biological Basis of Schizophrenia," *Social Work* 32, no. 2 (1987): 115–21.

41. A. Stone, "Where Will Psychoanalysis Survive?" *Harvard Magazine*, January/February 1997.

42. The 1995 Hopwood Decision by the United States Fifth Circuit Court of Appeals stated that the University of Texas could not use any form of racial or ethnic classifications for affirmative action purposes in admissions or in the awarding of scholarships supported by public funds. The decision applied to all publicly supported colleges and universities in the Fifth Circuit region.

43. D. Stoesz, "The End of Social Work," in *Social Work in the 21st Century*, ed. M. Reisch and E. Gambrill (Thousand Oaks, CA: Pine Forge, 1997): 368–75, 1987.

44. R. M. Kanter, "Restoring People to the Heart of the Organization," in *The Organization of the Future*, ed. F. Hasselbein, M. Goldsmith, and R. Beckard (San Francisco: Jossey-Bass, 1996): 139–50.

45. Government Accounting Office, *Child Welfare: States Progress in Implementing Family Preservation and Support Services*, HEHS-97-34 (Washington, DC: GAO, 18 February 1997).

Chapter 3: Social Work's Century

The literature by social workers about social work is extensive, but surprisingly little has been written about it as a profession since the early years. The following provided some of the background for the analysis of this paper, but it is by no means a scholarly history of ideas. Many of the omitted references deal with the developments in welfare, but only fleetingly with the profession qua profession. I have also omitted detailed reference to some of the Council on Social Work Education commission reports, which deal at length with academic issues of governance and structure more than on the relationship, in anything other than broad generalities, between the profession and its environment,.

1. A. Johnson, ed., *National Conference of Charities and Corrections, 33d Annual Session* (Philadelphia: Fred Heer Press, 1906).
2. M. Richmond, *The Long View* (New York: Russell Sage Foundation, 1930).
3. J. Addams, *Twenty Years at Hull House* (New York: Macmillan, 1910).
4. W. Epstein, *The Dilemma of American Social Welfare* (New Brunswick, NJ: Transaction Publishers, 1993).
5. R. Morris, ed., *Encyclopedia of Social Work,* 16th ed. (New York: National Association of Social Workers, 1971).
6. S. Miller, "Human Services Professions," in *Encyclopedia of Social Work,* 16th ed. (New York: National Association of Social Workers, 1971): 982–98.
7. R. Lubove, *The Professional Altruist: The Emergence of Social Work as a Career 1880–1930* (Cambridge: Harvard University Press, 1970).
8. R. and M. Pumphrey, *The Heritage of American Social Work* (New York: Columbia University Press, 1970).
9. C. Chambers, *The Seed Time of Reform: American Social Service and Social Action* (Minneapolis: University of Minnesota Press, 1963).
10. P. R. Lee, *Social Work: Cause and Function* (New York: Columbia University Press, 1937).
11. Morris, op. cit. (see n. 5).
12. B. Coll, *Safety Net: Welfare and Social Security 1929–1979* 176–182 (New Brunswick NJ: Rutgers University Press, 1995).
13. *Statistical Abstract of the U.S. 1994* (Washington, DC: Government Printing Office, 1994).
14. National Association of Social Workers Memoranda: "Social Work Facts," 11 December 1996; "Social Welfare Myth Busters," 12 December 1996. Washington, DC.
15. Coll op. cit. 203–238.
16. H. Chaiklin, personal communication of various papers presented at conferences, especially that delivered at the Second Annual Criminal Justice Conference, October 1996.
17. G. Steiner, *The State of Welfare* (Washington, DC: The Brookings Institution, 1971).
18. H. Specht and R. Courtney, *Unfaithful Angels* (New York: Free Press, 1994).
19. W. Boehm, *Objectives for the Social Work Curriculum of the Future,* Vol. 1. (New York: Council on Social Work Education, 1970).
20. Epstien. op. cit. see note 4.

21. "The Knowledge Factory," *The Economist*, 4 October 1997.
22. S. Greenberg and T. Skocpol, *The New Majority: Toward a Popular Progressive Majority* (New Haven, CT: Yale University Press, 1997).
23. M. Abramovitz, *Decoding Welfare Reform*, pp 16–20 A Report to (New York City Chapter, National Association of Social Workers, 1997).

Chapter 4: Social Justice

1. National Association of Social Workers, *Code of Ethics* (Washington, DC: NASW, 1996); Council on Social Work Education, *The Handbook of Accreditation Standards and Procedures* (Alexandria, VA: CSWE, 1994).
2. C. Towle, *Common Human Needs* (Washington, DC: Social Security Bureau, 1945).
3. Ibid., 1.
4. D. G. Gil, *Unraveling Social Policy*, 4th ed. (Rochester, VT: Schenkman Books, 1990; 1st ed. 1973).
5. Ibid., 19.
6. J. F. Longres, *Human Behavior in the Social Environment*, 2d ed. (Itasca, IL: F.E. Peacock Publishers, 1995), 13–14.
7. J. Fugueira-McDonough, "Policy Practice: The Neglected Side of Social Work Intervention," *Social Work* 38 (1993): 179–88; J. Rawls, *A Theory of Justice* (Cambridge: Belknap Press of Harvard, 1971).
8. Fugueira-McDonough, op. cit. (see n. 7): 180, 185.
9. A. Murdach, "Beneficence Re-Examined: Protective Intervention in Mental Health," *Social Work* 41 (1996): 26–32; United Nations Convention on the Rights of the Child, 1989.
10. W. S. Korr, "The Current Legal Environment," in *Dimensions of State Mental Health Policy*, ed. C. G. Hudson and A. J. Cox (New York: Praeger, 1991).
11. *Lessard v. Schmidt*, (349 F. Supp. 1078 (1972); *Price v. Shepard*, (239 N.W. 2d 905 (1976).
12. D. Brieland, B. Fallon, W. S. Korr, and D. Bretherton, "Freedoms, Entitlements, Protections, and Parents' Rights: An Analysis of the UN Convention on the Rights of the Child," *Children Australia* (1991).
13. J. F. Handler, *The Poverty of Welfare Reform* (New Haven, CT: Yale University Press, 1995).
14. *Shapiro v. Thompson*, (394 U.S. 618 (1969).
15. *Goldberg v. Kelly*, (397 U.S. 254 (1970).
16. *Townsend v. Swank*, (404 U.S. 282 (1971).
17. Warren Burger, Chief Justice, (404 U.S. 292 (1971) in *Townsend v. Swank*, n. 16 above.
18. W. A. Reynolds, "For Students on Welfare, Degrees Pay Dividends," *Chronicle of Higher Education* XLIII (1997): A 68.
19. *Wyman v. James*, (400 U.S. 309 (1971).

Notes

20. National Conference of State Legislators, "Top 14 List of Welfare Innovations," November 1997.

Chapter 5: Social Work and Health Care

1. C.P. Emerson, "Medical Social Services of the Future," *Hospital Social Services* 1, no. 4 (November 1919).
2. Ibid.
3. MacKenzie, M.T. "Medical Social Service and the Hospital Organization," *Hospital Social Services*. 1(2): 95.
4. S.S. Goldwater, "Who Started Hospital Social Services? The Time, 1636—The Place, Paris—The Man, Vincent de Paul," *Hospital Social Service* (August 1919): 235–237.
5. I.M. Cannon, *On the Social Frontiers of Medicine* (Cambridge: Harvard University Press, 1952), ch. 1.
6. A. Deutsch, *The Mentally Ill in the United States* (New York: Columbia University Press, 1956).
7. A. Flexner, "Is Social Work a Profession?" *Proceedings of the National Conference of Charities and Correction* Baltimore (1915), 587.
8. D.K. Rosner, "A Once Charitable Enterprise" doctoral dissertation submitted, Harvard University, 1978).
9. J. Leiby, *A History of Social Welfare and Social Work in the United States* (New York: Columbia University Press, 1978, 74.
10. M.T. MacEachern, *Hospital Organization Management* (Chicago: Physician Record 1940), 109–12.
11. J. Axinn and H. Levin, *Social Welfare: A History of the American Response to Need* (New York: Harper and Row, 1975), 94.
12. E. Friedson, *Professional Dominance: The Social Structure of Medicine* (Chicago: Aldine, 1970), 88.
13. Flexner, op. cit. (see n. 7).
14. M. Richmond, *Social Diagnosis* (New York: Russell Sage Foundation, 1917).
15. H. Rehr and G. Rosenberg, "Access to Social-Health Care: Implications for Social Work," in *Access to Social Health Care*, ed. H. Rehr (Lexington, MA: Ginn Press, 1986), 80.
16. M. M. Melum, "Hospitals Must Change, Control Is the Issue," *Hospitals*, March 1 (1989) 67–72.
17. *Hospitals*, (July 1992).
18. J.S. Campy, *Reengineering Management* (New York: Harper Business, 1995).
19. R. Bergman, "Reengineering Health Care," *Hospitals and Health Networks*, (5 February 1995), 28–36.
20. V.A. Ancona-Berk and T.C. Chalmers, "An Analysis of the Costs of Ambulatory and Inpatient Care," *American Journal of Public Health*, 76, no. 9 (September 1986): 1102–04.

Notes

21. E.P. Simon, N. Showers, S. Blumenfield, G. Holden, and X. Wu, "Delivery of Home Care Services After Discharge: What Really Happens," *Health and Social Work,* 20, no. 1 (1995): 5–14.
22. U.S. Department of Health and Human Services, *Healthy People 2000: National Heart Promotion And Disease Prevention Objectives,* DHHS Pub. no. (PHS), 912-50212 (Washington, DC: GPO, 1990).
23. Ibid.
24. R.S. Miller and H. Rehr, *Social Work Issues in Health Care,* (Englewood Cliffs, NJ: Prentice-Hall, 1983), 258.
25. Revision based on a presentation by Ronda Kotelchuk at the Doreis Siegel Memorial Colloquium, New York, April 2, 1992.
26. B. Berkman, "The Emerging Health Care World: Implications for Social Work Practice and Education," *Social Work,* 41, no. 5 (1996): 542–55.
27. The preceding come, in part, from the *Special Report of the Health Care Reform Task Force,* Society for Social Work Administrators in Health Care, American Hospital Association (August 1993).
28. A.J. Kahn, "Theory and Practice of Social Planning." New York: Russell Sage (1969), P.N.A.
29. Washington Business Group in Health, *Social Workers and the Case Management of Catastrophic Care.* Report prepared for the National Center for Social Policy and Practice (Silver Spring, MD: National Association of Social Workers, 1988).
30. P. DeJong and S.D. Miller, "How to Interview for Client Strengths," *Social Work* 40, no. 6 (1995): 729–36.
31. The content derives from the *Model of the Division of Social Work,* Department Of Community Medicine, Mount Sinai School of Medicine (rev. April, 1981).
32. H. Rehr and G. Rosenberg, "Today's Education for Today's Health Care Social Work Practice," *Clinical Social Work Journal* 5, no. 4 (1977): 242–48.

Chapter 6: Social Work: Conceptual Frameworks

1. American Association of Social Workers, "Social Case Work—Generic and Specific: A Report of the Milford Conference" (New York, 1931). Although the conference was held in 1928, the conference report was published three years later.
2. H. L. Witmer, *Social Work* (New York: Farrar and Rhinehart, 1942).
3. Ibid., 121.
4. K. De Schweinitz, cited in R. E. Smalley, *Theory for Social Work Practice* (New York: Columbia University Press, 1967), 4.
5. E. V. Hollis and A. L. Taylor, *Social Work Education in the United States* (New York: Columbia University Press, 1951).
6. Ibid., 59.

Notes

7. H. Bartlett, National Association of Social Workers commission on Social Work Practice. Bartlett, H., "Toward *Clarification* and Improvement of Social Work Practice," *Social Work*, no. 3, 1958: 5–9.
8. W. E. Gordon, "A Critique of the Working Definition," *Social Work*, no. 7 4 (1962): 3–13.
9. National Association of Social Workers, op. cit. (see n. 7).
10. Gordon, op. cit. (see n. 8), 5.
11. Ibid., 9.
12. Ibid., 11.
13. Ibid., 226.
14. W. W. Boehm, *Objectives of the Social Work Curriculum of the Future* (New York: Council on Social Work Education, 1959).
15. Ibid., 226.
16. H. M. Bartlett, *The Common Base of Social Work Practice* (New York: National Association of Social Workers, 1970).
17. M. E. Richmond, *Social Diagnosis* (New York: Russell Sage Foundation, 1917).
18. M. A. Cannon, "Where the Changes in Social Case Work Have Brought Us," in *Readings in Social Case Work: 1920–1938,* ed. F. Lowry (New York: Columbia University Press, 1939), 112.
19. G. Hamilton, *Theory and Practice of Social Casework* (New York: Columbia University Press, 1940).
20. Bartlett, op. cit. (see n. 16), 92–93.
21. Ibid., 191–92.
22. Ibid., 190.
23. L. Videka-Sherman, "Meta-analysis of Research on Social Work Practice in Mental Health," *Social Work* 33, no. 4 (1988): 325–38.
24. A. Minahan and S. Briar, "Introduction to the Special Issue," *Social Work* 22, no. 5 (1977): 339.
25. "Conceptual Frameworks", *Social Work* 22, no. 5 (1977): 338–44.
26. S. Briar, "In Summary," *Social Work* 22, no. 5 (1977): 415–16, 444.
27. Ibid., 416.
28. "Conceptual Frameworks," op. cit. (see n. 25), 382.
29. Ibid., 385.
30. W. E. Gordon and M. L. Schutz, "A Natural Basis for Social Work Specialization," *Social Work* 22, no. 5 (1977): 422–27.
31. "Conceptual Frameworks II: Special Issue on Conceptual Frameworks," *Social Work* 26, no. 1 (1981): 5–96.
32. Ibid., 6.
33. "Conceptual Frameworks." op. cit. (see n. 25).
34. D. Brieland, "Definition, Specialization, and Domain in Social Work," *Social Work* 26, no. 1 (1981): 79–83.
35. S. Briar, "Needed: A Simple Definition of Social Work," *Social Work* 26, no. 1 (1981): 83–84.

36. C. Levy, "On Comments, Courses, and Conceptual Frameworks," *Social Work* 27, no. 2 (1982):

37. R. C. Crouch, "Social Work Defined," *Social Work* 24 (1979): 46–48.

38. A. D. Murdach, "Defining From the Other End," *Social Work* 26, no. 4 (1981): 339–40.

39. B. L. Haar, "Letter," *Social Work* 26, no. 1 (1981): 340.

40. R. L. Edwards, "Introduction," *Encyclopedia of Social Work,* 19th ed., Vol. 1 (Washington, DC: National Association of Social Workers, 1995): 1–5.

41. Council on Social Work Education, *The Handbook of Accreditation Standards and Procedures* (Alexandria, VA: CSWE, 1994).

42. National Association of Social Workers, *Code of Ethics* (Washington, DC: NASW, 1996).

43. L. Margolin, *Under the Cover of Kindness* (Charlottesville, VA: University Press of Virginia, 1997), 5.

44. Ibid., 2, 5.

45. Ibid., 2–3.

Chapter 7: School Reform

1. F. Newmann and G. Wehlage, *Successful School Restructuring* (Madison, WI: National Center on Organization and Restructuring, 1995).

2. M. A. Vinovskis, "An Analysis of the Concept and Uses of Systemic Educational Reform," *American Educational Research Journal* 33, no. 1 (1996): 83–85.

3. P. Lipman, "Restructuring in Context: A Case Study of Teacher Preparation and the Dynamics of Ideology, Race and Power," *American Educational Research Journal* 34, no. 1 (1997): 3.

4. J. G. Dryfoos, *Full-Service Schools: A Revolution in Health and Social Services for Children, Youth, and Families* (San Francisco: Jossey-Bass, 1994).

5. W. M. McLaughlin and M. A. Irby, *Urban Sanctuaries: Neighborhood Organizations in the Lives and Futures of Inner-City Youth* (San Francisco: Jossey-Bass, 1994).

6. F. Furstenberg et al., "Adolescent Mothers and Their Children in Later Life," *Family Planning Perspective* 19, no. 4 (1987): 142–52.

7. J. A. Ladner and R. M. Gourdine, "Adolescent Pregnancy in the African American Community," in *Health Issues in the Black Community,* eds., R. Braithwaite and S. Taylor (San Francisco: Jossey-Bass, 1992), 219.

8. D. Prothrow-Stith and M. Wiessman, *Deadly Consequences* (New York: HarperCollins, 1991).

9. A. W. Brown and R. M. Gourdine, "Teenage Black Girls: Coming of Age in an Urban Environment," *Journal of Human Behavior and the Social Environment,* no. 2/3 (1998): 105–24.

10. R. A. Astor, "Perceptions of School Violence as a Problem and Reports of Violent Events: A National Survey of School Social Workers," *Social Work* 48, No. (1997); 101–112.

Notes

11. H. Hill et al., "Sociocultural Factors in the Etiology and Prevention of Violence Among Ethnic Minority Youth," in *Reason to Hope: A Psychosocial Perspective on Violence and Youth*, ed., L. Ebron, J. Gentry, and M. Schelegal (Washington, DC: American Psychological Association, 1995).

12. H. Hill and W. Winters, *Safe Start: A Culturally Based Comprehensive Violence Prevention Intervention for the Elementary School* (Washington, DC: Howard University Center for Research on the Education of Students Placed at Risk, 1996).

13. M. C. Rist, "The Shadow Children," *American School Board Journal* (Jan. 1990): 19–23.

14. National Association of State Directors of Special Education, *Comparison of Key Issues: Current Law and Amendments* (Washington, DC: NASDSE, 1997).

15. Prothrow-Stith and Wiessman op. cit. (see n. 8).

16. E. L. Bassuk, L. Rubin, and A. S. Lauriat, "Characteristics of Sheltered Homeless Families," *American Journal of Public Health* 76, (1986): 1097–1101.

17. Ibid.

18. C. Jackson, "An Overview of Welfare Reform in Michigan," *Institute for Children and Poverty* 2 (summer/fall 1997): 84.

19. National Association of State Directors of Special Education, op. cit. (see n. 14).

20. W. S. Clay, "Inclusion "How Should Inclusion Be Defined and Why Inclusion Should Not Be a General Policy for All Special Education Students," available on-line at *http://san 183.sang. Wmich. edu/SPED603/paper.clay.html.* (June 14, 1998.)

21. P. Allen-Meares et al., *Social Work Services in Schools,* 2d ed. (Boston: Allyn and Bacon, 1996), 145.

22. Ibid.

23. "Citizens for an Educated America," No on 227: Analysis by the Legislative Analyst, available on-line at *http://www. Noonunz.org/whatanalysis.html.*

24. P. Constable, "Region a Melting Pot of Bilingual Ed Programs" *The Washington Post,* 23 July 1998, A01.

25. California State Proposition 187, "Illegal Aliens; Ineligibility for Public Services, Nov. 1994," available on-line at *http://cwis.usc.edu/Library/Ref/Ethic/prop-187.TXT.* (Feb. 1998).

26. D. Tyack, "Schooling and Social Diversity," in *Toward a Common Destiny: Improving Race and Ethnic Relations in America,* ed. W. D. Hawley and A. W. Jackson (San Francisco: Jossey-Bass, 1995), (3–38).

27. Ibid.

28. J. A. Banks, "Multicultural Education and the Modification of Students," Racial Attitudes, *Toward a Common Destiny,* op. cit. (see n. 26), 317–18.

29. W. G. Winters, *African American Mothers and Urban Schools: The Power of Participation* (New York: Lexington Books, 1993), 86.

30. C. Billings-Ladson, *The Dream Keepers: Successful Teachers of African American Children* (San Francisco: Jossey-Bass, 1994).

31. J. M. Smith, *A Qualitative Analysis of the Howard University School of Social and Education Collaboration Project* (Washington, DC: Howard University School of Social Work and Education Collaboration, 1996).

Notes

32. L. Costin, *The Visiting Teacher Movement with Special Reference to Administrative Relationships* 2d ed (New York: Joint Committee on Methods of Preventing Delinquency, 1925); L. Costin, "An Analysis of the Tasks in School Social Work," *Social Services Review* 433 No. 3 (1969), 274–285.

33. W. G. Winters and F. Easton, *The Practice of Social Work in Schools: An Ecological Perspective* (New York: Free Press, 1983), 14.

34. A. Maslow, *Motivation and Personality* (New York: Harper, 1954).

35. E. Martinez-Brawley, "Knowledge Diffusion and Transfer of Technology: Conceptual Premises and Concrete Steps for Human Services Innovators," *Social Work* 40, (1995). 670–682.

36. S. Conley, "Review of Research on Teacher Participation on School Decision Making," in *Review of Research in Education 17,* ed. G. Grant (Washington, DC: American Educational Research Association, 1991).

37. B. Malen, R.T. Ogawa, and J. Kranz, "What Do We Know About School-Based Management? A Case Study of Literature—a Call for Research," in *Choice and Control in American Education: The Practice of Choice, Decentralization and School Restructuring, vol. 11,* ed. W. H. Clune and J. F. Witte (New York: Falmer Press, 1990), 20.

38. Lipman, op. cit. (see n. 3).

39. M. A. Raywid, "Rethinking School Governance," in *Restructuring Schools: The Next Generation of Educational Reform,* ed. R. Elmore (San Francisco: Jossey-Bass, 1990); G. Whelage, G. Smith, and P. Lipman, "Restructuring Urban Schools: The New Futures Experience," *American Educational Research Journal* 29, no. 1 (1992): 51–93.

40. Lipman, op. cit. (see n. 3); Winters, op. cit. (see no. 29).

41. Whelage, Smith, and Lipman, op. cit. (see no. 39).

42. A. C. Lewis and A. T. Henderson, *Urgent Message: Families Crucial to School Reform* (Washington, DC: Center for Law and Education, 1997).

43. A. Liberman, ed., *Schools as Collaborative Cultures* (New York: Falmer Press, 1990); J. Q. Easton et al., *Local School Council Governance: The Third Year of Chicago School Reform* (Chicago: Chicago Panel of Public School Policy and Finance, 1993).

44. Liberman, op. cit. (see n. 43); C. H. Weiss, *Shared Decision Making About What? A Comparison of Schools With and Without Teacher Participation* (Cambridge: Harvard University National Center for Educational Leadership, September 1992).

45. Dryfoos, op. cit. (see n. 4); B. Gray, *Obstacles to Success in Education Collaborations,* in *School Community Connections: Exploring Issues for Research and Practice,* ed. L. C. Rigsby, M. C. Reynolds, and M. C. Wang, (San Francisco: Jossey-Bass 1995); Lewis and Henderson, op. cit. (see n. 42); Winters, op. cit. (see n. 29).

46. U.S. Department of Education and U.S. Department of Housing and Urban Development, "Connecting community building and education reform: Effective school/community partnerships, Forum, Washington, D.C., Jan. 1998.

Notes

47. Dryfoos, op. cit. (see n. 4), 41.

48. Allen-Meares et al., op. cit. (see n. 21).

49. Hill and Winters, op. cit. (see n. 12).

50. L. M. Bambara, N. A. Kvacky-Mitchell, and S. Iacobelli, "Positive Behavioral Support for Students With Severe Disabilities: An Emerging Multi-Component Approach for Addressing Challenging Behaviors, *Social Psychology Review* 23, no. 23 (1994): 263–78.

51. *The Washington Post*, 6 July 1998, A 10.

52. Ibid.

53. "School Development Program," *Newsline* 6, no. 3 (spring 1998).

54. Lewis and Henderson, op. cit. (see n. 42).

55. H. H. Arvey and A. Tijerina, "The School of the Future," in *Exploring Issues for School Community Connections Research and Practice*, ed. L. C. Rigsby, M. C. and Reynolds, and M. C. Wang (San Francisco: Jossey-Bass, 1995).

56. Lewis and Henderson, op. cit. (see n. 42).

57. Annenberg Institute for School Reform, *Reasons for Hope: Voices for Change. A Report of the Annenberg Institute on Public Engagement for Public Education* (Providence, RI: Brown University, 1998).

58. Smith, op. cit. (see n. 31); Gray, op. cit. (see n. 45).

59. N. Chavkin, *Families and Schools in a Pluralistic Society* (Albany: State University of New York Press, 1993).

60. Dryfoos, op. cit. (see n. 4).

61. W. W. Krist and C. Kelly, "Collaboration to Improve Education and Children's Services" in *School Community Connections: Exploring Issues for Research and Practice*, ed. L. C. Rigsby, M. D. Reynolds, and M. C. Wang (San Francisco: Jossey-Bass, 1995).

62. W. C. Wang, G. D. Haertel, and H. J. Walberg, "The Effectiveness of Collaborative School Linked Services" in *School Community Connections*, op. cit. (see n. 61).

63. A. Hartman, foreword to *Social Work Services in Schools*, op. cit. (see n. 21).

64. Winters, op. cit. (see n. 29).

65. P. Burch and A. Palanki, *From Clients to Partners: Four Case Studies of Collaboration and Family Involvement in the Development of School-Linked Services* [Report No. 29] (Baltimore, MD: Johns Hopkins University Center on Families, Communities, Schools and Children's Learning, 1995); Lewis and Henderson, op. cit. (see n. 42).

66. J. G. Hopps, E. Pinderhughes, and R. Shankar, *The Power to Care: Clinical Practice Effectiveness with Overwhelmed Clients* (New York: Free Press, 1993).

67. Harman op. cit. (see n. 63).

68. Winters op. cit. (see n. 29), 3.

69. H. Specht and M. Courtney, *Unfaithful Angels: How Social Work Abandoned Its Mission* (New York: Free Press, 1993).

70. S. Sarason, *The Culture of the School and the Problem of Change*, 2d ed. (Boston: Allyn and Bacon, 1982).

71. J. L. Epstien and S. Dauber, "School Programs and Teacher Practices of Parent Involvement in Inner-City Elementary and Middle Schools," *Elementary School Journal* 91 (1991): 289–306; S. Sarason, *Parental Involvement and the Political Principle* (San Francisco: Jossey-Bass, 1995); K. Swick, *Teacher-Parent Partnerships to Enhance School Success in Early Childhood Education* (Washington, DC: National Education Association, 1991).

72. Ibid; op. cit. (see n. 26).

73. Lewis and Henderson, op. cit. (see n. 42).

Chapter 8: A Competence-Centered Perspective

1. Germain, C. G. and Gitterman, A. (1996). *The Life Model of Social Work Practice: Advances in Theory and Practice, (2nd ed.)*. New York: Columbia University Press.

2. Ibid no longer in use.

3. Kemp, S. P., Whittaker, J. K. and Tracy, E. M. (1997). *Person-Environment Practice: The Social Ecology of Interpersonal helping*. New York: Aldine de Gruyter; Maluccio, A. N. (1999). "Action as a Vehicle for Promoting Competence," In Compton, B. R. and Galaway, B. (1999). *Social Work Processes, (6th ed.) (pp. 354–65)*. Pacific Grove, CA: Brooks/Cole.

4. Germain, C. G. and Gitterman, A. (1996). *The Life Model of Social Work Practice: Advances in Theory and Practice, (2nd ed.)*. New York: Columbia University Press.

5. Kemp, S. P., Whittaker, J. K. and Tracy, E. M. (1997). *Person-Environment Practice: The Social Ecology of Interpersonal helping*. New York: Aldine de Gruyter; Maluccio, A. N. (1999). "Action as a Vehicle for Promoting Competence," In Compton, B. R. and Galaway, B. (1999). *Social Work Processes, (6th ed.) (pp. 354–65)*. Pacific Grove, CA: Brooks/Cole.

6. Rapp, C. A. The Strength Model: Case Management with People Suffering Severe and Persistent Mental Illness New York: Oxford University Press, 1998; Saleebey, D. D., ed., *The Strengths Perspective in Social Work Practice, 2d. (New York: Longman, 1997)*.

7. Maluccio, A. N. ed., (1981). *Promoting Competence in Clients: A New/Old Approach to Social Work Practice, New York: Free Press*.

8. Gilligan, C. (1993). *In a Different Voice: Psychological Theory and Women's Development* Cambridge: Harvard University Press.

9. Erikson, E. H. (1963). *Childhood and Society*, 2d ed. New York: W. W. Norton.

10. Devore, W. & Schlesinger, E. G. (1996). *Ethnic-Sensitive Social Work Practice*. (4th ed.). Boston: Allyn and Bacon; Okun, B. F. (1986). *Understanding Diverse Families: What Practitioners Need to Know* New York: Guilford Press.

11. McFadden, J. E. & Downs, S. W. "Family Continuity: The New Paradigm in Permanence Planning," *Community Alternatives-International Journal of Family Care, 7(1)*, 39–59.

12. Maluccio, A. N., Fein, E. & Olmstead, K. A. (1986). *Permanency Planning for*

Notes

Children: Concepts and Methods London and New York: Routledge, Chapman and Hall.

13. Laird, J. (1995). Family-Centered Practice in the Postmodern Era," *Families in Society: The Journal of Contemporary Human Services, 76(3),* 150–162.

14. Fanshel, D. & Shinn, E. (1978). *Children in Foster Care: A Longitudinal Investigation* (p. 96). New York: Columbia University Press, 96.

15. Davis, I. et al., (1996). Parental Visiting and Foster Care Reunification. *Children and Youth Services Review, 18(415),* 363–382.

16. Fein, E. Maluccio, A. N. & Kluger, M. (1990). *No More Partings: An Examination of Long-term Foster Family Care* Washington, DC: Child Welfare League of America; Hopps, J. G. Pinderhughes, E. & Shankar, R. (1995). *The Power to Care: Clinical Practice with Overwhelmed Clients* New York: Free Press.

17. Kagan, S. L. (1993). *Integrating Services for Children and Families: Understanding the Past to Shape the Future* New Haven, CT: Yale University Press.

18. Everett, J. E., Chipungu, S. S. & Leashore, B. R., (1991). *Child Welfare: An Africentric Perspective* New Brunswick, NJ: Rutgers University Press.

19. Boyd-Franklin, N. (1989). *Black Families in Therapy: A Multisystem Approach* New York: Guilford Press, 43.

20. Pelton, L. H. (1994). "The Role of Material Factors in Child Abuse and Neglect," in *Protecting Children from Abuse and Neglect: Foundations for a New National Strategy,* ed. Melton G. B. and Barry F. D. New York: Guilford Press, 131–81.

21. Jansson, B. S. (1994). *Social Welfare Policy: From Theory to Practice* (Pacific Grove, CA: Brooks/Cole.)

22. Saleebey, op. cit. (see n. 6).

23. Pinderhughes, E. (1995). Empowering Diverse Populations: Family Practice in the 21st Century. *Families in Society: The Journal of Contemporary Human Services, 76(3),* 131–40.

24. Solomon, B. (1976). *Black Empowerment: Social Work in Oppressed Communities* New York: Columbia University Press.

25. Gamble, D. N. & Weil, M. O. (1995). Citizen participation. In Edwards, R. L. & Hopps, J. G. (Eds.). (1995). *Encyclopedia of Social Work.* (19th ed. Vol. 1). Washington, D.C.: National Association of Social Workers Press. 483–94.

26. Warsh, R. Maluccio, A. N. & Pine, B. A. (1994). *Teaching Family Reunification: A Sourcebook* Washington, D.C.: Child Welfare League of America.

27. Kufeldt, K. (1994). "Inclusive Foster Care: Implementation of the Model," in *Current Perspectives on Foster Family Care for Children and Youth,* ed. B. McKenzie Toronto: Wall and Emerson, 84–111.

28. Barth, R. P. & Berry, M. (1994). "Implications of Research on the Welfare of Children under Permanency Planning, in *Child Welfare Review,* Vol. 1, ed. Barth, R. P., Berrick, J. D. and Gilbert N. New York: Columbia University Press), 323–68.

29. Maluccio, A. N., Krieger R., & Pine, B. A. eds., (1990). *Preparing Adolescents for Life After Foster Care: The Central Role of Foster Parents* Washington, D.C.: Child Welfare League of America.

30. Blythe, B., Salley, M. R., & Jayaratne, S. (1994). "A Review of Intensive Family Preservation Services Research," *Social Work Research*, no. 4 (1994): 213–24.

31. Anderson, G. R., Ryan, A. S. & Leashore, B. R. eds., (1997). *The Challenge of Permanency Planning in a Multicultural Society* New York: Haworth Press.

32. Pine, B. A., Warsh R., & Maluccio, A. N. (1998). "Participatory Management in a Public Child Welfare Agency: A Key to Effective Change." *Administration in Social Work 22(1)*, 19–32.

Chapter 9: Restoring Communities

1. W. J. Wilson, *The Truly Disadvantaged: The Inner City, the Underclass, and Public Policy* (Chicago: University of Chicago Press, 1987).

2. H. J. Gans, "Deconstructing the Underclass: The Term's Dangers as a Planning Concept," *APA Journal* (1990): 271–77.

3. R. Aponte, "Conceptualizing the Underclass: An Alternative Perspective," Urban Poverty Project, University of Chicago (paper presented at the annual meeting of the American Sociological Association, 1998).

4. C. Jencks and P. E. Peterson, eds., "Is the American Underclass Growing?" in *The Urban Underclass* (Washington, DC: The Brookings Institution, 1991), 28–102.

5. D. S. Massey and M. Eggers, "The Ecology of Inequality: Minorities and the Concentration of Poverty, 1970–1980," *American Journal of Sociology* 95, no. 5 (1990): 1153–88.

6. K. Auletta, *The Underclass* (New York: Vintage Books, 1982).

7. E. R. Ricketts and I. Sawhill, "Defining and Measuring the Underclass," *Journal of Policy Analysis and Management* 7, no. 2 (1998): 316–25.

8. See note 4 above.

9. R. B. Mincy, I. V. Sawhill, and D. A. Wolf, "The Underclass: Definition and Measurement," *Science* 248 (1990) 450–53. Volume 248 nuaya 4954

10. P. A. Jargowsky and M. Bane, "Ghetto Poverty in the United States, 1970–1980," in *The Urban Underclass*, op. cit. (see n. 4), 235–73.

11. M. Hughes, "Formation of the Impacted Ghetto: Evidence From Large Metropolitan Areas, 1970–1980," *Urban Geography* 11, no. 3 (1990): 2655–84.

12. See note 10 above.

13. J. Chow and C. J. Coulton, "Was There a Social Transformation of Urban Neighborhoods in the 1980s?" *Urban Studies* 35, no. 8 (1998): 1359–75.

14. J. D. Kasarda. "Inner-City Concentrated Poverty and Neighborhood Distress: 1970–1990." *Housing Policy Debate* 4 (1993): 253–302.

15. P. A. Jargowsky, *Poverty and Place: Ghettos, Barrios, and the American City* (New York: Russell Sage Foundation, 1997).

16. D. S. Massey and M. Eggers, "The Spatial Concentration of Affluence and Poverty During the 1970s," *Urban Affairs Quarterly* 29, no. 2 (1993): 299–315.

17. A. J. Abramson, M. S. Tobin, and M. R. VanderGoot, "The Changing Geogra-

phy of Metropolitan Opportunity: The Segregation of the Poor in U.S. Metropolitan Areas, 1970 to 1990," *Housing Policy Debate* 6, no. 1 (1995): 45–72.

18. C. J. Coulton et al., "Geographic Concentration of Affluence and Poverty in 100 Metropolitan Areas," *Urban Affairs Review* 32, no. 2 (1996): 186–216.

19. J. D. Kasarda et al., "Central City and Suburban Migration Patters: Is a Turnaround on the Horizon?" [Housing Policy Debate 8, no. 2 (1997): 307–58.]

20. R. Reich, *The Work of Nations: Preparing Ourselves for the 21st Century* (New York: Knopf, 1991).

21. D. Rusk, *Cities Without Suburbs* (Washington, DC: Woodrow Wilson Center Press, 1993).

22. M. Orfield, *Metropolitics: A Regional Agenda for Community and Stability* (Washington, DC: The Brookings Institution, 1997).

23. C. Abbot, "The Portland Region: Where City and Suburbs Talk to Each Other and Often Agree," [Housing Policy Debate 8, no. 1 (1997): 11–52].

24. See note 22 above. 24a. R. A. Simons and D. S. Sharkey, "Jump-Starting Cleveland's New Urban Housing Markets: Do the Potential Fiscal Benefits Justify the Public Subsidy Costs?" *Housing Policy Debate* 8 (1997): 143–72.

25. J. M. Downs, "The Challenge of Our Declining Big Cities," *Housing Policy Debate* 8, (1997): 359–408. ·

26. See note 19 above.

27. W. J. Wilson, *When Work Disappears: The World of the New Urban Poor* (New York: Knopf, 1996).

28. B. Bluestone and B. Harrison, *The Deindustrialization of America: Plant Closings, Community Abandonment, and the Dismantling of Basic Industry* (New York: Basic Books, 1982).

29. J. D. Kasarda, "Urban Industrial Transition and the Underclass," *Annals of the American Academy* of Political and Social Sciences 501, January 1989: 26–47.

30. See note 14 above.

31. G. C. Galster and R. B. Mincy, "Understanding the Changing Fortunes of Metropolitan Neighborhoods, 1980 to 1990," *Housing Policy Debate* 4, no. 3 (1993): 1–50.

32. C. Jencks and S. Mayer, "The Social Consequences of Growing Up in a Poor Neighborhood," *Inner-City Poverty in the United States,* ed. L. E. Lynn and M. G. H. McGeary, (Washington, D.C.: National Academy Press, 1990).

33. H. J. Holzer, "The Spatial Mismatch Hypothesis: What Has the Evidence Shown?" *Urban Studies* 28 (1991): 105–22. V. 28 n. 1

34. J. Kain, "The Spatial Mismatch Hypothesis: Three Decades Later," *Housing Policy Debate* 3, no. 2 (1992): 371–460.

35. J. Kirschenman and K. M. Neckerman, "We'd Love to Hire Them, but . . .": The Meaning of Race for Employers," in *The Urban Underclass,* op. cit. (see n. 4), 203–33.

36. S. Rapheal, M. A. Stoll, and H. J. Holzer, *Are Suburban Firms More Likely to Discriminate Against African Americans?* Discussion paper, University of Wisconsin at Madison, Institute for Research on Poverty, 1998, 1160–98.

Notes

37. M. Hughes, "Employment Decentralization and Accessibility: A Strategy for Stimulating Regional Mobility," *Journal of the American Planning Association* 57, no. 3 (1991): 288–98.

38. See note 32 above.

39. M. Tienda, "Poor People and Poor Places: Deciphering Neighborhood Effects on Poverty Outcomes," *Macro-Micro Linkages in Sociology,* ed. J. Huber (Newbury Park, CA: Sage, 1991), 244–62.

40. J. E. Rosenbaum and S. J. Popkin, "Employment and Earnings of Low-Income Blacks Who Move to Middle-Class Suburbs," in *The Urban Underclass,* op. cit. (See n. 4), 342–56.

41. J. E. Rosenbaum, "Black Pioneers: Do Their Moves to the Suburbs Increase Economic Opportunity for Mothers and Children?" *Housing Policy Debate* 2 (1991): 1179-213.

42. J. Brooks-Gunn, G. Duncan and L. Aber, eds., *Neighborhood Poverty: Context and Consequences for Children* (New York: Russell Sage Foundation, 1997).

43. C. J. Coulton, "Effects of Neighborhoods on Families and Children: Implications for Services," *Children and Their Families in Big Cities* (1996): 87-120.

44. I. G. Ellen and M. A. Turner, "Does Neighborhood Matter? Assessing Recent Evidence," *Housing Policy Debate* 8 (1997): 833-66. V. 8 n. 4

45. F. Furstenberg, "How Families Manage Risk and Opportunity in Dangerous Neighborhoods," in *Sociology and the Public Agenda,* ed. W. J. Wilson (Newbury Park, CA: Sage, 1993), 231–58.

46. J. Garbarino et al., *Children in Danger: Coping With the Consequences of Community Violence* (San Francisco: Jossey-Bass, 1992).

47. J. Korbin and C. Coulton, "Understanding the Neighborhood Context for Children and Families: Combining Epidemiological and Ethnographic Approaches," in *Neighborhood Poverty: Context and Consequences for Children,* op. cit. (see n. 42), 1997.

48. C. J. Coulton, J. Korbin, and M. Su, *Neighborhoods and Child Maltreatment: A Multi-Level Study of Resources and Controls* (Cleveland, OH: The Center on Urban Poverty and Social Change, Mandel School of Applied Social Sciences, Case Western Reserve University, 1998).

49. L. M. Burton, D. A. Obeidallah, and K. W. Allison, "Ethnographic Insights on Social Context and Adolescent Development Among Inner-City African-American Teens," in *Essays on Ethnography and Human Development,* ed. R. Jessor, A. Colby and R. Shweder (Chicago: University of Chicago Press, in press).

50. See note 47 above.

51. See note 45 above.

52. R. J. Sampson, S. W. Raudenbush, and F. Earls, "Neighborhoods and Violent Crime: A Multilevel Study of Collective Efficacy," *Science* 277, no. 5328 (1997): 918-24.

53. T. D. Cook, S. C. Shagle, and S. M. Degirmencioglu, "Capturing Social Process for Testing Mediational Models of Neighborhood Effects." *Neighborhood Poverty* 2 (1997): 94–119.

54. R. N. Bellah et al., *Habits of the Heart: Individualism and Commitment in American Life* (Berkeley: University of California Press, 1985).

55. J. Jacobs, *The Death and Life of Great American Cities* (New York: Vintage Books, 1963).

56. R. D. Putnam, "The Prosperous Community: Social Capital and Public Life," *American Prospect* 13 (1993): 35–42.

57. F. Fukuyama, *Trust* (New York: Free Press, 1995).

58. R. D. Putnam, "Bowling Alone," *American Prospect* 13 (1995): 36–42.

59. Pew Research Center, *Trust and Citizen Engagement in Metropolitan Philadelphia: A Case Study* (Philadelphia: Pew Research Center, 1997).

60. Committee for Economic Development, *Rebuilding Inner-City Communities: A New Approach to the Nation's Urban Crisis* (New York: Committee for Economic Development, 1995).

61. See note 59 above.

62. S. Saegert and G. Winkel, "Social Capital and the Revitalization of New York City's Distressed Inner-City Housing," *Housing Policy Debate* 9, no. 1 (1968): 17–60.

63. See note 59 above.

64. See note 57 above.

65. See note 52 above.

66. A. Portes and P. Landolt, "The Downside of Social Capital," *American Prospect* 26 (1996): 18–21.

67. M. Warner, *Social Capital Construction and the Role of the Local State.* (Ithaca, NY: Cornell University, Department of City and Regional Planning, 1998).

68. A. J. Kahn and S. B. Kamerman, eds., *Children and Their Families in Big Cities.* (New York: Columbia University Press, 1996).

69. Ibld.

70. L. B. Schorr, *Common Purpose: Strengthening Families and Neighborhoods to Rebuild America.* (New York: Anchor/Doubleday, 1997).

71. R. Nathan, *Hard Road Ahead: Block Grants and the Devolution Revolution.* (Albany, NY: Nelson A. Rockefeller Institute of Government, 1995).

72. M. Weisman, "Welfare Reform in the United States: A Background Paper," *Housing Policy Debate* 7(4) (1996): 595–648.

73. J. R. Wolch, "Community-Based Human Service Delivery," *Housing Policy Debate* 7 (1996): 649–72.

74. L. J. Gallagher et al., eds., *One Year After Federal Welfare Reform: A Description of State Temporary Assistance for Needy Families (TANF) Decision as of October 1997.* (Washington, DC: The Urban Institute, 1998).

75. R. Halpern, *Rebuilding the Inner City: A History of Neighborhood Initiatives to Address Poverty in the United States.* (New York: Columbia University Press, 1995).

76. B. Katz, "Connecting Community Building to Metropolitan Solutions," *Shelterforce* 14 (Jan./Feb. 1998): 8–9.

Notes

77. T. J. Bartik, *Who Benefits From State and Local Economic Development Policies?* (Kalamazoo, MI: W. E. Upjohn Institute for Employment Research, 1991).
78. See note 22 above.
79. See note 75 above.
80. M. Katz, *The Undeserving Poor: From the War on Poverty to the War on Welfare.* (New York: Pantheon, 1989).
81. See note 75 above.
82. D. S. Massey and N. A. Denton, *American Apartheid: Segregation and the Making of the Underclass.* (Cambridge: Harvard University Press, 1993).
83. See note 75 above.
84. Ibid.
85. Ibid.
86. P. Marris and M. Rein. *Dilemmas of Social Reform: Poverty and Community Action in the United States.* (London: Routledge and Kegan Paul, 1967).
87. F. Seebohm, *Report of the Committee on Local Authority and Allied Personal Social Services.* (London: Her majesty's Stationary Office, 1968).
88. See note 70 above.
89. A. K. Johnson, "The Revitalization of Community Practice: Characteristics, Competencies, and Curricula for Community-Based Services," *Journal of Community Practice,* Vol. 5 (1998): 37–62.
90. P. L. Clay, *Community Development Corporation: An Assessment of Vision and Practice.* (Cambridge: MIT Press, 1997).
91. M. Sullivan, *More Than Housing: How Community Development Corporations Go About Changing Lives and Neighborhoods.* (New York: Community Development Research Center, Graduate School of Management and Urban Policy, New School for Social Research (1993).
92. Ibid.
93. Ibid.
94. A. Vidal, *Rebuilding Communities: A National Study of Urban Community Development Corporations* (New York: New School for Social Research, 1992).
95. Ibid.
96. See note 90 above.
97. See note 91 above.
98. B. Harrison, and M. Weiss, *Workforce Development Networks: Community-Based Organizations and Regional Alliances* (New York: Sage 1998).
99. See note 89 above.
100. See note 60 above.
101. Roundtable on Comprehensive Community Initiatives for Children and Families, *Voices From the Field: Learning From the Early Work of Comprehensive Community Initiatives* (Washington, DC: The Aspen Institute, 1997),
102. A. Naparstek and D. Dooley, "Countering Urban Disinvestment Through Community Building Initiatives," *Social Work* 42, n. 5 (1997): 506–14.
103. M. W. Stagner and M. A. Duran, "Comprehensive Community Initiatives:

Principles, Practice, and Lessons Learned," *Children and Poverty*, V. 7. n. 2 (1997): 132–40.

104. T. Burns and G. Spilka, *Rebuilding Communities Initiative* (Baltimore: The Annie E. Casey Foundation, 1997).

105. D. Nelson, "The Path of Most Resistance: Lessons Learned From New Futures," *Children and Their Families in Big Cities*, This is a chapter in a book (1996): 163–84.

106. S. Milligan, M. Nario-Redmond, and C. Coulton, *The 1995–1996 CCBI Baseline Progress Report.* (Cleveland, OH: Center on Urban Poverty and Social Change, Mandel School of Applied Social Sciences, Case Western Reserve University, 1997).

107. See note 98 above.

108. D. R. Dupper and J. Poertner, "Public Schools and the Revitalization of Impoverished Communities: School-Linked, Family Resource Centers," *Social Work* 42 no. 5 (1997): 415–22.

109. See note 70 above.

110. A. Naparstek, D. Dooley, and R. Smith. *Community Building in Public Housing: Ties That Bind People and Their Communities* (Washington, DC: U.S. Department of Housing and Urban Development, 1997).

111. P. Brown and S. Garg. *Foundations and Comprehensive Community Initiatives: The Challenges of Partnerships* (Chicago: Chapin Hall Center for Children, University of Chicago, 1997).

112. See note 101 above.

113. R. Stone, ed., *Core Issues in Comprehensive Community-Building Initiatives* (Chicago: Chapin Hall Center for Children, University of Chicago, 1996.)

114. See note 110 above.

115. See note 103 above.

116. See note 110 above.

117. W. Pitcoff, "Collaborating for Change," *Shelterforce* 14 January/Feb issue (1998): 2–16.

118. See note 101 above.

119. R. J. Chaskin, M. Joseph, and Chipenda-Dansokho, "Implementing Comprehensive Community Development: Possibilities and Limitations," *Social Work* 42(5) (1997): 435–44.

120. See note 105 above.

121. See note 106 above.

122. See note 117 above.

123. See note 119 above.

124. See note 60 above.

125. See note 119 above.

126. See note 106 above.

127. See note 70 above.

128. J. Kretzmann and J. McKnight, *Building Communities From the Inside Out: A*

Notes

Path Toward Finding and Mobilizing a Community's Assets (Evanston, IL: Center for Urban Affairs and Policy Research, Neighborhood Innovations Network, 1993).

129. D. Page-Adams, and M. Sherraden, "Asset Building as a Community Revitalization Strategy," *Social Work* 42 no. 5 (1997): 423–34.
130. See note 128 above.
131. C. Finn, P. Zorita, and C. Coulton, "Assets and Financial Management Among Poor Households in Extreme Poverty Neighborhoods," *Journal of Sociology and Social Welfare* 21(4) (1994): 75–94.
132. M. Sherraden, *Assets and the Poor: A New American Welfare Policy.* (Armonk, NY: M. E. Sharpe, 1991).
133. See note 129 above.
134. S. Milligan et al., *Implementing a Theories-of-Change Evaluation in the Cleveland Community-Building Initiative* (Cleveland, OH: Center on Urban Poverty and Social Change, Mandel School of Applied Social Sciences, Case Western Reserve University, 1996).
135. See note 70 above.
136. See note 80 above.
137. J. Nowak, "Expanding Community Development," *Shelterforce* 14 (Jan/Feb 1998): 13–15.
138. See note 107 above.
139. See note 137 above.
140. C. J. Coulton, L. Leete, and N. Bania, *Housing, Transportation, and Access to Suburban Jobs by Welfare Recipients in the Cleveland Area.* (Washington, DC: The Urban Institute, in press).
141. See note 22 above.
142. D. Rusk, "St. Louis Congregations Fight Urban Sprawl," *Shelterforce* 14 (Jan/Feb 1998): 21–22.
143. See note 22 above.
144. C. Abbot, "The Portland Region: Where City and Suburbs Talk to Each Other and Often Agree," *Housing Policy Debate* 8 (1997): 11–52.
145. See note 27 above.
146. See note 42 above.
147. See note 46 above.
148. See note 52 above.
149. See note 59 above.
150. P. Adams and K. Nelson, *Reinventing Human Services: Community- and Family-Centered Practice* (New York: Aldine de Gruyter, 1995).
151. See note 110 above.
152. G. S. Finney, *Building From Strength: Replication as a Strategy for Expanding Social Programs That Work.* (Philadelphia: The Conservation Company, 1993).
153. K. Nelson and M. Allen, "Family-Centered Social Services: Moving Toward System Change," *Reinventing Human Services* (1995).

Notes

154. J. Connell et al., *New Approaches to Evaluating Community Initiatives: Concepts, Methods, and Contexts* (New York: The Aspen Institute, 1995).
155. See note 60 above.

Chapter 10: State Social Welfare

1. D. Stoesz and H. Karger, *Restructuring the American Welfare State* (Lanhan, MD: Rowan and Littlefield, 1993).
2. J. Midgley, *Social Development: The Developmental Perspective in Social Welfare* (Newbury Park, CA: Sage, 1995).
3. D. Iatridis, "Critical Social Policy," in *Handbook of Social Policy*, ed. J. Midgley et al. (Newbury Park, CA: Sage, in press); T. Weisskopf, "Economic Perspectives on Privatization in Russia: 1990–1994," in *Privatization in Central and Eastern Europe: Perspectives and Approaches,* ed. D. S. Iatridis and J. Hopps (Westport, CT: Praeger, 1998), 104–21; L. Popescu, "State and Market in Romanian Social Policy," in *Privatization in Central and Eastern Europe,* 155–68.
4. N. Ginsberg, "Institutional Racism and Local Authority Housing," *Critical Social Policy 24* (1989); I. Gough, *The Political Economy of the Welfare State* (Basingstoke: Macmillan, 1979); D. Iatridis, "Neoconservatism Reviewed," *Social Work Journal* 28, no. 2 (March/April, 1983): 101–7; D. Iatridis, "A Global Approach to Privatization," in *Privatization in Central and Eastern Europe,* op. cit. (see n. 3), 3–25; P. Leonard, *Postmodern Welfare* (Beverly Hills, CA: Sage, 1977); M. Specher, "Privatization, Competition and Structural Change in Eastern Europe," in *Privatization in Central and Eastern Europe,* op. cit. (see n. 3); R. M. Solow, "Guess Who Pays for Workfare?" *New York Review of Books* (5 November 1998, 27–28, 36–37); C. Jencks, "The Hidden Paradox of Welfare Reform," *American Prospect,* (May/June 1997): 33–40; P. Elderman, "The Worst Thing Bill Clinton Has Done," *Atlantic Monthly,* (v. 279 March 97 pp. 43–46); W. J. Wilson, *When Work Disappears: The World of the New Urban Poor* (New York: Knopf, 1996); S. K. Danziger and S. Danziger, "Will Welfare Recipients Find Work When Welfare Ends?" in *Welfare Reform: An Analysis of the Issues,* ed. I. V. Sawhill (Washington, DC: Urban Institute, 1995), 41–44. L. Gibbs et al., "A Measure of Critical Thinking about Practice, *Research in Social Work Practice* 5, no. 2 (1995): 193–204.
5. Midgley, op. cit. (see n. 2); J. Midgley, "The American Welfare State in International Perspective," in *American Social Welfare Policy: A Pluralist Approach,* 3rd ed., ed. H. J. Karger and D. Stoez (New York: Longman, 1998), 434–78.
6. N. Ginsburg, *Division of Welfare: A Critical Introduction to Comparative Social Policy.* (New York: Sage, 1992).
7. V. George and N. Manning, *Socialism, Social Welfare and the Soviet Union* (Boston: Routledge and Kegan Paul, 1980); N. Manning, "Social Policy in the USSR and the Nature of Soviet Society," *Critical Social Policy* (winter 1984):75–87.
8. Leonard, op. cit. (see n. 4); P. Leonard, "Postmodernism, Socialism and Social

290

Notes

Welfare," *Journal of Progressive Human Services* 6, no. 2 (1995): 3–19.

9. Iatridis, op. cit. (see n. 3).

10. R. Frydman and A. Rapaczynski, *Privatization in Eastern Europe: Is the State Withering Away?* (Budapest: Central European University Press, 1994).

11. J. Miller, "Learning from the Southeast Asian Crisis," *Dollars and Sense* (November/December 1998):12–15.

12. R. E. Scott, "Asia's Crisis and the U.S. Economy," *Dollars and Sense* (November/December 1998): 14.

13. D. E. Sanger, "U.S. Plans to Send Millions to Shield Brazil's Economy," *The New York Times*, 24 October 1998, p. 1.

14. Privatization Review, *Privatization International*, 64 (1994):28–29; Reuters, *International Herald Tribune*, 8 August 1995, p. 13.

15. Reuters, *Cape Town Times*, 11 February 1994, p. 1.

16. P. Marer and S. Zecchini, *The Transition to a Market Economy* (Paris: Organization for Economic Cooperation and Development (OECD), 1991); Iatridis and Hopps, op. cit. (see n.3).

17. G. A. Corina and S. Sipos, *Children and the Transition to the Market Economy* (Brookfield, Brookfield, VT: Avebury, 1991); Iatridis and Hopps, op. cit. (see n. 3).

18. Frydman and Rapaczynski, op. cit. (see n. 10).

19. A. Bass, "Weld to Privatize Acute Care for Uninsured Mentally Ill," *The Boston Globe*, 25 January 1995, p. 1.

20. Ibid.; G. Judson, "Hartford Plays to End the Private Management of Its Public Schools," *The New York Times*, 24 January 1996, p. B1; "School Privatizers in Retreat," *The New York Times*, 12 February 1996, p. A4.

21. G. W. Bowman, S. Hakim, and P. Seidenstad, eds., *Privatizing Correctional Institutions* (New Brunswick, NJ: Transaction Publishers, 1993).

22. S. B. Garland, "A Rich New Business Called Poverty," *Business Week*, 19 May 1997, 132–34.

23. N. Bernstein, "Giant Companies Entering Race to Run State Welfare Programs: Powers Like Lockheed Explore New Profit Area," *The New York Times* Sept 15, 1996 see 1 page one column one 1996, p.

24. A. H. Munnel, "Privatization Plans Hit Women Hardest," *The Boston Globe*, 3 November, p. A17.

25. F. F. Piven and R. A. Cloward, "Welfare Reform and the New Class War," in *Myths About the Powerless: Contesting Social Inequalities*, ed., M. B. Lykes et al. (Philadelphia: Temple University Press, 1996), 72–86; F. F. Piven and R. A. Cloward, *Regulating the Poor* (New York: Vintage, 1971); F. F. Piven and R. A. Cloward, *Poor People's Movement* (New York: Vintage, 1977); F. F. Piven and R. A. Cloward, *Regulating the Poor: The Function of Public Welfare* (1972); Ginsburg, op. cit. (see n. 6); B. L. Fenby, "Feminist Theory, Critical Theory and Management's Romance with the Technical," *Affilia* 6, no. 1 (spring 1991): 20–37; K. B. Tyson, "A New Approach to Relevant Scientific for Practitioners: The Heuristic Paradigm," *Social Work 37:* 541 (1992); M. Abramovitz, "Challenging the Myths of Welfare Reform from a Woman's Perspective," *Social Jus-*

tice 21, no. 1 spring (1994): 17–21; M. Abramovitz, "Under Attack, Fighting Back: Women and Welfare in the United States," *New York Monthly* 25 (1996); I. Gough, *The Political Economy of the Welfare State* (Basingstoke: Macmillan, 1979); D. Taylor, ed., *Critical Social Policy: A Reader* (London: Sage, 1996); D. Taylor, "Citizenship and Social Order," *Critical Social Policy,* 26 (fall); J. Forester, *Critical Theory, Public Policy, and Planning Practice: Toward a Critical Pragmatism* (Albany: State University of New York Press, 1993); D. Riffe, S. Lacy, and F. Fico, *Analyzing Media Messages: Using Quantitative Content Analysis in Research* (Mahwah, NJ: Lawrence Erlbaum, 1998); Iatridis, op. cit. (see n. 3); B. Dubois, "Passionate Scholarship: Notes on Values, Knowing and Method," in *Theories of Women's Studies II,* ed. G. Bowles and R. Dvelli-Klein (Berkeley, CA: University of California, 1981); B. Renard, *Housing Reform in Socialist Economies* (Washington, DC: The World Bank, 19).

26. J. H. Turner, "In Defense of Positivism," *Sociological Theory* 3 (1985): 24–30; P. Ammassori, "Epistemology," in *Encyclopedia of Sociology,* vol. 1, ed. E. F. Borgatta (New York: Mcmillan, 1992), 550–54; W. L. Kolb, "Science," in *Dictionary of the Social Sciences,* ed. J. Gould and W. L. Kolb (New York: Free Press of Glencoe, 1964), 620–22; F. Adler, "Positivism," in *Dictionary of the Social Sciences,* 520–22; Tyson, op. cit. (see n.25); Iatridis, op. cit. (see n. 3); H. Raymond, "Sociologist Sees Intellectual Peril," *The New York Times* (15 December 1968), p. 11; D. Lerner and H. D. Lasswell, *The Policy Sciences in the United States* (Paris: A. Colin, 1951); J. Eckstein, "Political Science and Public Policy," in *Contemporary Political Science: Toward Empirical Theory,* ed. I. de Sola Pool (New York: McGraw-Hill, 1968), 143; L. Cseh-Czombathy, *Collection of Sociological Studies* (Budapest: Institute for Social Sciences and Institute for Sociological Research of the Hungarian Academy of Sciences, 1986).

27. T. Vema, "The Poor Get Poorer," (21 July 1996,) A-16.

28. R. Albelba and C. Tilly, "Unnecessary Evil: Why Inequality Is Bad for Business," *Dollars and Sense* (1995): 18–21.

29. A. Glyn and D. Miliband, "Paying for Inequality: The Economic Cost of Social Injustice," *Institute of Public Policy Research,* (1994).

30. C. J. Coulton, "Restoring Communities within the Context of the Metropolis," in J. G. title, ed., J. G. Hopps et al. (city: pub, 1995) New York, Free Press, 1995.

31. Wilson, op. cit. (see n. 4).

32. Solow, op. cit. (see n. 4); Jencks, op. cit. (see n. 4); Elderman, op. cit. (see n. 4); Wilson, op. cit. (see n. 4); Danziger and Danziger, op. cit. (see n. 4).

Chapter 11: Eclecticism Is Not a Free Good

1. For an elaboration of the arguments and observations in this paragraph, see D. J. Tucker, "Eclecticism Is Not a Free Good: Barriers to Knowledge Development in Social Work," *Social Service Review* 70 (September 1996): 400–434, especially pp. 401–08.

2. R. L. Simpson, "Is Research Utilization for Social Workers?" *Journal of Social*

Service Research 2 (winter 1978): 143–57; S. A. Kirk, "The Puzzles of Peer Perusal," *Social Work Research and Abstracts* 29 (June 1993): 3–4; G. O. Haworth, "Social Work Research, Practice and Paradigms," *Social Service Review* 58 (September 1984): 343–57; W. E. Gordon, "Social Work Revolution or Evolution," *Social Work* 28 (May 1983): 181–85.

3. H. Specht, "Social Work and the Popular Psychotherapies," *Social Service Review* 64 (September 1990): 345–57; J. C. Wakefield, "Why Psychotherapeutic Social Work Don't Get No Re-Specht?" *Social Service Review* 66 (March 1992): 141–51; H. Specht, "Author's Reply: A Less Complex Statement of Social Work's Mission," *Social Service Review* 66 (March 1992): 152–59.

4. J. T. Pardeck, "Are Social Work Editorial Boards Competent? Some Disquieting Data with Implications for Research on Social Work Practice," *Research on Social Work Practice* 2 (October 1992): 487–96; J. G. Hopps, "A Response to Pardeck: From the Past Editor of *Social Work*," *Research on Social Work Practice* 2 (October 1992): 497–98; J. R. Schuerman, "A Response to Pardeck: From the Editor of the *Social Service Review*," *Research on Social Work Practice* 2 (October 1992): 499–500; F. G. Reamer, "A Response to Pardeck: From the Editor-in-Chief of the *Journal of Social Work Education*," *Research on Social Work Practice* 2 (October 1992): 501–04; A. E. Fortune, "More Is Not Better—Manuscript Reviewer Competence and Citations: From the Past Editor-in-Chief of the *Journal of Social Work Education*," *Research on Social Work Practice* 2 (October 1992): 505–10; D. Lindsey, "Improving the Quality of Social Work Journals: From the Editor of *Children and Youth Services Review*," *Research on Social Work Practice* 2 (October 1992): 515–24; W. M. Epstein, "A Response to Pardeck: Thumb Therapy for Social Work Journals," *Research on Social Work Practice* 2 (October 1992): 525–28; J. T. Pardeck, "The Distinction and Achievement Levels of Social Work Editorial Boards Revisited," *Research on Social Work Practice* 2 (October 1992): 529–37.

5. W. Epstein, "Social Work in the University," *Journal of Social Work Education* 31 (spring/summer 1995): 281–92; C. Glisson, "The State of the Art of Social Work Research: Implications for Mental Health," (paper presented to NIMH Conference on Building Social Work Knowledge for Effective Mental Health Services and Policies, Bethesda, MD, 1995); W. C. Klein and M. Bloom, "Social Work as Applied Social Science: A Historical Analysis," *Social Work* 39 (July 1994): 421–31.

6. M. B. Heineman, "The Obsolete Scientific Imperative in Social Work Research," *Social Service Review* 55 (September 1981): 371–97; J. R. Schuerman, "Debate with Authors: The Scientific Imperative in Social Work Research," *Social Service Review* 56 (March 1982): 44–46; W. W. Hudson, "Scientific Imperatives in Social Work Research and Practice," *Social Service Review* 56 (June 1982): 246–58; L. L. Geismar, "Comments on 'The Obsolete Scientific Imperative in Social Work Research,'" *Social Service Review* 56 (June 1982): 311–12; M. H. Pieper, "The Future of Social Work Research," *Social Work Research and Abstracts* 21 (winter 1985): 3–11; E. J. Mullen, "Methodological Dilemmas in

Notes

Social Work Research," *Social Work Research and Abstracts* 21 (Winter 1985): 12–20; W. M. Epstein, "Science and Social Work," *Social Service Review* 60 (March 1986): 145–60; C. Peile, "Research Paradigms in Social Work: From Stalemate to Creative Synthesis," *Social Service Review* 62 (March 1988): 1–19.

7. D. R. Baker, "A Structural Analysis of the Social Work Journal Network: 1985–1986," *Journal of Social Service Research* 15 (1992): 153–68.

8. P. Doreian, "Structural Equivalence in a Psychology Journal Network," *Journal of the American Society for Information Science* 36 (November 1985): 411–17; P. Doreian and T. J. Fararo, "Structural Equivalence in a Journal Network," *Journal of the American Society for Information Science* 36 (January 1985): 28–37.

9. Baker, op. cit. (see n. 7), 164. It is also worth noting here that Doreian and Fararo's network study of citation patterns in sociology found a core-periphery structure, similar to Baker's finding for social work. Doreian's later study of citation patterns in psychology revealed a different structure, one characterized by a less dominant central core of generalist journals, with more interchange at the periphery between specialist journals. Doreian speculated that differences between journal network structures is probably an important predictor of the intellectual state of a field; the centralized form of journal network structure, as found in social work and sociology, could characterize an unproductive, more fragmented discipline, whereas a more decentralized structure, as found in psychology, could characterize a healthy and productive field. See Doreian and Fararo (n. 8) and Doreian (n. 8).

10. K. M. Cheung, "Interdisciplinary Relationships between Social Work and Other Disciplines: A Citation Study," *Social Work Research and Abstracts* 26 (September 1990): 23–29.

11. J. Pfeffer, "Barriers to the Advance of Organizational Science: Paradigm Development as a Dependent Variable," *Academy of Management Review* 18 (October 1993): 606.

12. M. Fraser et al., "Social Work and Science: Many Ways of Knowing," *Social Work Research and Abstracts* 27 (December 1991): 5–15.

13. Ibid., 13.

14. Glisson, op. cit. (see n. 5).

15. Ibid., 7. Interestingly, Merlin Taber and Iris Shapiro, in a study published thirty years before Glisson's study, also found a wide range of topics covered in a sample of 124 articles from three core journals over a forty-year period, with only three topics achieving the rank of accounting for 10 percent of the articles. In a similar vein, Michael Howe and John Schuerman, in a study published twenty years ago on trends in the literature from 1957 to 1972 as reflected in three major social work journals, found increased theoretical eclecticism in the social treatment literature in social work. See M. W. Howe and J. R. Schuerman, "Trends in Social Work Literature: 1957–72," *Social Service Review* 48 (June 1974): 279–85; and M. Taber and I. Shapiro, "Social Work and Its Knowledge Base: A Content Analysis of Periodical Literature," *Social Work* 10 (October 1965): 100–106.

16. This point is suggested by John Miner, who, prompted by concern for the low level of paradigm development in organization science, studied the connection between rated importance, usefulness, and validity of thirty-two theories in organization science. Based on a finding of no connection between the three variables, he proposed the development of a new discipline so as to better integrate the study of organizations. See J. B. Miner, "The Validity and Usefulness of Theories in an Emerging Organizational Science," *Academy of Management Review* 9 (April 1984): 296–306.

17. Haworth, op. cit. (see n. 2). Also, see R. F. Zammuto and T. Connolly, "Coping with Disciplinary Fragmentation," *The Organizational Behavior Teaching Review* 9 (1984): 30–37, for a similar argument in the case of organization science. For clinical social work, Katherine Kendall alludes to this issue when, in introducing Turner's text on social work treatment, which identifies some twenty-two different theories of clinical practice, she asks: "At what point does diversity become anarchy?" K. A. Kendall, "Foreword," *Social Work Treatment: Interlocking Theoretical Approaches*, 3d ed., ed. Francis Turner (New York: Free Press, 1986), xiii–xvi.

18. I use the terms *manuscript evaluation time lag* and *editorial time lag* interchangeably to refer to the time lag between the submission of a manuscript to a journal and the editorial decision to accept or reject it.

19. Data on the psychology journals were obtained from the published annual reports of the American Psychology Association (APA), excepting for the data on manuscript evaluation time lags. These data were obtained directly from APA's publication department. For sociology, data for *American Sociological Review* and *Journal of Health and Social Behavior* were obtained from the published annual reports of the American Sociological Association. For the two remaining sociology journals, *Social Forces* and *Social Problems,* data were obtained from the annual reports of the editors. For the social work journals, data were obtained directly from journal editors or their staff. Other data sources included a variety of published author's guides to journals dating back to 1977. These included American Psychological Association, *Journals in Psychology,* 4th ed. (Washington, DC: American Psychological Association, 1993); M. D. Gordon, *A Study of the Evaluation of Research Papers by Primary Journals in the U.K.* (Leicester, England: Primary Communications Research Center, University of Leicester, 1978); C. B. Howery, *Publishing Options: An Author's Guide to Journals,* 3d ed. (Washington, DC: American Sociological Association, 1993); W. H. Loke, *A Guide to Journals in Psychology and Education* (Metuchen, NJ: Scarecrow Press, 1990); A. Markle and R. C. Rinn, *Authors Guide to Journals in Psychology, Psychiatry and Social Work,* (New York: Haworth Press, 1977); H. N. Mendelsohn, *An Author's Guide to Social Work Journals* (Silver Spring, MD: National Association of Social Workers, 1983), *An Author's Guide to Social Work Journals,* 2d ed. (Silver Spring, MD: National Association of Social Workers, 1987), and *An Author's Guide to Social Work Journals,* 3d. ed. (Silver Spring, MD: National Association of Social Workers,

1992); A. Y. Wang, *Author's Guide to Journals in the Behavioral Sciences.* (Hillsdale, NJ: Lawrence Erlbaum, 1989).

20. D. Lindsey, "Distinction, Achievement, and Editorial Board Membership," *American Psychologist* 31 (November 1976): 799–804; D. Lindsey, "The Operation of Professional Journals in Social Work," *Journal of Sociology and Social Welfare* 5 (March 1978): 273–98; Baker op. cit. (see n. 7); Glisson, op. cit. (see n. 5); Fraser et al., op. cit. (see n. 12); T. Pardeck et al., "Distinction and Achievement Levels of Editorial Board Members of Psychology and Social Work Journals," *Psychological Reports* 68 (1991): 523–27; Cheung, op. cit. (see n. 10).

21. Acceptance rates were standardized across the journals by subtracting from unity the figure obtained by dividing the number of papers published over a two-year period by the number of submissions received over a two-year period, with the latter lagged one year.

22. For Time 1 data, $F_{2,13} = 2.53$, which is not significant at the .05 level. For Time 2 data, $F_{2,13} = 6.31$, significant at the .01 level. The Student-Newman-Keuls procedure, a post hoc test on difference between two means, found that for Time 2, the acceptance rates for social work and sociology differed from each other, but those for social work and psychology and for psychology and sociology did not. Note that data on the *Journal of Social Work Education* were included in this analysis. I will provide full details on the analysis on request.

23. It is important to remember that overall, the acceptance rates reported in Table 1 are all low when compared to acceptance rates for the more paradigmatically developed physical sciences. To illustrate, I performed a one-way analysis of variance on data for Time 1 acceptance rates but added to the analysis additional data on average acceptance rates for five physical science journals: *Genetics, Industrial and Engineering Chemistry Fundamentals, Industrial and Engineering Chemistry Process, Journal of the American Chemistry Society,* and *Physical Review Letters.* The additional data, reported in Lowell L. Hargens's study of rejection rates for thirty physical and social science journals ("Scholarly Consensus and Journal Rejection Rates," *American Sociological Review* 53 [February 1988], 141, 150) were average acceptance rates for each of the five journals for the period, 1980–1983. I selected these five journals because they had the lowest acceptance rates of the fourteen physical science journals in the Hargens sample of thirty physical and social science journals. The overall mean for the five physical science journals was .58 compared to overall means of .13, .20, and .27 for sociology, psychology, and social work, respectively. The results were highly significant ($F_{3,17} = 26.31$, p < .0001), showing the acceptance rates for the physical science journals as significantly higher than the acceptance rates for the social work, sociology, and psychology journals. Full details of this analysis are available from the author.

24. In the case of the journals studied here, I measured changes in submissions only for journals on which I had six or more years of data. For these, I divided the sum of a journal's 1992 and 1993 submissions by the sum of two earlier

years for which I had data, with none extending back beyond 1983. On average, submissions to social work journals decreased by 30 percent, with two journals having decreases of over 30 percent. Only one journal experienced an increases in number of submissions, but at a modest level of 9 percent over a six-year period.

25. Editors of social work journals, similar to what Hargens found for editors in sociology and psychology, appear more often to complain of a dearth of publishable papers among new submissions than of an abundance (Hargens, op. cit. [see n. 23], 141). For example, John Schuerman, editor of *Social Service Review*, in responding to Pardeck's criticism that social work editorial board members are comparatively incompetent, opined that an examination of a sample of material appearing in social work journals would probably reveal that much of it was inadequate. He then went on to observe that the main reason for this "was not the incompetence of those making publication decisions; the principal factor determining the quality of the work published is the quality of the work submitted. Journals reflect the state of the work in the field." See Schuerman, op. cit. (n. 4), 500.

26. This is generally the case for the six core social work journals examined here. The number of papers each published per year varied only very modestly between 1983 and 1993. The average total number of papers published by these six journals in 1983–1984 and in 1992–1993 was 228 and 213, respectively, an overall average decrease of just over 6.5 percent. By the same token, there is some variation in this pattern when a larger group of journals is examined. Here, there is a modest overall increase in the number of articles published per year. At the same time, some individual journals decreased the number of articles published annually by as much as 30 percent.

27. Editors generally suggest that they play a mainly unobtrusive role in the peer review process. At the same time, however, and as one editor noted, the presence of dissensus in the peer-review process tends to increase an editor's power by providing evaluative material from which an editor can draw regardless of reviewers' recommendations.

28. In a similar vein, informal discussions with some editors indicated that, faced with fewer new manuscripts, there was some increased effort to adjust the decision framework from one presupposing that submitted papers should not be published to one presupposing that they should. This was done by recruiting reviewers favorably predisposed to providing authors with helpful comments and criticism, or by an editor taking a more active role in interpreting reviewers' comments to authors. In both cases, the apparent intent is to increase the numbers of publishable papers by providing advice and encouragement on revisions and resubmissions.

29. J. Fischer, "The Social Work Revolution," *Social Work* 26 (May 1981): 199–207.

30. H. Zuckerman and R. K. Merton, "Patterns of Evaluation in Science: Institutionalization, Structure and Functions of the Referee System," *Minerva* 9 (January 1971): 66–100; Hargens, op. cit. (see n. 23), 139–51.

31. For Time 1 data, $F_{2.13} = 32.43$, significant at the .0001 level; for Time 2 data, $F_{2.13} = 5.93$, significant at the .02 level. Results from the Student-Newman-Keuls test on the difference between means reveal that the length of editorial time lags for sociology and psychology do not differ significantly from each other. However, the editorial time lags for both sociology and psychology are significantly shorter than social work's editorial time lags. I will provide full details on the analysis on request.

32. S. E. Zimbalist, *Historic Themes and Landmarks in Social Welfare Research.* (New York: Harper and Row, 1977), 406–7. In his concluding chapter, Zimbalist notes that there have been wide swings in research emphasis over the years, with "an excessive tendency for social work to go 'overboard' with the latest wave of research when one succeeds in catching on in this generally research-resistant profession." He goes on to observe: "Perhaps the periodic over-enthusiasm is fed by the relative neglect of research at other times, so that the one extreme is a reaction to the other. In any case, there has been an obvious readiness to embrace a promising research approach as a potential panacea and ready solution to the highly intractable and deep-seated ills. We saw this long ago in the research on the causes of poverty, in the social survey movement, in the drive for social work measurement, and more recently in the study of the multiproblem family. Closer study of the dynamics and sources of such oscillations in research interest and activity should be rewarding. What is clearly needed is a more evenly balanced and steady commitment to research and research criticism throughout the profession over the long haul."

33. W. B. Arthur, M. E. Yu, and M. K. Yu, "Path-Dependent Processes and the Emergent of Macro-Structure," *European Journal of Operational Research* 30 (June 1987): 294–304.

34. P. A. David, "Clio and the Economics of QWERTY," *Economic History* 75 (May 1985): 332–37; W. B. Arthur, "Competing Technologies, Increasing Returns, and Lock-In by Historical Events," *Economic Journal* 99 (March 1989): 116–31; W. B. Arthur, "Positive Feedbacks in the Economy," *Scientific American* 262 (February 1990): 92–99.

35. T. Eggertsson, "The Economics of Institutions: Avoiding the Open Field Syndrome and the Perils of Path Dependence," *Acta Sociologica* 36 (1993): 223–37; D. C. North, *Institutions, Institutional Change and Economic Performance* (Cambridge: Cambridge University Press, 1990); Pfeffer, op. cit. (see n. 11).

36. J. B. Lodahl and G. Gordon. "Funding the Sciences in University Departments," *Educational Record* 54 (winter 1973): 74–82.

37. Arthur, "Positive Feedbacks" (see n. 34); North, op. cit. (see n. 35).

38. For example, see Task Force on Social Work Research, *Building Social Work Knowledge for Effective Services and Policies: A Plan for Research Development* (Bethesda, MD: National Institute of Mental Health, 1991).

39. National Science Board, *Knowledge into Action: Improving the Nation's Use of the Social Sciences* (Washington, DC: National Science Foundation, 1969), 44–50.

40. Ibid., xiii.

41. M. Fraser, J. M. Jensen, and R. E. Lewis. "Training for Research Scholarship in Social Work Doctoral Programs," *Social Service Review* 65 (December 1991): 597–613; Fraser et al., op. cit. (see n. 12).

42. J. M. England, *A Patron for Pure Science* (Washington, DC: National Science Foundation, 1982).

43. Glisson, op. cit. (see n. 5). This is not to deny that benefits in the form of pay and status will accrue to the minority who do manage to publish, or that the more gifted and experienced members of a given field will be more efficient in moving their work into the public realm. Regardless, low acceptance rates and longer time lags still suggest higher levels of wasted effort overall than is likely to be present in fields in which there is more certainty about relevant problems and approaches. Moreover, there is the additional consideration in social work that, historically, practitioners have contributed a good portion of published articles. There is some evidence, however, that the trend in recent years is toward faculty contributing an increasing percentage of all journal articles. One possible reason for this is a change in the structure and operation of service delivery systems, with more emphasis on productivity specific to the requirements of employing organizations. See R. M. Grinnell and M. L. Royer, "Authors of Articles in Social Work Journals," *Journal of Social Service Research* 6, no. 3/4 (1983): 147–54; S. A. Kirk and K. J. Corcoran, "The $12,000.00 Question: Does It Pay to Publish?" *Social Work* 34 (July 1989): 379–81; B. A. Thyer and K. J. Bentley, "Academic Affiliations of Social Work Authors: A Citation Analysis of Six Major Journals," *Journal of Social Work Education* 22, no. 3/4 (1986): 67–73; B. A. Thyer et al., "Academic Affiliations of Social Work Journal Articles: A Publication Productivity Analysis," *Journal of Social Service Research* 18, no (1994): 153–67.

44. Simpson, op. cit. (see n. 2), 147.

45. Pfeffer, op. cit. (see n. 11), 611.

46. Simpson, op. cit. (see n. 2); R. K. Merton, "The Matthew Effect in Science," *Science* 159 (January 1968): 56–63; J. A. Stewart, "Achievement and Ascriptive Processes in the Recognition of Scientific Articles," *Social Forces* 62 (September 1983): 166–89.

47. Merton, op. cit. (see n. 46). In this regard, it is interesting to note that in a study of the productivity of social work doctoral graduates, Green, Hutchinson, and Sar found that nearly "50 percent of all reported conference presentations and refereed journal articles were directed to non social work conferences and journals." R. G. Green, E. D. Hutchinson, and B. K. Sar, "Evaluating Scholarly Performance: The Productivity of Graduates of Social Work Doctoral Programs," *Social Service Review* 66 (September 1992): 441–66, quote on 457.

48. Pfeffer, op. cit. (see n. 11), 610.

49. Pardeck et al., op. cit. (see n. 20); Pardeck "Are Editorial Boards Competent?" (see n. 4); Lindsey "Operation of Professional Journals" (see n. 20); D. Lindsey,

Notes

The Scientific Publication System in Social Science (San Francisco: Jossey-Bass, 1978); W. M. Epstein, "Confirmational Response Bias among Social Work Journals," *Science, Technology, and Human Values* 15 (winter 1990): 9–38; and "The Obligation of Intellectuals," *Science, Technology, and Human Values* 15 (spring 1990): 244–47; W. C. Klein and M. Bloom. "Studies of Scholarly Productivity in Social Work Using Citation Analysis," *Journal of Social Work Education* 28 (fall 1992): 291–99.

50. Pfeffer, op. cit. (see n. 11), 610.
51. Andrew Abbott observes: "The ability of a profession to sustain its jurisdiction lies partly in the power and prestige of its academic knowledge." See A. Abbott, *The Systems of Professions* (Chicago: University of Chicago Press, 1988), 53–54. For similar views, see D. A. Schon, *The Reflective Practitioner: How Professionals Think in Action.* New York: Basic Books, 1983); E. Freidson, *Professionalism Reborn* (Chicago: University of Chicago Press, 1994).
52. S. Cole, "The Hierarchy of the Sciences," *American Journal of Sociology* 89 (July 1983): 111–39.
53. For example, we read papers in journals, give credit for publications in prestigious journals, and think more highly of people who have received grants, fellowships, awards, and memberships in prestigious organizations—all based on the evaluations of others. Ibid., 137.
54. Ibid., 138.
55. Ibid.
56. Pardeck "Are Editorial Borads Competent?" (see n. 4); Klein and Bloom, op. cit. (see n. 49); Pardeck et al., op. cit. (see n. 20); Lindsey, "Editorial Board Membership" (see n. 20).
57. Hopps, op. cit. (see n. 4); Reamer op. cit. (see n. 4); Fortune, op. cit. (see n. 4).
58. R. Whitley, "The Establishment and Structure of Science as Reputational Organizations," in *Scientific Establishments and Hierarchies,* ed. N. Elias, H. Martin, and R. Whitley (Dordrecht, Holland: D. Reidel Publishing, 1982), 313–57.
59. One example is the emergence in the late 1970s of organizational ecology in organization science. Greeted initially with hostility and questions about its relevance, organizational ecology's selection approach to studying dynamic change and its use of longitudinal, population-level research designs, are now broadly accepted. In addition, the scope of organization science has expanded to acknowledge an important place for macrotheories of organization. A second example is the bifurcation of social studies' departments in England in the early 1950s into the separate but related fields of social work and social administration (now social policy), and the subsequent emergence of consensus about the orientation of each field, as well as about the appropriateness of the separation itself. Finally, Pfeffer argues that over the past thirty years, political science has emerged as one of the more paradigmatically developed social sciences, based on increased consensus among political scientists about such factors as appropriate units of analysis and basic assumptions about human nature. For further elaboration, see W. R. Scott, *Organizations: Rational, Nat-*

ural, and Open Systems, 3d. ed. (Englewood Cliffs, NJ: Prentice Hall, 1992); R. A. Parker, "Social Ills and Public Remedies," in *Man and the Social Sciences,* ed. W. A. Robson (Beverly Hills, CA: Sage, 1972), 113–29; R. Mishra, "The Academic Tradition in Social Policy: The Titmuss Years," in *The Goals of Social Policy,* ed. M. Bulmer, J. Lewis, and D. Piachaud (London: Unwin Hyman, 1989), 64–83; R. Pinker, "Social Work and Social Policy in the Twentieth Century," in *The Goals of Social Policy,* 84–107; Pfeffer, op. cit. (see n. 11), 615.

60. J. K. Benson, "A Framework for Policy Analysis," in *Interorganizational Coordination: Theory, Research, and Implementation,* ed. D. L. Rogers and D. A. Whetten. (Ames: Iowa State University Press, 1982), 137–76.

61. C. B. Germain and A. Gitterman, *The Life Model of Social Work Practice* (New York: Columbia University Press, 1980); A. Brower, "Can the Ecological Model Guide Social Work Practice?" *Social Service Review* 62 (September 1988): 411–29.

62. Neither have they been studied from the point of view of understanding dynamic change processes that obtain at other aggregated levels of analysis. I elaborate on this in the following section.

63. J. D. Thompson, *Organizations in Action* (New York: McGraw-Hill, 1967); J. Child, "Organization Structure, Environment and Performance: The Role of Strategic Choice," *Sociology* 6 (1972): 1–22; J. Pfeffer and G. R. Salancik, *The External Control of Organizations* (New York: Harper and Row, 1978).

64. M. T. Hannan and J. Freeman, "The Population Ecology of Organizations," *American Journal of Sociology* 82 (March 1977): 929–64.

65. This argument is elaborated in a later article. See M. T. Hannan and J. Freeman, "Structural Inertia and Organizational Change," *American Sociological Review* 49 (April 1984): 149–64.

66. For relevant reviews, see G. R. Carroll, "Organizational Ecology," *Annual Review of Sociology* 10 (1984): 71–93; J. V. Singh and C. J. Lumsden, "Theory and Research in Organizational Ecology," *Annual Review of Sociology* 16 (1990): 161–95; D. J. Tucker, J. A. C. Baum, and J. V. Singh, "The Institutional Ecology of Human Service Organizations," in *Human Services as Complex Organizations,* ed. Y. Hasenfeld (Newbury Park, CA: Sage, 1992), 47–72; J. A. C. Baum, "Organizational Ecology," in *Handbook of Organization Studies,* ed. S. Clegg, C. Hardy, and W. Nord (London: Sage, 1997), 77–114.

67. M. T. Hannan, "Social Change, Organizational Diversity, and the Life Course," in *Social Structures and Human Lives,* ed. M. W. Riley (Beverly Hills, CA: Sage, 1988), 161–74; A. S. Miner, "Organizational Evolution and the Social Ecology of Jobs," *American Sociological Review* 56 (1991): 772–85; A. S. Miner, "Seeking Adaptive Advantage: Evolutionary Theory and Managerial Action," in *Evolutionary Dynamics of Organizations,* ed. J. A. C. Baum and J. V. Singh (Oxford: Oxford University Press, 1994), 76–89; R. A. Burgelman and B. S. Mittman, "An Intraorganizational Ecological Perspective on Managerial Risk Behavior, Performance, and Survival: Individual, Organizational, and Environmental Effects," in *Evolutionary Dynamics of Organizations,* 53–75; H. Aldrich, "New

Notes

Paradigms for Old: The Population Perspective's Contribution to Health Services Research," *Medical Care Review* 44 (fall 1987): 257–77; D. J. Tucker, "Progress and Problems in Population Ecology," in *Evolutionary Dynamics of Organizations*, 327–33.

68. Germain and Gitterman, op. cit. (see n. 61), 5.
69. R. Morris and D. Anderson, "Personal Care Services: An Identity for Social Work," *Social Service Review* 49 (July 1975): 157–74; R. A. Parker, "Tending and Social Policy," in *A New Look at the Personal Social Services*, ed. E. M. Goldberg and S. Hatch (London: Policy Studies Institute, 1981), 17–34.
70. For an overview, see Tucker, Baum, and Singh, op. cit. (see n. 66).
71. For one of the very few studies of this genre pertaining to social work and the human services, see R. L. Warren, S. M. Rose, and A. F. Bergunder, *The Structure of Urban Reform* (Lexington, MA: D. C. Heath, 1974).
72. F. E. Emery and E. L. Trist, *Towards a Social Ecology* (London: Plenum, 1973); R. Boyd and P. J. Richerson, *Culture and the Evolutionary Process* (Chicago: University of Chicago Press, 1985); J. A. C. Baum and J. V. Singh, "Organizational Hierarchies and Evolutionary Processes: Some Reflections on a Theory of Organizational Evolution," in *Evolutionary Dynamics of Organizations* (see n. 67), 3–20.
73. T. Kuan. "The Structure of Scientific Revolution" (Chicago: University of Chicago Press (1962). See also P. Hoyningen-Huene, *Reconstructing Scientific Revolutions* (Chicago: University of Chicago Press, 1993), chap. 4.
74. Ibid., 132–36.
75. Zimbalist, op. cit. (see n. 32).
76. Hoyningen-Huene, op. cit. (see n. 73); Gordon, op. cit. (see n. 2); Fischer, op. cit. (see n. 29); L. Laudan, *Progress and Its Problems* (Berkeley: University of California Press, 1977).
77. Tucker, Baum, and Singh, op. cit. (see n. 66).
78. D. J. Tucker and L. F. Hurl, "An Ecological Study of the Dynamics of Foster Home Entries," *Social Service Review* 66 (December 1992): 617–41; D. J. Tucker, L. F. Hurl, and H. Ford, "Applying Organizational Ecology to the Study of the Family: The Case of Who Persists in Providing Foster Care," *Journal of Marriage and the Family* 56 (November 1994): 1005–18; L. F. Hurl and D. J. Tucker. "Constructing an Ecology of Foster Care: An Analysis of the Entry and Exit Rates of Foster Homes," *Journal of Sociology and Social Welfare* 22 (September 1995): 89–119.
79. A. C. Baum and V. Singh, "Organizational Hierarchies," in Evolutionary Dynamics of Organizations. New York (Oxford University Press (1994) 10–11.
80. B. T. Pentland, "Organizing Moves in Software Support Hotlines," *Administrative Science Quarterly* 37 (December 1992): 527–48.
81. Ibid. See also B. T. Pentland and H. H. Rueter, "Organizational Routines as Grammers of Action," *Administrative Science Quarterly* 39 (September 1994): 484–510. For an earlier, classic statement that reflects a similar perspective, see M. Polanyi, *Personal Knowledge* (Chicago: University of Chicago Press, 1958).

Another relevant study that invokes the idea of routines as a basis for analyzing family processes is D. Reiss, *The Family's Construction of Reality* (Cambridge: Harvard University Press, 1981).

82. Eggertsson, op. cit. (see n. 35), 224.
83. Abbott, op. cit. (see n. 51), 102.
84. A. Halter and E. Gullerud, "Academic Mergers in Social Work Programs: Autonomy or Disharmony," *Journal of Social Work Education* 31 (spring/summer 1995): 269–80.

Chapter 12: Social Efficiency and Social Work Research

1. W. M. Epstein, "Randomized Controlled Trials in the Human Services," *Social Work Research and Abstracts* 29, no. 3 (1993): 3–10.
2. T. L. Haskell, *The Emergence of Professional Social Science* (Urbana: University of Illinois Press, 1977) and "Justifying the Rights of Academic Freedom in the Era of Power/Knowledge," in *The Future of Academic Freedom*, ed. L. Menand (Chicago: University of Chicago Press, 1996), acknowledging his debt to F. E. Abbot, *Scientific Theism* (New York: ASM Press, 1885) and *Way out of Agnosticism* (New York: ASM Press, 1890) for the term "community of the competent," and to P. P. Wiener, *Evolution and the Founders of Pragmatism* (Philadelphia: University of Pennsylvania Press, 1972), who trace the notion of competence to the founding of the European university and the modern American university at the end of the nineteenth century. Competence in the context of social work and social service research refers to the development of objective, coherent tests (e.g., science) of practice. The goal of competence is for Haskell the expert authority that warrants the gift of communal autonomy—academic freedom—to defy "the primacy of the political" ("Justifying the Rights," 80).
3. Haskell, *The Emergence of Professional Social Science* (see n. 2).
4. J. Fischer, "Is Casework Effective: A Review," *Social Work* 18, no. 1 (1973): 19.
5. B. Wootton, *Social Science and Social Pathology* (London: George Allen and Unwin, 1959); S. Segal, "Research on the Outcome of Social Work Therapeutic Interventions: A Review of the Literature," *Journal of Health and Social Behavior* 13 (March 1972): 3–17.
6. Wooton, op. cit. (see n. 5), 328.
7. Segal, op. cit. (see n. 5), 15.
8. K. M. Wood, "Casework Effectiveness: A New Look at the Research Evidence," *Social Work* 23 (November 1978): 437–58.
9. E. E. Schwartz and W. C. Sample, "First Findings from Midway," *Social Service Review* 41 (June 1967): 113–51.
10. R. A. Wilson, "An Evaluation of Intensive Casework Impact," *Public Welfare* 25 (October 1967): 301–6.
11. See R. Lubove, *The Professional Altruist* (Cambridge: Harvard University Press, 1965); W. Dryden and C. Feltham, *Psychotherapy and Its Discontents* (Bucking-

ham, England: Open University Press, 1992); M. Macmillan, *Freud Evaluated* (Cambridge: MIT Press, 1997); P. Kline, *Psychology Exposed or the Emperor's New Clothes* (London: Routledge, 1988).

12. J. Fischer, "Has Mighty Casework Struck Out?" *Social Work* 18, no. 4 (1973): 107–10.

13. R. R. Ravetz, *Scientific Knowledge and Its Social Problems* (New York: Oxford University Press, 1979).

14. J. Fischer, "The Social Work Revolution," *Social Work* 26, no. 3 (1981): 199–209.

15. Ibid.

16. Epstein, op. cit. (see n. 1).

17. J. Fischer, "Does Anything Work?" *Journal of Social Service Research* 1, no. 3 (1978): 215–44; W. M. Epstein, *The Dilemma of American Social Welfare* (New Brunswick, NJ: Transaction Publishers, 1993).

18. W. J. Reid and P. Hanrahan, "Recent Evaluations of Social Work: Grounds for Optimism." *Social Work* 27, no. 4 (1982): 328–40.

19. Ibid., 331.

20. A. Rubin, "Practice Effectiveness: More Grounds for Optimism," *Social Work* 30, no. 6 pp 469–476 (1985):

21. See for example R. M. Berger and S. D. Rose, "Interpersonal Skill Training with Institutionalized Elderly Patients," *Journal of Gerontology* 32:2 (1977): 346–53.

22. L. I. Stein and M. A. Test, "Alternatives to Mental Hospital Treatment," *Archives of General Psychiatry* 37 (April 1980): 392–412.

23. Epstein, op. cit. (see n. 17), 89.

24. R. J. Thomlison, "Something Works: Evidence from Practice Effectiveness Studies," *Social Work* 29, no. 1 (1984): 51–56; B. Sheldon, "Social Work Effectiveness Experiments: Review and Implications," *British Journal of Social Work* 16, no. 2 (1986): 223–42.

25. Thomlison, op. cit. (see n. 24), 52.

26. N. Krasnegor, "Analysis and Modification of Substance Abuse: A Behavioral Overview," *Behavior Modification* 4 (January 1980): 49.

27. J. Phillips and R. Ray, "Behavioral Approaches to Childhood Disorders," *Behavior Modification* 4 (January 1980): 3–34.

28. M. Kovacs, "Treating Depressive Disorders," *Behavior Modification* 3 (October 1979): 496–517.

29. A. Stunkard and M. Mahoney in *Handbook of Behavior Modification and Behavior Therapy*, ed. H. Leitenberg (Englewood Cliffs, NJ: Prentice-Hall, 1976).

30. Sheldon, op. cit. (see n. 24).

31. A. E. Bergin, "The Evaluation of Therapeutic Outcomes," in *Handbook of Psychotherapy and Behavior Change*, ed. S. L. Garfield and A. E. Bergin (New York: John Wiley, 1971); A. E. Bergin and M. J. Lambert, "The Evaluation of Therapeutic Outcomes," in *Handbook of Psychotherapy and Behavior Change*, ed. S. L. Garfield and A. E. Bergin, (New York: John Wiley, 1978).

Notes

32. M. L. Smith, G. V. Glass, and T. I. Miller, *The Benefits of Psychotherapy* (Baltimore MD: Johns Hopkins University Press, 1980).

33. W. M. Epstein, "Technology and Social Work, Part 1: The Effectiveness of Psychotherapy," *Journal of Applied Social Sciences* 8, no, 2 (1984): 155–75; W. M. Epstein, *The Illusion of Psychotherapy* (New Brunswick, N.J.: Transaction Publishers, 1995).

34. L. Videka-Sherman, "Meta-analysis of Research on Social Work Practice in Mental Health," *Social Work* 33, no. 4 (1988): 325–38.

35. J. L. Edelson and M. Sayers, "Relative Effectiveness of Group Treatments for Men Who Batter," *Social Work Research and Abstracts* 26, no. 2 (1990): J. A. Hall and S. D. Rose, "Evaluation of Training in Groups for Parent-Adolescent Conflict," *Social Work Research and Abstracts* 23, no. 1 (1987): 3–8; R. W. Toseland, "Long-Term Effectiveness of Peer-Led and Professionally Led Support Groups for Caregivers," *Social Service Review* 64, no. 2 (1990): 308–27; M. A. Kirkham and R. F. Schilling II, "Life Skills Training with Mothers of Handicapped Children," *Journal of Social Service Research* 13, no. 2 (1989): R. M. Tolman and S. D. Rose, "Teaching Clients to Cope with Stress: The Effectiveness of Structured Group Stress Management Training," *Journal of Social Service Research* 13, no. 2 (1989): 45–66.

36. K. M. Gorey, "Effectiveness of Social Work Intervention Research: Internal Versus External Evaluations," *Social Work Research* 20, no. 2 (1996): 119–28. For Gorey, "prestigious" simply means that the journal accepted less than 50 percent of submitted articles. Since this fact confers no standing on a journal even within social work, perhaps "discriminating" might be the more appropriate term. Gorey concluded that "more than three-quarters of clients participating in [a social work] intervention do better than the average client who does not" (124).

37. An effect size is the difference of means between the control and experimental group divided by the standard deviation of the control.

38. Gorey, op. cit. (see n. 36), 120.

39. See the estimates of placebo effect sizes in L. M. Prioleau, M. Murdock, and N. Brody, "An Analysis of Psychotherapy versus Placebo Studies," *Behavioral and Brain Sciences* 6, (1983): 275–310; Smith, Glass, and Miller, op. cit. (see n. 32); M. Lambert, F. D. Weber, and J. D. Sykes, "Psychotherapy versus Placebo Therapies: A review of the Meta-analytic Literature" (poster paper presented at the annual Meeting of the Western Psychological Association, Phoenix, Arizona, 1993).

40. M. R. Burt and L. H. Blair, *Options for Improving Care of Neglected and Dependent Children* (Washington, DC: Urban Institute, 1971); M. R. Burt and R. R. Balyeat, *A Comprehensive Emergency System for Neglected and Abused Children* (New York: Vantage Press, 1977).

41. M. A. Jones, *A Second Chance for Families: Five Years Later* (New York: Child Welfare League of America, 1985); M. A. Jones, R. Neuman, and A. Shyne, *A Second Chance for Families: Evaluation of a Program to Reduce Foster Care* (New York: Child Welfare League of America, 1976).

42. V. Pike, "Permanent Planning for Foster Care: The Oregon Project," *Children Today* 5:1 (1976): 22–25; A. Emlen et al., *Barriers to Planning for Children in Foster Care* (Portland, OR: Regional Research Institute for Human Services, Portland State University, 1976); A. Emlen et al., *Overcoming Barriers to Planning for Children in Foster Care* DHEW Publication N. (OHDS) 78-30138 (Washington, DC: U.S. Department of Health and Human Services, U.S. Children's Bureau, 1978); A. Emlen, et al., *Overcoming Barriers to Planning for Children in Foster Care* (Portland, OR: Regional Research Institute for Human Services, Portland State University, 1977); J. Lahti, "A Follow-up Study of Foster Children in Permanent Placements," *Social Service Review* 4 (1982): 556–71; J. Lahti et al., *A Follow-up Study of the Oregon Project* (Portland, OR: Regional Research Institute for Human Services, Portland State University, 1978).

43. T. H. Stein, E. P. Gambrill, and K. T. Wiltse, *Children in Foster Homes: Achieving Continuity of Care* (New York: Praeger, 1978).

44. E. A. Sherman, R. Neuman, and A. W. Shyne, *Children Adrift in Foster Care: A Study of Alternative Approaches* (Washington, DC: Child Welfare League of America, 1973).

45. J. Schuerman, T. L. Rzepnicki, and J. H. Littell, *Putting Families First: An Experiment in Family Preservation* (New York: Aldine de Gruyter, 1994).

46. W. M. Epstein, "Social Science, Child Welfare, and Family Preservation: A Failure of Rationality in Public Policy," *Children and Youth Services Review* 19, no. 1/2 (1997): 41–60.

47. Schuerman, Rzepnicki, and Littell, op. cit. (see n. 45); P. H. Rossi, review of "Families in Crisis: The Impact of Intensive Family Preservation Services," *Children and Youth Services Review* 16, no. 5/6 (1994): 461–69; P. H. Rossi, *Evaluating Family Preservation Programs.* Report to the Edna McConnell Clark Foundation, 1991.

48. Rossi, "Families in Crisis," op. cit. (see n. 47), 464.

49. D. Fanshel and E. Shinn, *Children in Foster Care: A Longitudinal Investigation* (New York: Columbia University Press, 1978).

50. M. Bush, "The Public and Private Purposes of Case Records," *Children and Youth Services Review* 6 (1984): 1–18.

51. Epstein, op. cit. (see n. 46).

52. Epstein, *The Illusion of Psychotherapy* (see n. 33); W. M. Epstein, *Welfare in America: How Social Science Fails the Poor* (Madison: University of Wisconsin Press, 1997).

53. Smith, Glass, and Miller, op. cit. (see n. 32).

54. Ibid., 88.

55. P. Giblin, D. H. Sprenkle, and R. Sheehan, "Enrichment Outcome Research: A Meta-analysis of Premarital, Marital and Family Interventions," *Journal of Marital and Family Therapy* 11, no. 3 (1985): 257–71; K. Hahlweg and H. J. Markman, "Effectiveness of Behavioral Marital Therapy: Empirical Status of Behavioral Techniques in Preventing and Alleviating Marital Distress," *Journal*

of Consulting and Clinical Psychology 56, no. 3 (1988): 440–47; D. A. Shapiro and D. Shapiro, "Meta-analysis of Comparative Therapy Outcome Studies: A Republication and Refinement," *Psychological Bulletin* 93, no. 3 (1982): 581–604.

56. Prioleau, Murdoch, and Brody, op. cit. (see n. 39).
57. Smith, Glass, and Miller, op. cit. (see n. 32), 38.
58. S. Rachman, *The Effects of Psychological Treatment* (Oxford: Perragon Press, 1971).
59. Epstein, "Technology and Social Work" (see n. 33).
60. Kline, op. cit. (see n. 11); J. Masson, *Against Therapy: Emotional Tyranny and the Myth of Psychological Healing* (New York: Atheneum, 1988); A. S. Masten, "Family Therapy as a Treatment for Children: A Critical Review of Outcome Research," *Family Process* 18 no. 2 (1979): 303–35; R. M. Dawes, *House of Cards: Psychology and Psychotherapy Built on Myth* (New York: Free Press, 1994); M. L. Gross, *The Psychological Society* (New York: Random House, 1978).
61. I. Elkin et al., "National Institute of Mental Health Treatment of Depression Collaborative Research Program," *Archives of General Psychiatry* 46 (November 1989): 971–83; S. D. Imber et al., "Mode-Specific Effects Among Three Treatments for Depression," *Journal of Consulting and Clinical Psychology* 58, no. 3 (1990): 352–59; S. M. Sotsky et al., "Patient Predictors of Response to Psychotherapy and Pharmacotherapy: Findings in the NIMH Treatment of Depression Collaborative Research Program," *American Journal of Psychiatry* 148, no. 8 (1991): 997–1008.
62. W. M. Epstein, "The Ineffectiveness of Psychotherapy," in *Controversies in Psychotherapy and Counselling,* ed. C. Feltham (London: Sage, 64–74, 1999).
63. See the discussion of initial Seligman's *Consumer Reports* survey in *American Psychologist* 51, no. 10 (1996).
64. R. Martinson, "What Works—Questions and Answers about Prison Reform," *Public Interest* (April 1974): 22–54; Epstein, op. cit. (see n. 17).
65. J. Fitzgerald, P. Gottschalk, and R. Moffitt, "An Analysis of Sample Attrition in Panel Data: The Michigan Panel Study of Income Dynamics" (December 1996).
66. The evidence for the effectiveness of nontherapeutic care and systemic change strategies, particularly community organization and social development interventions including so-called empowerment strategies and the strengths perspectives, is more unformed but just as ambiguous. Indeed, there has yet to be any coherent and objective evaluation of community organization interventions in either the national or international context. Poorly matched comparison communities, reputational power analyses, subjective estimates of value, biased informers and researchers, "action" research, and short-term analyses have bedeviled every estimate of the impact of trained change agents on social systems. Moreover, the strengths perspective, more a theological mood than a series of definable services, has yet to mature to the point at which it can be operationally defined, let alone evaluated. See W. M. Epstein, "Economic De-

velopment and Social Welfare in the Third World: The End of Romance," *Journal of International and Comparative Social Welfare* 4 (1994): 107–37.

67. There are a few exceptions to the drab monotony of the child welfare literature's failure, in particular Schuerman, Rzepnicki, and Littell, op. cit. (see n. 47); D. Lindsey, *The Welfare of Children* (New York: Oxford University Press, 1994); Fanshel and Shinn, op. cit. (see n. 49).

68. Recognizing, of course, certain grave limitations. See, for example, Ravetz, op. cit. (see n. 13); I. L. Horowitz, *The Decomposition of Sociology* (New York: Oxford University Press, 1993); C. Norris, *What's Wrong with Postmodernism?* (Baltimore, MD: Johns Hopkins University Press, 1990); P. R. Gross and N. Levitt, *Higher Superstition: The Academic Left and Its Quarrels with Science* (Baltimore, MD: Johns Hopkins University Press, 1994). Nevertheless, the social sciences seem far more protective of cross-argumentation than social work, even boasting of robust competitive ideological schools.

69. Working America in the sense of L. Mishel, J. Bernstein, and J. Schmitt, *The State of Working America 1996–97* (Armonk, NY: M. E. Sharpe, 1997).

Index

Index

Index

Index

Index

Index

Index

State licensing, 31
State of Welfare, The (Steiner), 62
State social welfare
  future issues, 215–217
  postpositivism and, 214–215
  privatization and, 212–214, 218–219
  regionalism and, 210–212
  roles of government and state, 217–218
  social capital investments, 219–221
Stein, L. I., 254–255
Steiner, Gilberg, 62
Stewart B. McKinney Homeless Assistance
  Amendments Act (1990), 144
Subsidies for hiring welfare recipients, 85
Substance abuse, school reform and, 143
Supplemental Security Income (SSI), 30, 78
Supreme Court decisions, 79–83
Survey of Income and Program Participa-
  tion, 264

Taylor, Alice L., 124–125
Taylor, Graham, 28
Technology, role of, 109–110
Teenage mothers, restrictions on, 83
Teenage pregnancy, school reform and, 141
Temporary Assistance to Needy Families
  (TANF), 34, 74
Test, M. A., 254–255
Thomlison, R. J., 255
Towle, Charlotte, 74
Townsend v. Swank, 80–82
Tragedy of American Compassion, The
  (Olasky), 24
Truly Disadvantaged, The (Wilson), 176

Underclass, use of term, 177
Under the Cover of Kindness (Margolin), 136
Unfaithful Angels (Specht and Courtney),
  65
Unions, role of, 50
United Nations Convention on the Rights
  of the Child, 76
University of Chicago, 28, 46

University of Wisconsin conferences,
  129–131
Urban renewal. *See* Communities, restoring
Urban sprawl, 179–180, 200–202

Values, 129–130, 135–137
Veterans Administration Social Service, 57,
  92
Videka-Sherman, L., 255
Violence
  ethnic, 10
  family, 10
  how to prevent and manage, 9–11
  school reform and, 141–143
  workplace, 10
Visitacion Valley Middle School, 154

Warner, Amos, 27
War on Poverty, 54, 189–190
Wealth of Nations, The (Smith), 19
Welfare capitalism, use of term, 19
Welfare state
  reversing the (1980–1995), 63–66
  use of term, 19
Whelage, G., 151
Wickenden, Elizabeth, 55
Wilson, R. A., 251
Wilson, William Julius, 176–177
Winston, Ellen, 55
Winters, W. G., 149, 157
Witmer, Helen, 123–124
Women
  social work education for, 21–22
  as social workers, 23, 24–25, 39
Wood, K. M., 251
Wootton, B., 251
Workplace
  power sharing in, 12–13
  violence, 10
World War II, post, 209–210
Wyman v. James, 82–83

Zimbalist, S. E., 232, 244

tes

'A